SCHOLASTIC YEARBOOK

Illustrations by **PRIYA KURIYAN**

SCHOLASTIC
New York Toronto London Auckland
Sydney New Delhi Hong Kong

While the Editorial research team has made every attempt to authenticate the news and information that has been included in the Yearbook, we apologise for any unintentional errors or omissions.

Published by Scholastic India Pvt. Ltd.
A subsidiary of Scholastic Inc., New York, 10012 (USA).
Publishers since 1920, with international operations in Canada, Australia, New Zealand, the United Kingdom, India, and Hong Kong.

For information regarding permission, write to:
Scholastic India Pvt. Ltd.
A-27, Ground Floor, Bharti Sigma Centre
Infocity-1, Sector 34, Gurgaon 122001 (India)

This edition: October 2015

ISBN: 978-93-5103-997-6

Printed at Rave India, New Delhi

CONTENTS

EVENTS

☑ ALL MAJOR EVENTS

NOVEMBER 2014

Thousands of people gathered at the Brandenburg Gate in Berlin on November 9 to mark the 25th anniversary of the fall of the Berlin Wall in 1989. The Berlin Wall was built in 1961 to stop people from fleeing Communist East Germany.

A 104-storey building (tallest in the western hemisphere) named One World Trade Center, was opened in New York at the site of the twin towers destroyed in terrorist attacks on September 11, 2001.

Prime Minister Narendra Modi paid an official visit to Myanmar, Burma for the 12th India-ASEAN summit. He also spoke at the 9th East Asia Summit.

PM Modi visited Australia from November 15-18 to attend the G-20 summit and to meet BRICS heads of state. He addressed a joint session of the Australian parliament.

Modi also made a second visit to Nepal as Prime Minister to attend the 18th SAARC summit from November 25-27.

A suicide bomber detonated his vest at the Wagah border crossing in Pakistan after the daily parade on November 2. At least 61 people were killed and over 200 injured.

Indian Navy's torpedo recovery vessel, TRV-72 of the Astravahini class, sank off the coast of Visakhapatnam on November 6, killing one sailor.

The captain of the South Korean ferry, *MV Sewol*, that sank on April 16, 2014 killing over 300 passengers, a large number of which were school children, has been convicted of gross negligence and sentenced to 36 years in prison.

The deadly bubonic plague has killed 40 people in Madagascar and infected over 80 others, according to the World Health Organisation. In one of the deadliest outbreaks of the Bubonic and pneumonic plague in the Indian subcontinent, over 12.5 million people lost their lives in undivided India between 1896 and 1926.

The Indian Space Research Organisation has been chosen for the Indira Gandhi Prize for Peace, Disarmament and Development for the year.

UNESCO has declared the Rizal Monument in Manila, Machu Picchu in Peru, Camino de Santiago in Spain and the Dampier Archipelago in Australia as World Heritage Sites in Danger.

A robot probe launched by the European Space Agency finally landed on a comet on November 13. Probe Philae launched

in 2004 will provide some insights into the origin of the solar system.

Suzlon Energy has set up the world's tallest hybrid wind generator turbine at Kutch.

The death toll from the Ebola outbreak in the West African countries of Guinea, Liberia and Sierra Leone has risen to over 10,000, according to a WHO estimate.

PEOPLE METER

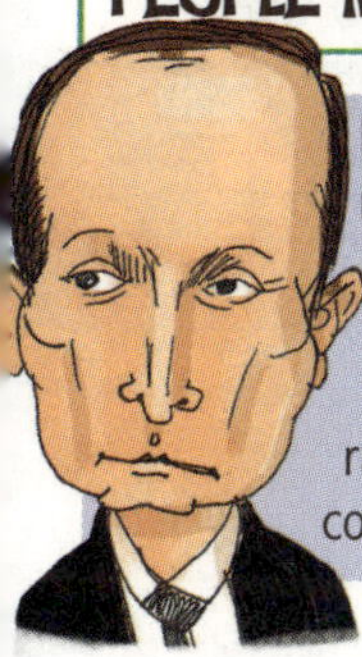

Prime Minister Modi was ranked 15th in the Forbes list of the world's most powerful people. Russian President Vladimir Putin was ranked No.1 for the second consecutive year.

Former Prime Minister of India, Dr. Manmohan Singh, was honoured by Japan with its highest imperial honour, The Grand Cordon of the Order of the Paulownia Flowers.

Former Egyptian President Hosni Mubarak was acquitted by an Egypt court of corruption and charges connected to the killing of 239 protesters during the Egypt uprising in 2011.

Former Uttar Pradesh Chief Secretary, Anoop Mishra, was appointed the new Secretary-General of the Lok Sabha.

Indian tennis player Sania Mirza was named United Nations Goodwill Ambassador for the South Asian Region by UN Women.

DIED

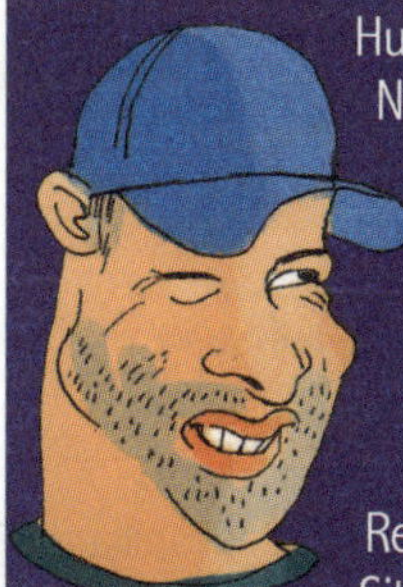

Australian cricketer, Phillip Hughes, died on November 27 following a head injury sustained while facing a short-pitched delivery from New South Wales paceman Sean Abbott.

Renowned Kathak dancer, Sitara Devi, also known as the Kathak queen, winner of Sangeet Natak Akademi Award, Padma Shri and Kalidas Samman died on November 25, at the age of 94.

Sadashiv Amrapurkar, Hindi and Marathi film actor, died on November 3.

DECEMBER 2014

An AirAsia Airbus Flight 8501 en route to Singapore from Surabaya in Indonesia crashed into the Java Sea owing to bad weather on December 28, killing all 155 passengers and seven crew.

On December 16, seven gunmen attacked an Army Public School in Peshawar, Pakistan, killing 151 people, including 132 children between the ages of eight and eighteen. The gunmen are believed to be affiliated with the Tehrik-i-Taliban. The gunmen entered the school and opened fire on the school staff and children. Pakistan Army's Special Services Group (SSG) killed all the seven terrorists.

An oil tanker sank in river Shela after colliding with a cargo vessel and caused an oil spillage that threatened wildlife in the Sundarbans forest.

Indian officials said that a Pakistani fishing boat blew itself up on December 31 after being chased by an Indian Coast Guard patrol.

A fire broke out on the Italian-owned car ferry *Norman Atlantic* shortly after it left a Greek port on its way to southern Italy on December 28. It was carrying 499 people, which included passengers and crew. Eventually, more than 400 people were rescued, with 13 believed to have died in the incident.

Floods and landslides in Sri Lanka caused by heavy rains in late December left 39 people dead.

A volcano on Mount Gamalama in eastern Indonesia erupted on December 19, spewing clouds of hot ash up to 2000 metres into the sky. Four hikers were injured following the volcanic eruption.

On December 15 a gunman in Sydney, Australia, Man Haron Monis, held ten customers and eight employees hostage at a Lindt chocolate cafe. After a 17-hour standoff, the police stormed the cafe and managed to free the hostages. Monis was killed in the raid.

The first prototype (NP1) of indigenously designed and developed 4th plus generation Naval Light Combat Aircraft (LCA) was successfully tested from a shore-based ski-jump facility at INS Hansa, Goa.

Delhi University launched the Dharohar-Gyanodaya Express from Safdarjung railway station on a study tour to the north eastern states of India.

ICRISAT launched a low-cost combination phone and tablet computer called 'GreenPHABLET powered by the GreenSIM' to benefit smallholder farmers.

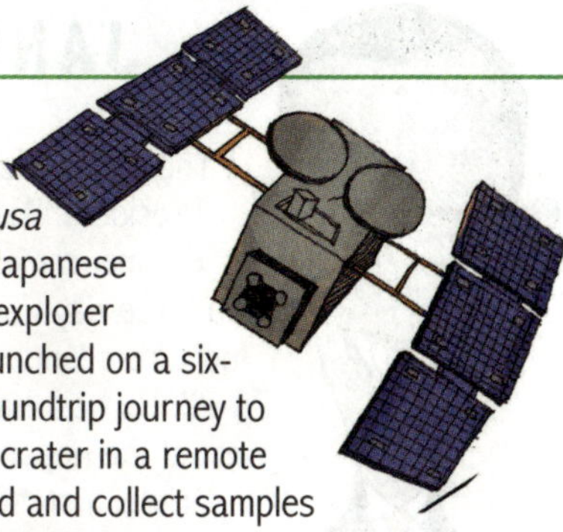

Hayabusa 2, the Japanese space explorer was launched on a six-year roundtrip journey to blow a crater in a remote asteroid and collect samples with the aim of gathering clues to the origin of earth.

PEOPLE METER

Dr. K. Radhakrishnan, Indian space scientist and head of the Indian Space Research Organisation, was chosen as one of the top ten scientists of 2014 by the prestigious journal *Nature*.

Shailesh Nayak became the new chairman of Indian Space Research Organisation, taking over from outgoing chief, Dr. K Radhakrishnan.

Indian woman boxer, Laishram Sarita Devi, was handed a one-year ban by the International Boxing Association for refusing to accept her bronze medal at the Asian Games 2014.

PETA India named the former Supreme Court judge, KS Radhakrishnan, as Man of the Year 2014 and the Bollywood actress Jacqueline Fernandez as Woman of the Year 2014.

Indian mountaineering twins Tashi and Nungshi Malik conquered Mt. Vinson Massif, the highest peak in Antarctica.

They have become the first twins in the world to have climbed all the seven highest peaks in seven continents.

Richard Rahul Verma has been appointed as the next United States ambassador to India. The post fell vacant after the resignation of Nancy Powell in March 2014. He is the first Indian-American chosen for the post.

Anil Sinha was appointed as the new Director General of Central Bureau of Investigation following the retirement of former chief Ranjit Sinha.

DIED

AR Antulay, the first and only Muslim Chief Minister of Maharashtra, passed away on December 2.

German-born American actress, and Academy Award winner, Luise Rainer (*The Great Ziegfeld*, *The Good Earth*) died of pneumonia at the age of 104.

JANUARY 2015

The United States President, Barack Obama, came on a three-day visit to India from January 25-27. He was the chief guest at the Republic Day parade, a first for a US President. He was accompanied by his wife, Michelle Obama.

Lithuania has become the 19th member of the Eurozone (the economic region that is formed by those member countries of the European Union that have adopted the Euro). Its currency earlier was the Litas.

The headquarters of satirical weekly Charlie Hebdo in Paris was attacked by terrorists resulting in the death of 12 persons. Four of France's best-known satirical cartoonists, including the magazine's editor, were among the dead.

Two balloonists, Troy Bradley of the US and Leonid Tiukhtyaev of Russia, crossed the Pacific Ocean in the Two Eagles gas balloon, surpassing the distance and duration records for straight gas balloons. They started from Japan on January 24 and landed in Mexico on January 31 after weather conditions changed the flight plan.

Sunni militants bombed a Shiite mosque in Pakistan's Sindh province killing 40 people and injuring 50 others.

Malaysia officially declared that the loss of Malaysia Airlines Flight 370 over the Indian Ocean was an accident, which implies that the victims' families can seek compensation.

The North American blizzard called Winter Storm Juno affected Canada and parts of the US, Greenland and Western Europe. The nor'easter disrupted transportation in several states.

The National Aeronautics and Space Administration has claimed that 2014 was the hottest year since record keeping began in 1880.

The eruption of the Hunga Tonga submerged volcano in the south Pacific Ocean, near Tonga, disrupted air travel and created a new island measuring one kilometre.

The Doomsday Clock has moved forward two minutes, leaving only three minutes from midnight due to the threat of global nuclear war and climate change. It is the closest it has been to midnight since 1987.

The new National Institution for Transforming India (NITI Aayog for short) has replaced the 65-year-old

Planning Commission. NITI will include leaders of India's 29 states and seven union territories.

India's first floating solar power plant was installed in Kolkata, by Vikram Solar in collaboration with Arka Renewable Energy College.

Vistara, the new airline of Tata SIA Airlines, commenced commercial operations by making its maiden flight from Delhi to Mumbai.

The first canister-based trial of India's most potent missile Agni-V was successfully carried out from Wheeler Island.

PEOPLE METER

Maithripala Sirisena was sworn in as the seventh President of Sri Lanka.

HS Brahma was appointed the new Chief Election Commissioner to take over from retiring CEC VS Sampath.

Wing Commander Pooja Thakur, became the first woman to lead a ceremonial Guard of Honour held on arrival of Barack Obama.

Kalyan Singh, the Governor of Rajasthan, was given the additional charge of Governor of Himachal Pradesh after Urmila Singh retired from her post.

Shekhar Sen, the eminent singer and theatre director was appointed Chairman of Sangeet Natak Akademi.

AS Kiran Kumar, the Director of Space Application Centre, Ahmedabad, was chosen to be the Chairman of Indian Space Research Organisation and the Space Commission and also became the new Secretary of the Department of Space.

Pahlaj Nihalani was appointed the new Chairman of Central Board of Film Censors to fill the vacancy following the resignation of Ms Leela Samson.

Robert Mugabe, the President of Zimbabwe, became the Chairman of the African Union on rotational basis among the five geographical regions of Africa.

DIED

Cartoonist RK Laxman, India's 'Common Man' died on January 26 at the age of 94.

Vasant Gowarikar, the former chief of Indian Space Research Organisation (ISRO), also known as 'Father of Indian Monsoon Model', passed away on January 2.

Subhash Ghisingh, the founder-leader of the movement for a separate homeland for the Gorkhas in northern Bengal, died on January 29.

FEBRUARY 2015

Elections were held for the Delhi Legislative Assembly on February 7. The Aam Aadmi Party won an absolute majority, winning 67 of the total 70 seats. Delhi had remained under President's Rule from February 2014 to March 2015 after Arvind Kejriwal, who became the chief minister after the December 2013 state elections, resigned after 49 days in power. This is Kejriwal's second term as chief minister.

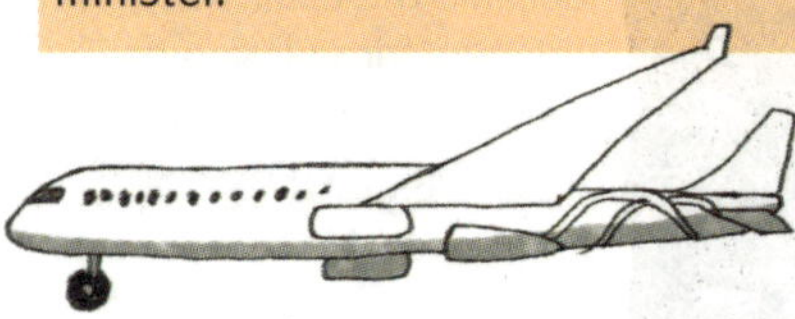

A TransAsia Airways Flight 235 crashed into the Keelung River on February 4, shortly after takeoff from Taipei Airport in Taiwan. The plane was flying with 58 passengers and 5 crew, of which there were 35 survivors.

A ferry carrying 100 passengers capsized in the Padma River in Bangadesh after colliding with a trawler. Sixty-six people are believed to have died in the accident.

The Islamic State of Iraq and Syria (ISIS) is believed to have burned more than 100,000 books and manuscripts in Mosul, Iraq.

A private bus with around 55-60 passengers plunged into a 150-ft deep gorge in the Dhar district of Madhya Pradesh, killing 10 passengers and injuring 33 others.

Two people were killed in a pile-up involving 100 cars on a bridge in South Korea that connects Incheon and the capital, Seoul, to the airport on Yongjing island. Heavy fog is believed to have caused the pile-up.

The Telephone Regulatory Authority of India (TRAI) announced that mobile subscribers will be able to retain the same mobile number throughout India (Pan-India Mobile Number Portability) from May 3 onwards.

The world's largest solar power plant with a capacity of 750 MW (larger than 550-megawatt Desert Sunlight solar project in California) is being set up in Rewa, Madhya Pradesh.

The painting of two Tahitian girls titled *Nafea Faa Ipoipo*, or *When Will You Marry?* by Paul Gauguin, the French artist, sold for $300 million, making it the most expensive work of art ever sold.

The NASA spacecraft, New Horizons, launched in 2006, returned its first images of Pluto and its largest moon, Charon.

Mountaineers claim to have found the wreckage of the LAN Chile Flight 210 that disappeared in the Andes on April 3, 1961. The crash stunned the sporting world as among those killed were eight members and two coaches of a Chilean football team.

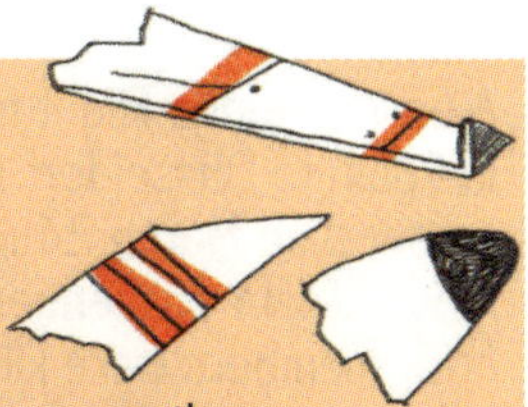

PEOPLE METER

Dr. Rajendra K Pachauri, the Chairperson of the Intergovernmental Panel on Climate Change, stepped down from his post following allegations against him.

Sergio Mattarella, the Italian constitutional court judge and politician, was chosen to be the 12th President of Italy (since the Second World War) for a seven-year term.

Yogaraj C.P, the Indian Yoga teacher in Hong Kong, set a Guinness World record for Longest Yoga Marathon (Male) by performing for 40 hours and demonstrating more than 1500 asanas.

Indian Economist and Nobel laureate Amartya Sen was awarded the newly instituted Charleston-EFG John Maynard Keynes Prize in recognition of his outstanding contribution to society.

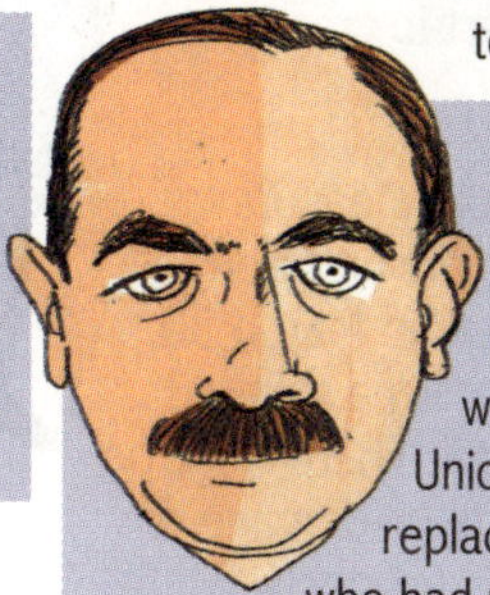

L.C Goyal, the secretary in the Union Ministry of Rural Development, was appointed Union Home Secretary replacing Anil Goswami who had resigned earlier.

DIED

American actor Leonard Nimoy, best known for his role as Spock from the Star Trek series, died at the age of 83.

Carl Djerassi, the US scientist considered the father of the birth control pill, died on January 30.

MARCH 2015

A Germanwings Flight from Barcelona in Spain to Düsseldorf in Germany, crashed on March 24 in the French Alps. All 144 passengers and six crew members were killed. It is believed that the crash was deliberately caused by the co-pilot, Andreas Lubitz. Lubitz locked the pilot out of the cockpit before starting a descent that caused the aircraft to crash into a mountain.

A powerful earthquake measuring 7.5 on the Richter scale hit Papua New Guinea on March 30, generating a small tsunami. There were no reports of damage or loss of property.

At least 38 persons were killed and around 150 others injured when the engine and two coaches of the Dehradun-Varanasi Janta Express derailed near Bachhrawan Railway station, about 50 km from the Uttar Pradesh state capital, Lucknow.

Prime Minister Modi visited the three Indian Ocean Island countries of Seychelles, Mauritius and Sri Lanka from March 10-14.

In a freak accident, two helicopters collided in Argentina. Three French sports personalities—Yachtswoman Florence Arthaud, Olympic swimmer Camille Muffat and Olympic boxer Alexis Vastine—were among the 10 people killed. The helicopters were involved in the filming of the TV survival show, *Dropped*. The show flies celebrities into rough terrain by helicopter and films their attempt to find food and shelter.

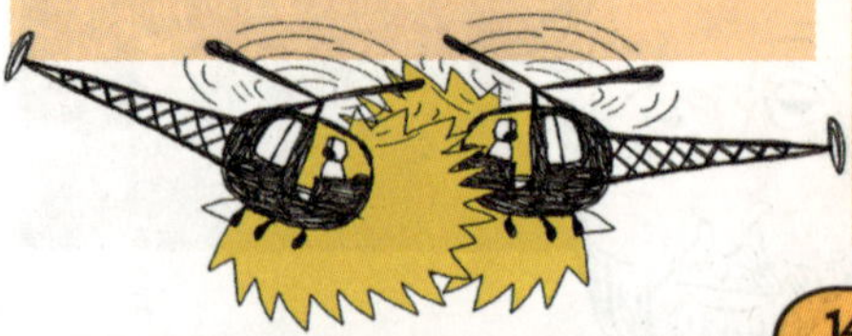

A nine-foot high bronze statue of Mahatma Gandhi was unveiled by the Union Finance Minister, Arun Jaitley, at the Parliament Square in London on March 14. The statue has been sculpted by Philip Jackson.

The Indian government censored the documentary *India's Daughter* depicting the Nirbhaya gang rape and murder.

A 2,300 year-old collection of silver coins and jewellery has been uncovered by travellers in a stalactite cave in Israel's Galilee region. These are believed to have been hidden there from the time of Alexander the Great of Macedonia. The discovery could be the first of its kind to be found from that period in this area.

The Norwegian Nobel Committee which awards the Nobel Peace Prize replaced its head, Thorbjørn Jagland, against his will, for the first time in its 114-year-old history. Kaci Kullmann Five succeeds Jagland who will still remain a member of the committee.

Soyuz-TMA-16M, carrying three crew members, was launched to the International Space Station. Russian cosmonaut Mikhail Korniyenko and American astronaut Scott Kelly are on a year-long mission to test the effects of long-term space habitation on the human body.

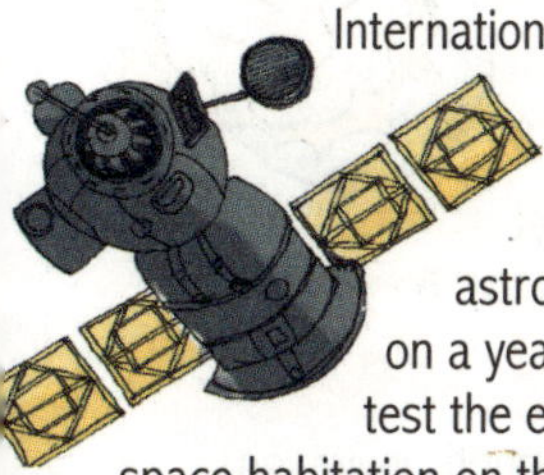

The new capital of Andhra Pradesh, Amaravathi, will be built near Vijayawada.

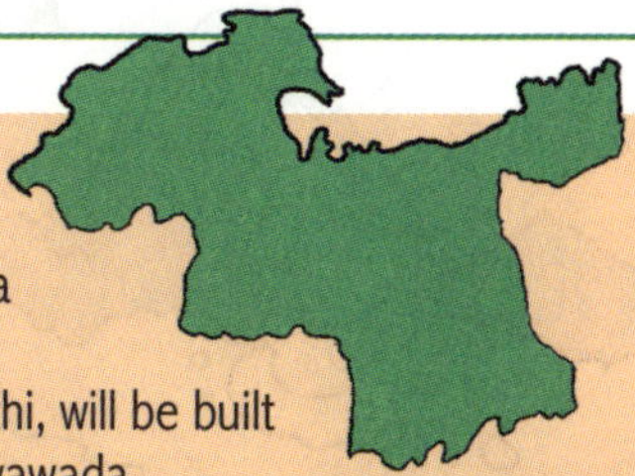

PEOPLE METER

Mufti Mohammad Sayeed, a candidate of the People's Democratic Party, took over as the Chief Minister of Jammu and Kashmir.

Vikas Swaroop, the author of *Q & A*, (the novel on which the film *Slumdog Millionaire* is based), was chosen to be the spokesperson of the Ministry of External Affairs.

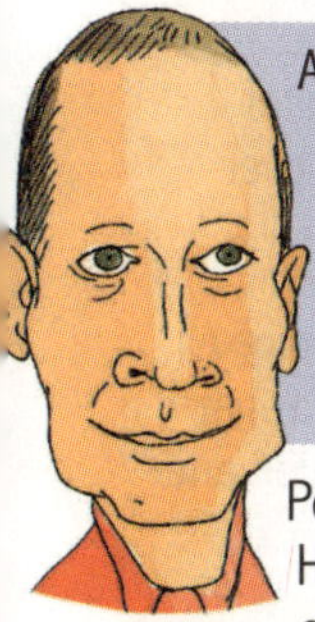

André Borschberg and Bertrand Piccard who founded the solar powered plane, Solar Impulse, made the first attempt to fly around the world from Al Bateen airport in Abu Dhabi.

Popular Hollywood star, Harrison Ford, had a narrow escape after he crash landed his single-engine Second World War-era training plane on a golf course in Los Angeles.

Arun Singh, the present Indian ambassador to France was appointed as the next Indian ambassador to the United States succeeding Mr. S Jaishankar.

Jagmohan Dalmiya was elected for the post of the new chairman of Board of Control for Cricket for the third time.

DIED

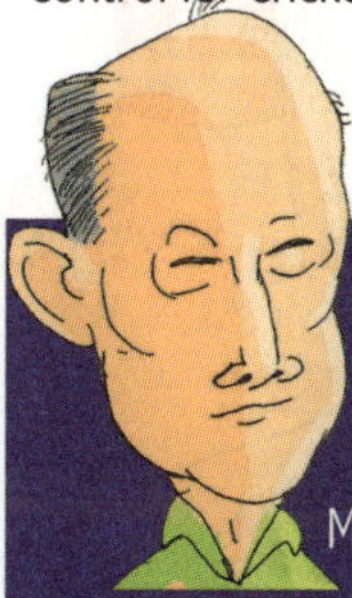

Lee Kuan Yew, the founder and first Prime Minister of Singapore died at the age of 91, on March 23.

Vinod Mehta, veteran journalist and editorial chairman of the Outlook group died on March 8.

Sam Simon, the co-creator of the animated television series, *The Simpsons,* died on March 8.

APRIL 2015

Nepal was hit by a 7.8 magnitude earthquake on April 25. The Gorkha earthquake killed more than 9,000 people and injured over 23,000 others and triggered an avalanche on Mount Everest that killed 19 people. It was the worst natural disaster to strike Nepal since the 1934 quake. Thousands were rendered homeless as entire villages were flattened. The Indian Army led a rescue and relief mission, Operation Maitri, in Nepal after the earthquake.

Prime Minister Modi visited France, Germany and Canada from April 9-17. This was his first visit to Europe as PM. Modi sought Canada's cooperation in some priority areas like energy and infrastructure.

A Trasmediterranea passenger ferry *Sorrento*, caught fire en route from Palma de Mallorca to Valencia in Spain. All 170 passengers were rescued.

Over 400 migrants died when their boat capsized in the Mediterranean. They were travelling from Libya to Italy when the mishap occurred.

The NASA spacecraft *Messenger* that was launched on August 3, 2004, to study the planet Mercury, crashed into the planet after exhaustion of its fuel on April 30.

Japanese Maglev (magnetic levitation) train, which is the fastest train in the world, set a new record of 603 kmph, beating its own 2003 record of 581 kmph.

Following the outbreak of civil war in Yemen, Saudi Arabia, spearheaded a coalition of nine Arab states that carried out airstrikes on Yemen as part of a military intervention codenamed Operation Decisive Storm.

In view of the worsening situation in Yemen, India shifted the Indian embassy from Yemen's capital Sana'a to Djibouti and evacuated over 4,741 Indians.

Vividh Bharati, the popular service of All India Radio, was launched in FM format by the Union Minister for Information and Broadcasting, Arun Jaitley.

Bhaskar Mahapatra's painting 'Tree of Life' was presented by Prime Minister Narendra Modi to French President Francois Hollande during his visit to the country.

Hagia Sophia, the museum in Istanbul, Turkey which once served as a church and a mosque witnessed the recital of Quran for the first time in 85 years.

The Government of Maharashtra has decided to set up a memorial to cartoonist R.K. Laxman in J.J. School of Arts.

PEOPLE METER

Hillary Clinton, the wife of the former President of the United States, Bill Clinton, is seeking a Democratic Party nomination for the 2016 US Presidential election.

Ratan Tata, the Indian industrialist acquired a stake in the Chinese smartphone maker Xiaomi, becoming the first Indian to do so.

Nasim Zaidi, the new Chief Election Commissioner of India, took over from outgoing CEC H.S. Brahma.

Venkadarath Saritha, a woman from Telangana and former driver with Azad Foundation's Sakha cabs, was appointed as the first woman driver by Delhi Transport Corporation.

Satya Nadella, the Indian-origin CEO of Microsoft, was honoured with the Champions of Change award by the US Government.

Rajeev Shukla, the former Minister of State in the Ministry of Parliamentary Affairs and Planning was appointed Chairman of the Governing Council of the Indian Premier League.

DIED

Günter Grass, the German novelist, poet, playwright and recipient of the 1999 Nobel Prize in Literature passed away on April 13.

Richie Benaud, the former Australian cricket all-rounder and commentator, died on April 10.

JB Patnaik, the former Chief Minister of Odisha (and also former Governor of Assam), passed away on April 21.

MAY 2015

An intense heat wave in India claimed over 2000 lives. The government instructed hospitals to treat heatstroke as an emergency. This heat wave was the deadliest in over two decades.

Nepal was hit by another earthquake. The May earthquake measuring 7.3 on the Richter scale, struck near the Tibetan border, killing 66 people, including 17 in India and one in Tibet.

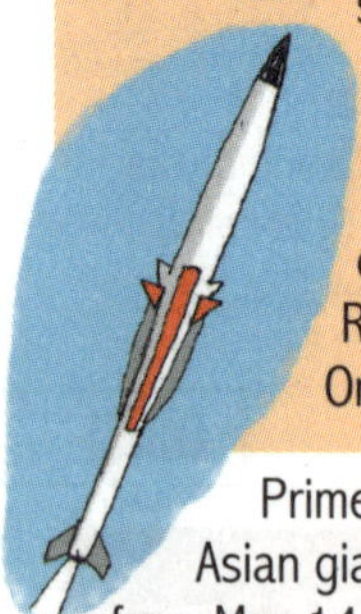

Akash, the indigenously developed surface-to-air missile with a range of 25 km, was inducted into the Army. The missile has been developed by the Defence Research & Development Organisation (DRDO).

Prime Minister Modi visited the Asian giants China and South Korea from May 14-19. Agreements and MOUs were signed with the two countries during the visit.

Storms, tornadoes and heavy rain from May 24-26 triggered record-breaking floods in Texas and Oklahoma in the United States. The storm system also produced deadly tornadoes in Mexico.

'Women of Algiers', a painting by Pablo Picasso, set a record for an artwork sold at an auction, by selling for $179.3 million at a Christie's auction.

The Conservative Party, led by David Cameron, won the general elections in the United Kingdom.

The historic city of Palmyra, in Syria, also a UNESCO World Heritage Site, has been seized by Islamic State militants.

A Mirage 2000 fighter aircraft was used by the Indian Air Force in a trial on Yamuna expressway to test it as a runway in case of an emergency.

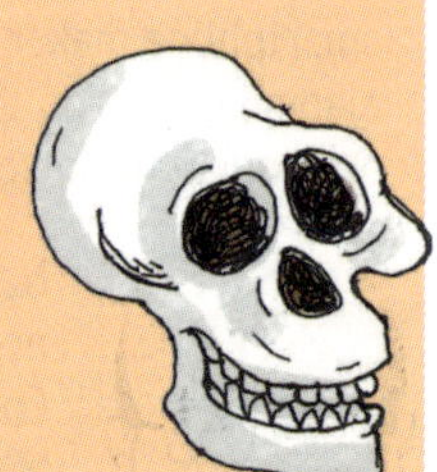

In Ethiopia, scientists discovered a new human ancestor species *Australopithecus deyiremeda* that lived alongside the famous 'Lucy' (*Australopithecus afarensis*) between 3.3 and 3.5 million years ago.

More than 1,34,000 saiga antelopes died in Kazakhstan over two weeks, leaving scientists and conservationists wondering about the cause of these unusual deaths and worried about the animal's future.

Bollywood star Salman Khan was sentenced to five years in jail on May 6 for killing a homeless man in 2002 in a hit-and-run driving incident in Mumbai. The man was among five people who were run over in the incident. Khan was charged with culpable homicide. However, the Bombay high court suspended his sentence and granted him bail.

PEOPLE METER

Sepp Blatter was elected to a fifth term as president of Fédération Internationale de Football Association (FIFA).

Draupadi Murmu, the former MLA and minister from Odisha, was sworn in as the first woman Governor of Jharkhand.

Mohammed Morsi, the former President of Egypt, was sentenced to death over his part in a mass prison break in 2011 that toppled Hosni Mubarak.

KV Kamath, the non-executive chairman of ICICI Bank and Infosys, has been chosen to head the BRICS Bank.

George Yeo, the former Singapore Foreign Minister was chosen to be the new Chancellor of the Nalanda University replacing Nobel laureate Amartya Sen.

DIED

Aruna Shanbaug, who was the focus of the euthanasia debate in India, died on May 18 at the age of 67. She was in a vegetative state since 1973 following a brutal rape in a Mumbai hospital.

Riley B. King (stage name BB King), the American Hall of Fame blues singer, songwriter and guitarist passed away on May 14 at the age of 89.

Amalendu Guha, eminent historian, economist and author of the acclaimed book *Planter Raj to Swaraj*, passed away on May 7.

Ruth Rendell, the well-known crime and mystery writer and creator of fictional Chief Inspector Wexford, passed away on May 2.

Amitabha Chowdhury, the acclaimed journalist and 1961 Magsaysay Award recipient for journalism and literature, passed away on May 1.

John F. Nash Jr., a mathematician who shared a Nobel in 1994 for work on modern economic theory was killed, along with his wife, in a car crash in New Jersey on May 23. He was 86.

Bangladesh and India sealed a historic land pact on June 7 that made the Land Boundary Agreement operational and allowed for the swapping of territories. This agreement enables tens of thousands of people living in border enclaves to choose their nationality. The pact was signed in the presence of Prime Minister Modi and his Bangladesh counterpart, Sheikh Hasina.

In one of the worst disasters at sea in China's history, a cruise ship that operated in the Three Gorges region of inland China capsized in rough weather on June 1, on the Yangtze river. Of the 454 people on board, 442 are believed to have died.

Greece plunged into a deep economic crisis after the European Union's bailout programme ended on June 30 with Greece failing to repay an International Monetary Fund loan.

India pledged $1 billion for earthquake reconstruction in Nepal, with a quarter of the amount in the form of grants. This was over and above the existing aid pledges to Nepal. Meanwhile, Nepal was hit by another major disaster on June 11 when heavy rainfall triggered landslides that buried six villages in Nepal's northeast and left at least 30 people dead and several missing.

The *SpaceX Falcon 9* rocket, carrying a Dragon space capsule which was launched from Cape Canaveral, Florida on June 28, exploded minutes after take-off.

The severe heat wave in the subcontinent continued with over 2000 people dying from dehydration and heat stroke in Pakistan.

Over 42 people were shot dead on June 24 by suspected Boko Haram gunmen, the Islamic extremist group which is based in northeastern Nigeria, in two attacks in villages in Nigeria's Borno state.

The first International Yoga Day was celebrated on June 21. Prime Minister Narendra Modi had suggested this date in his address at the UN as it is the longest day of the year in the Northern Hemisphere.

A Tunisian gunman opened fire at a beach resort in Sousse, Tunisia, on June 28 killing at least 38 foreign tourists, including Britons, Germans and Belgians.

North Korea has planted landmines in the demilitarised zone (DMZ) to prevent North Korean soldiers from fleeing to South Korea.

In a bizarre case, lions, tigers, bears and other wild animals escaped from a zoo in the Georgian capital of Tbilisi owing to flooding in the zoo premises that enabled them to break free of their enclosures and roam the streets.

Twenty-two Hindu pilgrims were killed when the van they were travelling in fell into the Dowleswaram dam in Andhra Pradesh on June 13.

There is a new virus on the run. The Middle East Respiratory Syndrome coronavirus (MERS) affected over 180 people in South Korea, with 36 succumbing to the viral attack.

On June 27, flammable starch-based powder exploded at a recreational water park in Bali, in New Taipei, Taiwan. The explosion at the Formosa Fun Coast left 12 people dead and over 500 injured.

At least 27 people were killed and over 200 injured following a suicide bombing at the Shia Imam Sadiq mosque in Kuwait City, Kuwait. The Islamic State of Iraq and the Levant claimed responsibility for the attack.

PEOPLE METER

Louisiana governor in the United States, Bobby Jindal, who is an Indian-American, is among the Republican contenders for the 2016 presidential elections.

Steffi Graf, the former German tennis star, has been appointed the Ayurveda brand ambassador of Kerala.

MS Dhoni became the only Indian sportsperson to figure in the *Forbes* magazine amongst the 100 highest-paid athletes in the world, a list that is led by American boxer Floyd Mayweather.

Surgeons at the M.D. Anderson Cancer Centre in Houston, led by Dr Jesse Selber, performed the world's first partial-skull and scalp transplant on 55-year-old James Boysen. The 12-doctor operation lasted 15 hours.

DIED

Christopher Lee, the British actor who became famous for his roles in *Star Wars* and *The Lord of the Rings* passed away on June 7.

Nek Chand, the creator of the Rock Garden in Chandigarh and Padma Shri awardee, died on June 12.

Praful Bidwai, journalist and columnist died on June 23. He was 66.

Charles Correa, architect and urban planner and recipient of the Padma Shri award died on June 16 at the age of 84.

Sister Nirmala, the head of the Missionaries of Charity organisation, since the death of Mother Teresa in 1997, passed away on June 23.

The World Wrestling Entertainment Hall of Famer Dusty Rhodes died at the age of 69.

Irwin Rose, the 2004 Chemistry Nobel Prize winning biochemist passed away on June 2.

JULY 2015

APJ Abdul Kalam, known also as the 'Missile Man of India', who had a remarkable career as an aerospace scientist and science administrator at the DRDO and the ISRO and who went on to become the 11th President of India in 2002, died on July 27 at the age of 83.

The United States and Cuba have resumed full diplomatic relations, five decades after they were severed in 1961, starting with reopening of embassies in each other's capitals, namely Washington and Havana.

A wildfire burning in San Bernardino County in California that started on July 18 burned over 3,500 acres of forests and destroyed 16 homes and other buildings. The fire also reached the freeway and burned over 60 passenger vehicles and tractor-trailers.

Twenty-nine people died in a stampede at the Godavari Maha Pushkaram festival at Rajahmundry in Andhra Pradesh on July 14. The stampede took place along the Godavari River.

Greek lawmakers have voted to approve an austerity bill that includes tax hikes and spending cuts to help the country recover from its economic crisis.

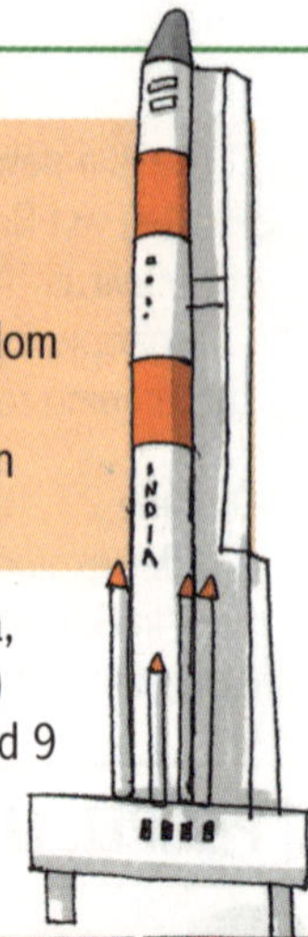

The Indian Space Research Organisation successfully launched five commercial satellites for the United Kingdom using the PSLV-C28 launch vehicle from the launch pad in Sriharikota on July 10.

The 7th BRICS (Brazil, Russia, India, China and South Africa) summit was held on July 8 and 9 in the Russian city of Ufa.

A five-day truce was declared in Yemen on July 25, 2015, as various aid groups, including Iran, tried to gain access to Yemen's ports and airports.

Taiwan held a large military parade in Taipei to commemorate the Second World War to highlight an old claim that its forces and not the Chinese Communists routed imperial Japan from China 70 years ago.

Nineteen army personnel were killed when an army train fell into a canal near Gujranwala in Pakistan following a bridge collapse on July 2.

British Petroleum has agreed to pay $18.7 billion as compensation to the United States Government and the five Gulf Coast states of Alabama, Florida, Louisiana, Mississippi and Texas for damages following the oil spill

triggered by the sinking of the Deepwater Horizon oil rig on April 20, 2010 in the Gulf of Mexico.

Yakub Memon, convicted of financing the 1993 Mumbai bombings was executed by hanging on July 30.

An animal skin parchment believed to be the world's oldest Quran from between 568 AD and 645 AD was found hidden inside the pages of a book in a library at the University of Birmingham in England.

Beijing (China) was chosen by the International Olympic Committee to host the 2022 Winter Olympics, becoming the first city to be awarded both summer and winter Games.

Hundreds of villagers were evacuated following the eruption of the Colima volcano in Mexico, the worst since the last big eruption in 1913.

PEOPLE METER

Peter Higgs, the 2013 winner of Physics Nobel prize, was awarded the Royal Society's Copley Medal (known as the world's oldest scientific prize) for his pioneering work on the theory of the Higgs boson.

Ajay Mathur, the Director-General, Bureau of Energy Efficiency, was appointed Director-General of The Energy and Resources Institute (also known as TERI).

Two Anglo-Indian members, George Baker, a BJP leader and actor from West Bengal, and Richard Hay, an economics professor from Kerala, have been nominated to the Lok Sabha by President Pranab Mukherjee.

Ram Sewak Sharma has been appointed Chairman of the Telecom Regulatory Authority of India.

DIED

Clive Rice, South Africa's first post-apartheid international cricket captain, passed away on July 28.

Jules Bianchi, the French Formula One driver, died on July 17 of critical head injuries sustained at last year's Japanese Grand Prix.

Nicholas Winton, the British humanitarian who rescued nearly 700 children, most of them Jewish, from Nazi-occupied Czechoslovakia on the eve of the Second World War in an operation known as the Czech Kindertransport, passed away on July 1.

Egyptian actor Omar Sharif died at the age of 83.

AUGUST 2015

A bombing inside the Erawan shrine in Bangkok, Thailand, on August 17 left 20 people dead and over a hundred injured.

In a double train tragedy, 31 people died when the Kamayani Janata Express train running from Mumbai to Varanasi was partially swept off a bridge while crossing flooded tracks in Madhya Pradesh. Within minutes of this first accident, an engine and four coaches of the Janata Express going to Mumbai from Jabalpur also derailed on the flooded tracks.

The Army was deployed in Gujarat following caste-related violence after police arrested a young leader who was demanding reservation in government jobs and colleges for the Patel community.

The interim Prime Minister of Greece, Vassiliki Thanou-Christophilou, also the country's first female prime minister, was sworn in on August 27. She will head the caretaker government that will oversee implementation of austerity measures.

A vintage jet aircraft crashed during a display at the Shoreham Airshow in England killing 11 people. This is the deadliest air show accident in UK since the Farnborough air show crash which killed 31 people in 1952.

A sinkhole in a northeastern Chinese city swallowed five pedestrians who were on the sidewalk when it suddenly caved in on August 27.

A series of explosions killed at least 44 people and injured hundreds of others at a container storage terminal at Tianjin port in China on August 12.

A Chinese stock market crash caused major aftershocks in Asian markets, including India, on July 27 and August 24 both termed as 'Black Monday'.

In fresh developments in the mysterious MH370 case—the plane that disappeared on March 8, 2014 while flying from Kuala Lumpur to Beijing—a part of the aircraft wing was found on the French Reunion Island in the Indian Ocean on August 5.

Cochin International Airport in Kerala became the first in the world to be powered totally by solar energy.

August 13 was marked as the Earth Overshoot Day for 2015, that is the day on which the world has exhausted nature's budget for the entire year (it was August 19 in 2014).

Google has created a new holding company called Alphabet Inc., on August 10, containing Google Inc. and Calico that

Alphabet

includes Google Ventures, Google Capital, Google X and other subsidiaries.

China has set up the world's largest mosquito factory in Guangzhou. The factory will release one million sterilised mosquitoes every week to dilute the population of dengue carrying insects with those that don't carry the disease.

PEOPLE METER

Ranil Wickremesinghe was sworn in as the new prime minister of Sri Lanka.

Aurangzeb Road in New Delhi has been renamed after the former President APJ Abdul Kalam.

Sebastian Coe, the British politician and former track and field athlete, was elected the President of International Association of Athletics Federation (IAAF) to succeed Lamine Diack of Senegal.

Amitabh Bachchan has been chosen as the state ambassador for the 'Save the Tiger' campaign and to promote tiger tourism in Maharashtra.

DIED

Khaled al-Assad, the 82-year-old Syrian archaeologist looking after ancient ruins of Palmyra in Syria for 40 years, was executed by Islamic State militants on August 18.

Suvra Mukherjee, wife of President Pranab Mukherjee, passed away on August 18. She was 74.

Niloy Chatterjee, the secular blogger and owner of website *Istishon.com* was hacked to death by unknown assailants in Bangladesh.

SEPTEMBER 2015

Prime Minister Narendra Modi was in the US for a five-day official visit from September 26-30. The highlights of his trip included speeches at the UN and G4 summits in New York, a summit meeting with US President Barack Obama on climate change, and a push for reform of the UN Security Council. He also met leaders of US tech giants Facebook and Microsoft and executives from 47 Fortune 500 companies.

The National Aeronautics and Space Administration has claimed that scientists have discovered evidence of 'flowing liquid water' on Mars. Although the water is highly poisonous, this is an extremely significant find as it indicates the possibility of life on Mars.

Over 1000 people were killed during a stampede on September 24 near Mecca, Saudi Arabia on the eve of Eid-al-Adha. The incident occurred during the ongoing Haj pilgrimage. Earlier, 107 people were killed when strong winds caused a construction crane to collapse on September 11 at the Masjid al-Haram, the Grand Mosque in Mecca. Most of those killed were Haj pilgrims.

An asteroid came hair-raisingly close to Earth on September 30. Space rock 2015 SZ2 was at a distance of just 309,000 miles which is about 1.3 times the distance from the Earth to the Moon. The asteroid was large enough to be able to destroy a city the size of London.

An interesting celestial event took place on September 28 when people in North and South America, Europe, Africa and the Middle East were witness to a 'blood moon' which is the combination of a supermoon and a lunar eclipse.

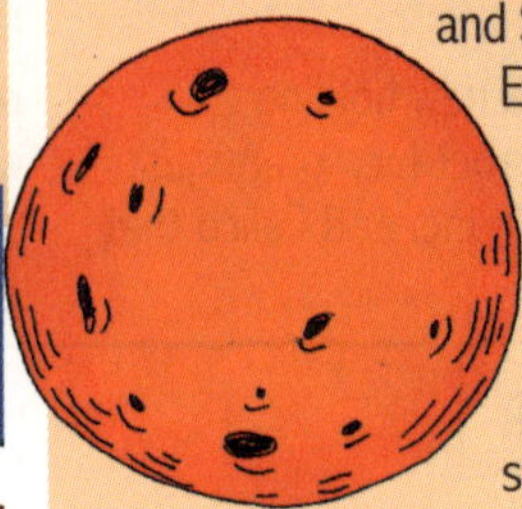

India experienced its worst outbreak of dengue fever in five years, with the number of dengue victims close to 20,000, at the beginning of September, as opposed to 10,000 in the previous year.

The German automaker, Volkswagen, was caught in a controversy over violation of emission norms in over 11 million Volkswagen and Audi models manufactured between 2009 and 2015.

Scientists have discovered the *Homo naledi*, a previously unknown species of early humans in a South African cave system. The species has a stature similar to small-bodied human populations. The fossils have still to be dated.

Chile was hit by an 8.3 magnitude earthquake on September 16. This was one of the largest in recent years. A tsunami alert was issued for Chile, Peru, New Zealand, Hawaii and California.

Indian American author-entrepreneur Prerna Gupta has launched an iPhone app called Hooked that features short fiction for Young Adult readers. Each book will be roughly 1,000 words and is designed to be read in about five minutes.

The Gandhi Peace Prize 2014 has been conferred on the Indian Space Research Organisation.

PEOPLE METER

Queen Elizabeth II became Britain's longest-reigning monarch (63 years and seven months). She surpassed her great-great-grandmother, Queen Victoria's record.

Pope Francis visited Cuba, the US and the United Nations from September 19 to 27. It was Pope Francis' first visit to both Cuba and the US.

Malcolm Turnbull, a former journalist, banker and lawyer, became Australia's 29th prime minister, replacing Tony Abbott. He won by a vote of 54-44.

Alexis Tsipras returned as the Prime Minister of Greece, winning 35 per cent of the vote, and 145 of 300 Parliament seats.

DIED

BCCI President Jagmohan Dalmiya died in Kolkata, on September 20.

Jackie Collins, the British-American romance novelist and author of *The World Is Full of Married Men*, passed away on September 19.

Popular Indian music composer and singer, Aadesh Shrivastava, died on September 5 at the age of 51.

Mohiniyattam dancer, Kalamandalam Satyabhama, died on September 13.

OCTOBER 2015

President Vladimir Putin of Russia escalated the stakes in his contest with the West over influence in West Asia on October 7, 2015, as Russian pilots carried out their first airstrikes in Syria. Russian warplanes and helicopter gunships dropped bombs north of the central city of Homs.

There was communal tension in Dadri, a town in Uttar Pradesh, after a 50-year-old man, Mohammad Akhlaq, and his son, Danish, were lynched, on September 28, by a mob following rumours that the family had consumed and stored beef in their house.

The Bihar State Assembly elections will be held in five phases in October and November 2015.

Fédération Internationale de Football Association (FIFA) has suspended Sepp Blatter, Michel Platini and Jerome Valcke from all football-related activities for 90 days following allegations of corruption.

Belarusian writer, Svetlana Alexievich, has won the Nobel Prize for Literature for her 'polyphonic writings'. Svetlana is the 14th woman to win the prize since it was first awarded in 1901.

In another tragic shooting incident in the US, this time in Oregon, 10 people were killed and nine injured in a mass shooting at the Umpqua Community College in Roseburg, Oregon. The 26-year-old shooter was a resident of Winchester.

The second edition of the Hero Indian Super League (ISL) for football began on October 3, 2015. The eight teams will play 61 matches over 79 days.

Two bomb explosions targeted a peace rally by leftist and Kurdish activists in the Turkish capital Ankara, killing 86 people and wounding 186.

Barely hours before the book launch of former Pakistan Foreign Minister Ahmed Kasuri's, *Neither a Hawk, Nor a Dove: An Insider's Account of Pakistan's Foreign Policy* on October 12, the main organiser and former journalist Sudheendra Kulkarni was abused and attacked with ink by political activists.

PEOPLE METER

Lawyer-turned-administrator Shashank Manohar has been elected as the BCCI President, following the passing away of Jagmohan Dalmiya.

KP Sharma Oli was elected Nepal's new prime minister, defeating Nepali Congress chief Sushil Koirala.

Bangalore author Shashi Deshpande resigned from the Sahitya Akademi's general council to protest against its silence on the murder of Kannada writer MM Kalburgi.

Brazilian football legend Pele set foot in Kolkata on October 11, after an interval of 38 years.

DIED

Music composer Ravindra Jain passed away on October 9, in Mumbai. The visually impaired musician, who overcame his disability to create memorable music for TV and films, was 71.

PEOPLE IN THE NEWS

☑ NATIONAL AND INTERNATIONAL NEWSMAKERS

NATIONAL

* Mohandas Karamchand Gandhi continues to be larger than life even 67 years after his death. In fact, more so. A nine-foot high bronze statue of Gandhi, sculpted by Philip Jackson, was unveiled at Parliament Square in London on March 14 by Arun Jaitley, the Union Finance Minister. Giving Gandhi company, though in another part of England, is the statue of Mohinder Singh Pujji, the longest surviving Indian fighter pilot. Pujji was among a group of 24 Indians who served in the British Royal Air Force during the Second World War.
* Prime Minister Narendra Modi deserves the "Globetrotting Leader of the Year Award". Modi visited 18 countries in the last year, including his much publicised recent trip to the US. As one periodical put it, "Modi has been one of the best salesmen India has ever had." And in keeping with this, Modi signed a slew of agreements and pacts—economic, environmental, political and more—wherever he went, logging both miles and smiles.
* The muffler man was back at the helm, the second time in two years, with the first lasting only 49 days. In elections held in February, Arvind Kejriwal's Aam Aadmi Party trounced all other parties in the polls to win an absolute majority. The party has been dogged by controversy right from the beginning. Starting with the removal of two senior members, Yogendra Yadav and Prashant Bhushan, from the political affairs committee; to the arrests of the law minister, Jitender Singh Tomar, for holding forged law degrees and of prominent party member, Somnath Bharti on charges of domestic violence; to the sacking of Food Minister Asim Ahmed Khan for allegedly demanding bribes from a builder; Kejriwal's Aam Aadmis have been hard at work doing damage control.
* The sudden and unfortunate passing away of former president, APJ Abdul Kalam, was mourned as a huge loss by the country. The People's President had charmed his way into people's hearts with his unassuming ways and accessible nature. He remained connected with students right till the end. Kalam was delivering a lecture at the Indian Institute of Management in Shillong, on July 27,

2015, when he suffered a massive cardiac arrest and collapsed. Besides being an eminent scientist, Kalam was also known as the 'Missile Man of India' owing to his association with India's military missile development programme. Incidentally, Wheeler Island, off the coast of Odisha, has been named after Kalam. The Integrated Test Range missile testing facility is located on the island.

* The Aruna Ramchandra Shanbaug case is unique in the annals of Indian legal history. Aruna was a nurse at the King Edward Memorial Hospital in Mumbai when she was assaulted in 1973. She remained in a vegetative state for 42 years after the assault. In 2011, the Supreme Court rejected a plea for euthanasia filed by Aruna's friend, journalist Pinki Virani. Nurses at the hospital looked after Aruna through her long battle to stay alive. Aruna died from pneumonia on May 18, 2015.

* One of India's most prominent environmental scientists, Dr Rajendra Kumar Pachauri, who was the chair of the Intergovernmental Panel on Climate Change (IPCC), and during whose tenure the organisation was awarded the Nobel Peace Prize, resigned from IPCC after allegations of misconduct by a junior colleague at the organisation based in New Delhi.

* After the Aarushi Talwar murder, media trials seem to have become par for the course, the most recent being the Sheena Bora murder case. That this murder remained undiscovered for over three years is not the only appalling detail—equally disconcerting is the fact that it implicates a high profile celebrity like the mother, Indrani Mukherjea, who is married to media baron, Peter Mukherjea. But ultimately what taxed the public mind the most was the convoluted family tree, which even the media had to devote considerable time and space to figure out.

* The disappearance of the Congress vice-president, Rahul Gandhi at the start of the crucial budget session of the Parliament in February gave rise to much speculation. Admittedly, Rahul was missing in action to reflect upon the future course of his party and perhaps prepare himself (as some believed) to take over as party president. Rahul returned after a 59-day sabbatical that included visits to Thailand, the UK, Italy and Burma.

INTERNATIONAL

- President Barack Obama and his wife Michelle Obama got a fair amount of media adulation when they visited India in January. Obama was the chief guest at the Republic Day parade, the first for a US president. Obama and Modi struck up quite a friendship and their strong sense of bonhomie did not go unnoticed. Wife Michelle did not have an official schedule of her own and no Indian first lady to keep her company. But her outfits created quite a buzz wherever she went. She stepped off Air Force One in a dress designed by Bibhu Mohapatra, an Indian designer who lives in New York.
- Queen Elizabeth II has surpassed the reign of her great-great-grandmother, Queen Victoria, to become Britain's longest serving monarch. The 89-year-old monarch has ruled for over 23,000 days. Long live the Queen!

- There is an interesting line-up of presidential candidates for the 2016 US presidential elections, including former president, Bill Clinton's wife, Hillary Clinton and real estate baron and television personality, Donald Trump. Trump announced his candidacy with characteristic flamboyance at the Trump Tower in New York City with the slogan "Make America Great Again". Interestingly, Indian-American Bobby Jindal is also on the list of hopefuls. Jindal is presently Louisiana governor.
- India is not the only country in Asia where dynasties are perpetuated. Bangladesh, Burma and Sri Lanka have also seen dynastic rule. Now traces of it can be seen in North Korea as well. North Korean leader Kim Jong-un's younger sister is a senior official in the ruling party and is playing an increasingly important role in supporting her brother's authoritarian rule and perpetuating the family dynasty that runs the country.
- There is always a great degree of mystery associated with bottles that contain messages and wash up on beaches and elsewhere, an idea further romanticised in Nicholas Sparks' novel, *Message in a Bottle*. A woman on vacation in Germany found what could perhaps be the oldest message in a bottle found to date. The bottle in question

contains a letter dated 1906 written by British marine biologist George Parker Bidder III.

- ✶ Prince William, the Duke of Cambridge and the elder son of Prince Charles and the late Lady Diana, has named his daughter Charlotte Elizabeth Diana, after her grandfather (Prince Charles), great grandmother (Queen Elizabeth) and grandmother (Lady Diana).
- ✶ The world's shortest man ever recorded, Chandra Bahadur Dangi, died from pneumonia in Nepal on September 3. He was 75. Dangi's height is listed in the Guinness World Records as 54.6 centimetres or 21.5 inches. Dangi was a primordial dwarf and broke the record of Gul Mohammed who was taller by 3 centimetres.

ART AND ENTERTAINMENT

- ✶ The common man lost his voice in the passing away of RK Laxman on January 26, 2015. Laxman's cartoons depicting the travails of the common Indian featured on the front page of *The Times of India* for more than five decades. The strips very effectively satirised Indian life and politics through the eyes of the 'Common Man' who stood for all Indians.
- ✶ After being engaged for around two years, Hollywood star Johnny Depp married actress Amber Heard on February 3 at their LA home. The two had met on the sets of *The Rum Diary*.
- ✶ Popular English actor and producer, Benedict Cumberbatch, married theatre director Sophie Hunter on February 13, 2015. The private ceremony took place at Church of St. Peter and St. Paul in Mottistone, located on the Isle of Wight in England.

- ✶ You have to watch your step, and more so if you're on stage, as singing sensation Madonna learned to her dismay. Madonna fell off the stage during her performance at the Brit Awards in London on February 25. Madonna was performing her new song *Living for Love* when she failed to loosen the cape from her matador costume before her dancers pulled it away.
- ✶ The author of the immensely popular Pulitzer prize-winning novel, *To Kill a Mockingbird*, Harper Lee, was in the news when it was announced in February that a sequel to her popular novel would be published 55 years after the first book. The new book,

Go Set a Watchman, a sequel by release date only, was written in the mid-1950s and is believed to be the first draft for Mockingbird.

★ Well-known Indian artist, Amrita Sher-Gil's self-portrait, painted when she was 19, sold for $2.92 million at an auction at Sotheby's, in New York, the highest ever for an Indian woman artist. Amrita, often referred to as India's Frida Kahlo, is one of the most eminent Indian painters and also one of the most expensive. Daughter of a Punjabi Sikh father and a Hungarian Jewish mother, Amrita died in 1941 at the young age of 28.

★ Bollywood weddings always grab headlines and the most talked-about Bollywood event of the year was the wedding of Shahid Kapoor and Delhi girl, Mira Rajput. And for those not invited to the wedding, there was social media, which put up enough updates and photographs of the various functions so that no one felt left out!

★ Superstar Salman Khan attempted to get into people's good books with his performance in the syrupy sweet tearjerker, *Bajrangi Bhaijaan*, even as he was in the law's bad books with a court judgement dated May 6 that sentenced him to five years in jail for killing a homeless man in a hit-and-run driving incident in Mumbai, in 2002. However, the Bombay High Court suspended the sentence and granted him bail till his appeal was decided and Salman was out of jail soon after. The speed of the exit was debated widely in the media.

BUSINESS

★ Time for some backslapping for Indians. Three Indian CEOs now run three of the biggest names in the global tech sector. This August, Sundar Pichai was named CEO of Google, joining Microsoft's Satya Nadella and Nokia's Rajeev Suri. Coincidentally, both Nadella and Suri have studied engineering at the Manipal Institute of Technology in Karnataka.

★ A prominent player in the healthcare sector, Shivinder Mohan Singh, and co-founder of one of India's foremost hospital chains, Fortis Healthcare Ltd., has decided to answer his inner calling at 40 and serve at the spiritual retreat Radha Soami Satsang Beas.

★ The flamboyant head of the United Breweries Group, Vijay Mallya, had further surprises in store for him in 2015. In an attempt to recover the

Rs. 6,800 crore that had been lent to him, a 17-member bank consortium took over the Kingfisher Airlines headquarters at Vile Parle in Mumbai. Spread over 17,000 square feet, Mallya's prized Kingfisher House is valued at Rs. 100 crore and is one of the prime properties of the airline which was once considered the most luxurious in India until its grounding in October 2012 and cancellation of the flying permit two months later.

- Universities and their governing bodies have been much in the news in 2015. It started with the controversy surrounding the stepping down of Nobel Prize-winning economist, Amartya Sen, from the chancellorship of Nalanda University. Later in the year, the appointment of Gajendra Chauhan as chairman of the Film and Television Institute caused a storm with students up in arms against the decision. Gajendra is popularly known for his role as Yudhisthira in the epic TV serial *Mahabharata*, telecast many years ago. More recently, news of BJP leader Subramanian Swamy being offered the post of vice chancellor of Jawaharlal Nehru University got a mixed response. The current vice chancellor SK Sopory retires in January 2016.
- One of India's most prominent women bankers, Naina Lal Kidwai, will retire in December 2015 after a 13-year stint with Hong Kong and Shanghai Banking Corporation (HSBC). She took over as CEO of HSBC India in 2007 and as Chairman of HSBC India in 2009. Post-retirement, Naina hopes to work in the area of women empowerment.

SPORTS

- The cricket circuit saw a fair number of controversies being stumped. The foremost, of course, was the one surrounding Lalit Modi, the ex-Indian Premier League commissioner, who was accused of bid rigging, accepting kickbacks, betting, money laundering and more. Amidst all this, Modi was found to have left India. Caught up in the controversy were the external affairs minister, Sushma Swaraj, and the Rajasthan chief minister, Vasundhara Raje Scindia. The appointment of Jagmohan Dalmiya as BCCI president in March brought more controversy in its wake so his sudden passing away on September 20 shocked one and all. Shashank Manohar has since taken over as BCCI president.

- ✶ The Boxing Fight of the Century was won by American boxer Floyd Mayweather Junior. Floyd defeated Manny Pacquiao from the Philippines to win the unified World Welterweight title. The match was valued at 300 million US dollars and is considered the richest boxing match in history. However, two months later, the World Boxing Organisation stripped Floyd of his title after he failed to pay the $200,000 sanctioning fee that was required to be paid.
- ✶ India's star boxer, MC Mary Kom, will hang up her boxing gloves after the Olympic Games in Rio in 2016. Post retirement, the 32-year-old boxer will concentrate on her boxing academy at Imphal, Manipur. Mary Kom is India's star pugilist, and has won many laurels for the country including the bronze medal at the London Olympics in 2012.
- ✶ Bhakti Sharma, the Indian Open swimmer, swam 1.4 miles in 52 minutes in one degree celsius temperature in the Antarctic Ocean. Besides setting a world record, Bhakti is also the youngest in the world to achieve this feat and the first Asian girl to do so. Bhakti has swum in all the five oceans of the world, besides swimming in or across eight other seas and channels. She was also awarded the Tenzing Norgay National Adventure Award in 2010.
- ✶ Indian boxer, Vijender Singh, has turned professional and will not represent India anymore. Vijender who won the bronze medal at the 2008 Olympic games has signed a multi-year deal with Queensberry Promotions as he forays into the world of pro-boxing.
- ✶ The Indian mountaineering twins Tashi and Nungshi Malik conquered Mt Vinson Massif, the highest peak in Antarctica, thus becoming the first twins in the world to have climbed all the seven highest peaks in the seven continents of the world. These twins have certainly gone to great heights and they've gone to them together!
- ✶ You don't always land where you want to. Especially if you are in a gas balloon! Tory Bradley of the US and Leonid Tiukhtyaev of Russia made a trans-pacific crossing in their Two Eagles gas balloon surpassing the distance and duration records for straight gas balloons. While they started the journey from Japan on January 24, weather conditions pushed them to a landing in Mexico on January 31 instead of US or Canada as per their original flight plan.
- ✶ Sania Mirza was back in action and how. Sania created history by becoming the first Indian woman to win a Women's Doubles Grand Slam trophy as she clinched the Wimbledon title with Martina Hingis.

AWARDS

☑ **INTERNATIONAL AND NATIONAL AWARDS**

NOBEL PRIZE

On November 27, 1895, Swedish inventor and philanthropist Alfred Nobel signed his last will and testament according to which a large chunk of his fortune was to be used to award those who 'shall have conferred the greatest benefit to mankind.' In his will, Nobel wanted prizes to be awarded for outstanding contributions in the fields of chemistry, physics, literature, peace and physiology or medicine. In 1968, a prize for economics was also established and endowed by Sweden's central bank, Sveriges Riksbank. These prizes are awarded annually by the Royal Swedish Academy of Sciences, the Swedish Academy, the Karolinska Institute and the Norwegian Nobel Committee. Following are this year's awardees:

- The **Nobel Peace Prize 2015** was awarded to **National Dialogue Quartet** "for its decisive contribution to the building of a pluralistic democracy in Tunisia in the wake of the Jasmine Revolution of 2011".
- The **Nobel Prize in Physics 2015** was awarded jointly to Japanese physicist **Takaaki Kajita** and Canadian astrophysicist **Arthur B. McDonald** "for the discovery of neutrino oscillations, which shows that neutrinos have mass".
- The **Nobel Prize in Chemistry 2015** was awarded jointly to **Tomas Lindahl**, **Paul Modrich** and **Aziz Sancar** "for mechanistic studies of DNA repair".
- The **Nobel Prize in Physiology or Medicine 2015** was awarded with one half jointly to **William C. Campbell** and **Satoshi Õmura** "for their discoveries concerning a novel therapy against infections caused by roundworm parasites" and the other half to **Youyou Tu** "for her discoveries concerning a novel therapy against Malaria".
- The **Nobel Prize in Literature 2015** was awarded to Belarusian author and journalist **Svetlana Alexievich** "for her polyphonic writings, a monument to suffering and courage in our time".
- The **Sveriges Riksbank Prize in Economic Sciences in Memory of Alfred Nobel 2015** was awarded to **Angus Deaton** "for his analysis of consumption, poverty, and welfare".

National Bravery Awards

The National Bravery Awards are awarded to children who perform exceptional acts of bravery against all odds. The awards are announced on Children's Day and are presented before Republic Day.

- **Bharat Award:** Resham Fatma, 16, fought an acid attack by her uncle.
- **Geeta Chopra Award:** Gunjan Sharma, 14, saved 10 school kids in the school bus from kidnappers.
- **Sanjay Chopra Award:** Devesh Kumar, 16, for fighting off chain-snatchers.
- **Bapu Gaidhani Award:** Monika (posthumous); Rumoh Meto; Riya Chaudhary (posthumous)

Other recipients: Aqil Mohammad N K, Anjith. P, Gaurav Kumar Bharti (posthumous), Hiral Jitubhai Halpati, Midhun PP, Ripa Das, Zeal Jitendra Marathe, Rajdeep Das, Stevenson Lawriniang, Ashwini Bandu Ughade, Gaurav Kumar Bharti, L. Brainson Singh, Labhanshu, G. Tooldev Sharma, Mhonbeni Ezung, Mesak K. Remnalalnghaka (posthumous), Sahanesh R, Balram Dansena, Vishal Becharbhai Katosna.

The Ramon Magsaysay Award

This award, instituted in the name of the late Philippines president, celebrates service and contribution to the development of the community.

- Anshu Gupta, India
- Sanjiv Chaturvedi, India
- Kommaly Chanthavong, Laos
- Ligaya Fernando-Amilbangsa
- Kyaw Thu, Myanmar.

Dronacharya Awards

- Naval Singh (Athletics para-sports coach)
- Anoop Singh (Wrestling coach)
- Swatantar Raj Singh (Boxing coach)
- Nihar Ameen (Swimming coach)
- Harbans Singh (Athletics)

The Padma Awards

The 'Padmas', the Padma Vibhushan, Padma Bhushan and Padma Shri, are India's highest civilian awards, awarded for exceptional and distinguished service in all fields and disciplines.

Padma Vibhushan

- Politician LK Advani
- Punjab Chief Minister Prakash Singh Badal
- Veteran actors Dilip Kumar and Amitabh Bachchan
- Social worker Dr D Veerendra Heggade
- Religious leader Jagadguru Ramanandacharya Swami Rambhadracharya
- Scientist Malur Ramaswamy Srinivasan
- Lawyer Kottayan K. Venugopa
- Businessman Karim Al Hussaini Aga Khan.

Padma Bhushan

- Political scientist Dr Subhash C Kashyap
- Classical vocalist Dr (Pandit) Gokulotsavji Maharaj
- Endocrinologist Dr Ambrish Mithal
- Vocalist Sudha Ragunathan
- Lawyer Harish Salve
- Cardiologist Dr Ashok Seth
- Journalist Rajat Sharma
- Wrestler Satpal Singh
- Humanitarian Shivakumara Swami
- Geologist Dr Kharag Singh Valdiya
- Canadian-American Mathematician Prof Manjul Bhargava.

Foreigners who received the Padma Bhushan include David Frawley (American teacher), Bill Gates (Co-founder of Microsoft Foundation), Melinda Gates (Philanthropist) and Saichiro Misumi (Japanese Indologist).

Padma Shri

Seventy five Padma Shri award recipients include film-maker Sanjay Leela Bhansali, badminton player PV Sindhu, lyricist and screenwriter Prasoon Joshi, humourist and column writer Tarak Mehta, writer and satirist Dr. Gyan Chaturvedi and cartoonist Pran Kumar Sharma among others.

The Grammy Awards

This American music award celebrates excellence in music across genres, from pop and folk to classical.

- Record of the Year, Song of the Year: Sam Smith - *Stay With Me*
- Best New Artist; Best Pop Vocal Album: Sam Smith - *In The Lonely Hour*
- Album of the Year: Beck - *Morning Phase*
- Best Pop Duo/Group Performance: A Great Big World With Christina Aguilera - *Say Something*
- Best Pop Solo Performance: Pharrell Williams - *Happy (Live)*
- Best Rock Album: Beck - *Morning Phase*
- Best Rock Song: Paramore - *Ain't It Fun*

MTV Music Video Awards

- Video of the Year: Taylor Swift feat Kendrick Lamar - *Bad Blood*
- Best Female Video and Best Pop Video: Taylor Swift - *Blank Space*
- Best Male Video: Mark Ronson feat Bruno Mars - *Uptown Funk*
- Best Rock Video: Fall Out Boy - *Uma Thurman*
- Artist to Watch: Trap Queen - *Fetty Wap*
- Best Direction: Kendrick Lamar (directed by Colin Tilley & The Little Homies) - *Alright*

The Sangeet Natak Akademi Awards

The Sangeet Natak Akademi is the country's premier association for the arts. The Akademi Fellowship (Akademi Ratna Sadasyata) and Akademi Award (Akademi Puraskar) are the most coveted national honours conferred on performing artists, gurus and scholars of the performing arts.

Sangeet Natak Akademi fellowships for the year 2014.

- Musicologist SR Janakiraman
- Filmmaker MS Sathyu
- Indian classical singer Vijay Kichlu
- Musician Tulsidas Borkar

The General Council also selected 36 artists from the fields of music, dance, theatre and puppetry for the Sangeet Natak Akademi Awards (Akademi Puraskar) for the year 2014.

Pulitzer Prize

Joseph Pulitzer was one of the most influential journalists of the late 19th and early 20th centuries in America. The Pulitzer Prizes for journalism, books, music and letters were instituted at the Columbia University, as per his will, in 1914.

Eric Lipton of *The New York Times; The Wall Street Journal* staff; *The New York Times* staff; *St. Louis Post-Dispatch* photography staff.

The Man Booker Prize

Hungarian author **László Krasznahorkai** for his literary works including *The Melancholy of Resistance.*

National Awards for Films

- Best Feature Film: *Court*
- Best Hindi Film: *Queen*
- Best Actress: Kangana Ranaut for *Queen*
- Best Actor: Vijay for *Nanu Avanalla Avalu* (Kannada)
- Best Direction: Srijit Mukherji for *Chotushkone* (Bengali)
- Best Music: *Haider* (Hindi); *Nineteen Eighty Three* (Malayalam)
- Best Popular Film: *Mary Kom*

Rajiv Gandhi Khel Ratna

- Sania Mirza (Tennis)

Commonwealth Short Story Prize

This year's Commonwealth Short Story Award was won by **Jonathan Tel** for his short story *The Human Phonograph*. The regional winners came from Nigeria, India, Trinidad & Tobago, Fiji and the UK and include **Siddhartha Gigoo** from India, **Lesley Nneka Arimah** from Nigeria, **Kevin Jared Hosein** from Trinidad and Tobago, and **Mary Rokonadravu** from Fiji.

The Golden Globe

Presented by the Hollywood Foreign Press Association (HFPA), these awards honour the best talent in film and television.

- Best Motion Picture - Drama: *Boyhood*
- Best Motion Picture - musical or comedy: *The Grand Budapest Hotel*
- Best Director: Richard Linklater, *Boyhood*
- Best Actor - Drama: Eddie Redmayne, *The Theory of Everything*
- Best Actor - Musical or Comedy: Michael Keaton, *Birdman*
- Best Actress - Motion Picture Drama: Julianne Moore, S*till Alice*
- Best Actress - Musical or Comedy: Amy Adams, *Big Eyes*
- Best TV series - Drama: *The Affair*
- Best TV series - Comedy or Musical: *Transparent*
- Best Mini-Series or Motion Picture Made for TV: *Fargo*
- Best Actor - Drama: Kevin Spacey, *House of Cards*
- Best Actress - Drama: Ruth Wilson, *The Affair*

Dhyan Chand Awards

- Romeo James (Hockey)
- Shiv Prakash Mishra (Tennis)
- TPP Nair (Volleyball)

The Laureus World Sports Awards

- World Sportsman of the Year: Novak Djokovic
- World Sportswoman of the Year: Genzebe Dibaba
- Laureus World Breakthrough of the Year Award: Daniel Ricciardo
- Laureus Comeback of the Year Award: Schalk Burger
- Laureus Sportsperson With a Disability: Tatyana McFadden.
- Team of the Year: Germany National Men's Football Team

FIFA Awards 2014

- FIFA Ballon d'Or Player of the Year: Cristiano Ronaldo
- FIFA Women's World Player of the Year: Nadine Kessler
- FIFA World Coaches of the Year for Men: German coach Joachim Low and compatriot
- FIFA World Coaches of the Year for Women: Ralf Kellermann

Dadasaheb Phalke Award

This year the award was given to veteran actor Shashi Kapoor.

The Oscars

Commonly known as the Oscars, the Academy Awards of Merit are awarded by the Academy of Motion Picture Arts and Sciences in Los Angeles for excellence in cinematic achievements in 24 categories. Instituted in 1929, they are the oldest media awards in the world.

- Best Picture, Best Director, Best Original Screenplay and Best Cinematography: *Birdman*
- Best Original Score, Achievement in Costume Design, Achievement in Makeup and Hairstyling and Best Production Design: *The Grand Budapest Hotel.*
- Best Actor: Eddie Redmayne, *The Theory of Everything.*
- Best Actress: Julianne Moore, *Still Alice.*

Arjuna Awards

- Naib Subedar Sandeep Kumar (Archery)
- M.R. Poovamma (Athletics)
- Kidambi Srikanth Nammalwar (Badminton)
- Mandeep Jangra (Boxing)
- Rohit Sharma (Cricket)
- Dipa Karmakar (Gymnastics)
- Sreejesh P.R. (Hockey)
- Manjeet Chhillar (Kabaddi)
- Abhilasha Shashikant Mhatre (Kabaddi)
- Sawarn Singh (Rowing)
- Anup Kumar Yama (Roller Skating)
- Jitu Rai (Shooting)
- S. Sathish Kumar (Weightlifting)
- Bajrang (Wrestling)
- Babita Kumari (Wrestling)
- Yumnam Sanathoi Devi (Wushu)
- Sharath M. Gayakwad (Para-Swimming)

Ashok Chakra

Major Mukund Varadarajan and Naik Neeraj Kumar laid down their lives while battling groups of militants in separate operations in Shopian and Kupwara districts of Kashmir respectively.

Tenzing Norgay National Adventure Awards

- Mountaineer Jot Singh (Indo-Tibetan Border Police)
- Ms. Arunima Sinha (Mountaineering)
- Wg. Cdr. Paramveer Singh (Aqua Sport)
- Lt. Col Satyendra Verma (Skydiving)
- Col. Satish Chander Sharma (Mountaineering)

MISCELLANEOUS AWARDS

- Indian scientist CNR Rao conferred Japan's highest award the Order of the Rising Sun, Gold and Silver Star.
- Distinguished journalist Vinod Mehta awarded the Yash Bharati Samman by the UP government.
- Filmmaker Adoor Gopalakrishnan awarded second Bishwaratna Dr. Bhupen Hazarika International Solidarity Award.

LITERARY AWARDS

- Indian author Anuradha Roy's novel *Sleeping on Jupiter* selected in the 2015 Man Booker Prize long list of 13 novels.
- Sanskrit scholar and author Prabhu Nath Dwivedi, chosen for the Sahitya Akademi Award for Sanskrit 2014.
- Eminent Hindi litterateur Kamal Kishore Goyanka, selected for the Vyas Samman for 2014 for his book *Premchand Kee Kahaniyo Kaa Kaalkramanusar.*
- Author Ali Smith chosen for the 2015 Baileys Prize (earlier known as Orange Prize) for the novel, *How to be Both.*

ART AWARDS

- Renowned Indian artist Syed Hyder Raza, conferred with the highest French civilian honour, the Commandeur de la Legion d'Honneur.

SPORTS AWARDS

- Former Indian hockey player Balbir Singh Senior, honoured with the Major Dhyanchand Lifetime Achievement Award.
- Former Indian cricket skipper Dilip Vengsarkar awarded the BCCI's Col. CK Nayudu Lifetime Achievement Award for 2013-2014.

BUSINESS AWARDS

- RBI Governor, Raghuram Rajan, named 'Governor of the Year' by the British magazine, *Central Banking.*

MUSIC AWARDS

- Renowned sarod maestro, Amjad Ali Khan, chosen for the Virasat award for 2015 instituted by Alva's Education Foundation.
- Music director duo, Pt. Shiv Kumar Sharma and Hariprasad Chaurasia, chosen for the Swaralaya Devarajan National Award for their contribution to the field of classical music.
- SP Balasubramaniam, the legendary playback singer, awarded the Harivarasanam Award instituted by the Kerala government.

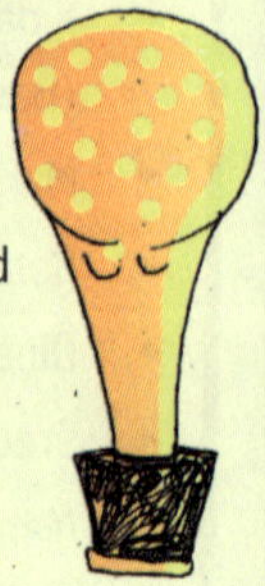

ENTERTAINMENT AWARDS

- Cinematographer in the Hindi and Marathi film industries Suryakant Lavande and veteran actress Shashikala awarded the V. Shantaram and Raj Kapoor Lifetime Achievement Awards.
- Indian actor Anil Kapoor along with Marathi actor Dilip Prabhavalkar awarded the prestigious Pandit Dinanath Mangeshkar Award 2015.

ENVIRONMENT AWARDS

- Renowned Indian ecologist, Madhav Gadgil, chosen for the prestigious 2015 Tyler Prize for Environmental Achievement, along with noted American marine ecologist Dr. Jane Lubchenc.
- Indian environmental activist, Rajendra Singh, chosen for the Stockholm Water Prize for his innovative water restoration efforts.

SCIENCE AND TECHNOLOGY

- Indian-origin scientist at the Massachusetts Institute of Technology, Sangeeta Bhatia, awarded the $2,50,000 Heinz award for her work in tissue engineering and disease detection.
- Co-creator of super heavy element 117 and professor at Saha Institute of Nuclear Physics, Susanta Lahiri, awarded the Hevesy Medal Award 2015.
- Mathematician from the Tata Institute of Fundamental Research, Amalendu Krishna, awarded the Ramanujan Prize for 2015.

INDIA

- ☑ INDIA
  - ☑ STATES AND UNION TERRITORIES
  - ☑ IMPORTANT OFFICE-HOLDERS
  - ☑ ORGANISATIONS AND COMMISSIONS
  - ☑ INDIAN POLITICS
  - ☑ OVERVIEW OF THE ECONOMY
  - ☑ COURT JUDGEMENTS
  - ☑ INDIAN HISTORY TIMELINE

Andhra Pradesh

- *Capital:* Hyderabad and Vijayawada; New capital to be located at Amaravathi
- *Date of formation:* October 1, 1953
- *Governor:* E.S.L. Narasimhan
- *Chief Minister:* Nara Chandrababu Naidu
- *Tourist attractions:* Visakhapatnam, Tirupati, Vijayawada, Nellore, Chittoor, Anantapur, Kurnool, Rajahmundry, Secunderabad, Bora caves, Araku valley

- *Festivals:* Sivaratri, Pongal, Vinayak Chaviti
- *Major dance and music forms:* Kuchipudi, Bhamakalpam, Dappu
- *Arts and crafts:* Kalamkari cotton, the Nakashis of Cheriyal village paint vibrantly coloured scrolls.
- *Languages:* Telugu, Urdu, English
- *Size:* 160,205 sq. km

- *Population:* 49,386,799
- *Rivers:* Godavari, Krishna, Wainganga, Tungabhadra, Chitravati, Musi, Banda, Papagni
- *Forests and wildlife sanctuaries:* Shivaram WS, Manjira WS, Nagarjunasagar-Srisailam
- *State animal:* Black buck
- *State bird:* Indian roller
- *State flower:* Water lily
- *State tree:* Neem
- Major crops: Jowar, rice, bajra

Factoids

- The Nehru Zoological Park established in 1959 is the biggest zoo in India.
- Cured and dried goatskin is coloured with vegetable dyes to make Tholu Bommalatta or leather puppets.

Arunachal Pradesh

- *Capital*: Itanagar
- *Date of formation*: February 20, 1987
- *Governor*: Jyoti Prashad Rajkhowa
- *Chief Minister*: Nabam Tuki
- *Tourist attractions:* Twang Hompa, Dirang, Bomdila
- *Festivals*: Losar, Si-Donyi, Reh, Mopin and Solung

- *Major dance and music forms*: Lion and Peacock dance, Ponung, Roppi, Wancho dance
- *Arts and crafts*: Monpas are especially good wood carvers, women in AP are expert weavers.
- *Languages*: Monpa, Miki, Aka, Sherdukpen, Apatani, Adi, Hill Miri
- *Size*: 83,743 sq. km
- *Population*: 1,383,727
- *Rivers:* Siang, Lohit, Kameg, Dikrong, Tirap, Dibang, Subansiri, Noa-Dihing, Kamlang
- *Forests and wildlife sanctuaries:* Namdapha NP, Monling NP
- *State animal:* Mithun
- *State bird*: Great Indian hornbill
- *State flower:* Foxtail orchid
- *State tree*: Hollong
- *Major crops*: Jhum

Factoids

- The mithun is considered a unit of wealth and is allowed to roam free till it is sacrificed and eaten on special occasions.
- Monpas, who are Buddhists, live in the mountains of western Arunachal Pradesh.

ASOM

- *Capital*: Dispur
- *Date of formation*: January 26, 1950
- *Governor*: Padmanabha Balakrishna Acharya
- *Chief Minister*: Tarun Gogoi
- *Tourist attractions:* Kamakhya temple, Umananda (Peacock Island), Navagraha (temple of nine planets), Basistha Ashram
- *Festivals*: Bihu, Sivaratri Mela, Baishagu
- *Major dance and music forms*: Bihu
- *Arts and crafts*: Jappi (traditional hat), toys made of clay, cork, wood and bamboo. Satras or monasteries to preserve art and culture.
- *Languages*: Assamese, Bodo, Karbi, Bengali
- *Size*: 78,438 sq. km
- *Population*: 31,205,570
- *Rivers:* Brahmaputra, Manas, Subansiri, Sonai
- *Forests and wildlife sanctuaries:* Kaziranga NP, Manas NP, Orang Sanctuary
- *State animal:* One-horned rhinoceros
- *State bird*: White-winged wood duck
- *State flower:* Foxtail orchid
- *State tree:* Hollong
- *Major crops*: Rice, jute, tea

Factoids

- It's name changed to Asom, in 2006.
- Tezpur was called the 'city of blood' after a mythical battle between Shiva and Vishnu filled it with blood.

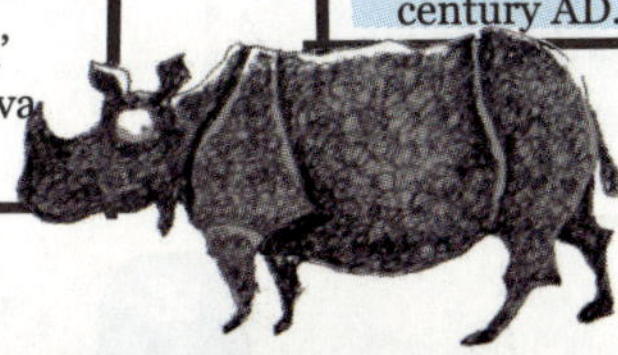

BIHAR

- *Capital*: Patna
- *Date of formation*: January 26, 1950
- *Governor*: Ram Nath Kovind
- *Chief Minister*: Nitish Kumar
- *Tourist attractions:* Rajgir, Nalanda, Vaishali, Pawapuri, Bodh Gaya, Vikramshila, Gaya, the ancient city of Pataliputra
- *Festivals*: Chatth Puja, Sama-Chakeva, Nag Panchami
- *Major dance and music forms*: Jat-Jatin dance of the Mithila region, Bidesia, the songs of Vidyapati, Chau Tribal dances
- *Arts and crafts*: Madhubani painting; Madhubani's marsh 'sikki' grass is used to make baskets, toys, dolls etc; Sujini kantha embroidery is a specialisation of Bihar.
- *Languages*: Hindi, Urdu, Santhali
- *Size*: 94,163 sq. km
- *Population*: 104, 099,452
- *Rivers:* Kosi, Ganga, Saryu, Gandak, Kamla, Panar, Saura, Pun-pun
- *Forests and wildlife sanctuaries:* Valmiki NP, Rajgir WS, Bhimbandh WS, Gautam Buddha WS, Udayapur WS
- *State animal:* Gaur
- *State bird*: Indian roller
- *State flower:* Kachnar
- *State tree:* Peepal
- *Major crops*: Paddy, wheat, maize

Factoids

- A peepal or bodhi tree in Bodh Gaya marks the spot where the Buddha achieved enlightenment.
- Nalanda University, a seat of Buddhist learning, was founded around the 5th century AD.

Chhattisgarh

- *Capital*: Raipur
- *Date of formation*: November 1, 2000
- *Governor*: Balram Das Tandon
- *Chief Minister*: Dr. Raman Singh
- *Tourist attractions:* Bastar, Chitrakote Falls, Kailash and Kutumsar Caves, Mahamaya Temple.

- *Festivals*: Pola, Nawakhai, Dussehra, Deepavali, Holi, Govardhan Pooja
- *Major dance and music forms*: Panthi, Raut Nacha and Soowa dances; Sohar, Bihav and Pathoni songs
- *Arts and crafts*: Iron crafting, lost wax method of metal casting, bhittichitras or murals.

- *Languages*: Hindi, Oriya, Marathi, Chhattisgarhi, Gondi, Korku
- *Size*: 1,35,191 sq. km
- *Population*: 25,545,198
- *Rivers:* Mahanadi, Indravati, Son, Pairi, Hasdo, Sabari

- *Forests and wildlife sanctuaries:* Kankerghati NP, Indravati NP, Kanger Valley NP
- *State animal:* Wild buffalo
- *State bird*: Hill myna
- *State tree*: Sal
- *Major crops*: Rice, wheat, niger

Factoids

- The ancient caves of Kutumsar, Kailash and Dandak in the Kanger forest have stunning limestone formations or stalagmites and stalactites.
- Approximately 90 languages and dialects are spoken in this state.

Goa

- *Capital*: Panaji
- *Date of formation*: May 30, 1987
- *Governor*: Mridula Sinha
- *Chief Minister*: Laxmikant Parsekar
- *Tourist attractions:* Anjuna, Arambol, Basilica of Bom Jesus, Se Cathedral

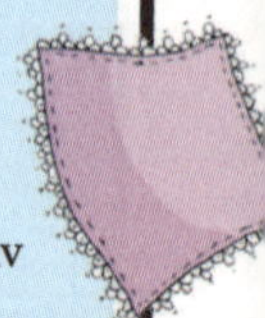

- *Festivals*: Carnival, Feast of St. Francis Xavier, Shigmotsav
- *Major dance and music forms*: Shigmo dance, Manddo, Durpod
- *Arts and crafts*: Terracotta or baked clay figurines, utensils etc; crochet tablecloths, curtains, covers, handkerchiefs; cane and bamboo fish traps, mats, baskets.

- *Languages*: Konkani, Marathi
- *Size*: 3,702 sq. km
- *Population*: 1,458,545
- *Rivers:* Mandovi, Zuari, Terekhol, Chapora, Sal, Talpona
- *Forests and wildlife sanctuaries:* Bondla WS, Morlem NP, Dr Salim Ali Bird Sanctuary, Cotigoa WS, Bhagwan Mahavir WS
- *State animal:* Gaur
- *State bird*: Black-crested bulbul
- *State tree:* Asna
- *Major crops*: Paddy, ragi, maize, cashew

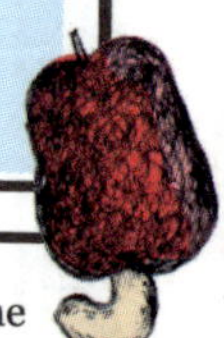

Factoids

- The Basilica of Bom Jesus holds the tomb of St Francis Xavier.
- Goa, Daman and Diu were liberated in 1961 and officially became a part of India in 1962.

GUJARAT

- *Capital*: Gandhinagar
- *Date of formation*: May 1, 1960
- *Governor*: O P Kohli
- *Chief Minister*: Anandiben Patel
- *Tourist attractions:* Gir NP, Somnath Temple, Dwarka, Palitana
- *Festivals*: Navratri, Kite Festival, Kutch Utsav
- *Major dance and music forms*: Bhavai
- *Arts and crafts*: Bandhani or tie-and-dye fabric; woven Patola fabric; rich embroidery by the Rabari tribals including Soof embroidery.
- *Languages*: Gujarati
- *Size*: 1,96,024 sq. km
- *Population*: 60,439,692
- *Rivers:* Sabarmati, Mahi, Narmada, Tapti, Banas, Saraswati, Damanganga
- *Forests and wildlife sanctuaries:* Gir NP, Wild Ass Sanctuary Kutchch, Nal Sarovar Bird Sanctuary, Velavadhar NP, Vansda NP
- *State animal:* Asiatic Lion
- *State bird*: Greater flamingo
- *State flower*: Galgota
- *State tree*: Mango
- *Major crops*: Groundnuts, cotton, tobacco

Factoids

- It is possible to climb down the richly carved step-wells or vavs of Gujarat.
- The ancient fort Uparkot was first built by the Mauryas.

HARYANA

- *Capital*: Chandigarh
- *Date of formation*: November 1, 1966
- *Governor*: Kaptan Singh Solanki
- *Chief Minister*: Manohar Lal
- *Tourist attractions:* Sultanpur NP, Rock Gardens
- *Festivals*: Gugga Naumi, Lohri, Basant Panchmi
- *Major dance and music forms*: Sarangi/Ras Leela, Phag Dance
- *Arts and crafts*: Shoes called tilla or kasuri juttis are made from buffalo and goat hide; panja dhurries
- *Languages*: Hindi, Punjabi, Urdu
- *Size*: 44,212 sq. km
- *Population*: 25,351,462
- *Rivers:* Yamuna, Ghaggar
- *Forests and wildlife sanctuaries:* Sultanpur NP, Kalesar NP, Simbalawara WS
- *State animal:* Blackbuck
- *State bird*: Black francolin
- *State flower:* Lotus
- *State tree*: Peepal
- *Major crops*: Sugarcane, groundnut, paddy, maize

Factoids

- Many invaders like the Huns and Alexander's army swept through Haryana.
- Gugga Naumi is a festival that is observed by both Hindus and Muslims. It honours Gugga Pir who could cure snake bites.

Himachal Pradesh

- *Capital*: Shimla
- *Date of formation*: January 25, 1971
- *Governor*: Acharya Dev Vrat
- *Chief Minister*: Virbhadra Singh
- *Tourist attractions:* Shimla, Kulu, Manali, Dharamsala
- *Festivals*: Pori, Fulaich
- *Major dance and music forms*: Mala dance, Rakshas Dance
- *Arts and crafts*: Pahari painting is done in the Basohli and Kangra styles; Kullu shawls and woollen caps are famous; the Chamba Rumal has Kangra style paintings embroidered on cloth.
- *Languages*: Hindi, Punjabi, Kinnauri, Pahari

- *Size*: 55,673 sq. km
- *Population*: 6,864,602
- *Rivers:* Ravi, Beas, Chenab, Sutlej, Yamuna
- *Forests and wildlife sanctuaries:* Pin Valley NP, Greater Himalayan NP, Renuka WS, Chail WS, Kalatope Khajjiar WS

- *State animal:* Snow leopard
- *State bird*: Western tragopan
- *State flower:* Pink rhododendron
- *State tree:* Deodar
- *Major crops*: Wheat, rice, maize, barley

Factoids

- The world's oldest democracy is believed to be a tiny, isolated village called Malana.
- Shimla was the summer capital of British India.

Jammu and Kashmir

- *Capital*: Srinagar (summer), Jammu (winter)
- *Date of formation*: October 26, 1947
- *Governor*: Narinder Nath Vohra
- *Chief Minister*: Mufti Mohammad Sayeed
- *Tourist attractions:* Dal Lake, Shalimar Bagh, Pahalgam Gulmarg, Vaishno Devi, Ladakh
- *Festivals*: Tihar, Navroz, Eid, Urs, Shab-e-Miraj

- *Major dance and music forms*: Kudd, Dogri/Pahari music, Hafixa, Bacha/Nagma dance
- *Arts and crafts*: Kar-i-kalamdan or the art of making lacquered pen cases out of paper pulp is a famous handicraft industry; Kashida embroidery.
- *Languages*: Urdu, Hindi, Punjabi, Dogri, Kashmiri, Balti, Ladakhi, Purig, Gurji, Dadri

- *Size*: 222,236 sq. km
- *Population*: 12,541,302
- *Rivers:* Chenab, Jhelum, Indus, Zanskar, Suru, Nubra, Shyok
- *Forests and wildlife sanctuaries:* Dachigam NP, Hemis High Altitude NP
- *State animal:* Hangul
- *State bird*: Black-necked crane
- *State flower:* Lotus
- *State tree:* Chinar
- *Major crops*: Paddy, wheat, fruit, saffron

Factoids

- The hangul or Kashmiri stag is the only species of European red deer found in India.
- In Ladakh, they believe in Bon which is an animistic religion in which the forces of nature are worshipped.

Jharkhand

- *Capital*: Ranchi
- *Date of formation*: November 15, 2000
- *Governor*: Draupadi Murmu
- *Chief Minister*: Raghubar Das
- *Tourist attractions:* Dassam Falls, Sun Temple, Birsa Zoological Park, Jamshedpur Industrial Area
- *Festivals*: Basant Panchami, Chhat Puja
- *Major dance and music forms*: Agni and Jhumar dances
- *Arts and crafts*: Large colourful masks made from the dark clay taken from the banks of the River Khakai; Jadu Patua is a form of scroll painting.
- *Languages*: Hindi, Urdu, Santhali
- *Size*: 79,714 sq. km
- *Population*: 32,988,134
- *Rivers:* Aon, Kosi, Ghagra
- *Forests and wildlife sanctuaries:* Betla (Palmau) NP, Hazaribagh Wildlife Sanctuary
- *State animal:* Elephant
- *State bird*: Asian koel
- *State flower:* Palash
- *State tree:* Sal
- *Major crops*: Paddy, wheat, maize

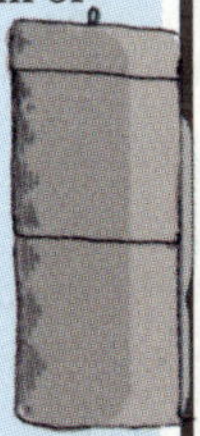

Factoids

- Dhanbad is also known as India's coal capital.
- Jharkhand's original inhabitants, the adivasis, revolted against British exploitation of their forests.

Karnataka

- *Capital*: Bengaluru
- *Date of formation*: November 1, 1973
- *Governor*: Vajubhai Vala
- *Chief Minister*: K Siddaramaiah
- *Tourist attractions:* Mysore City Palace, Chamundi Hill, Stone Chariot in Hampi
- *Festivals*: Kar Hunnive, Hampi Utsav
- *Major dance and music forms*: Simha Nutrya, Yakshagana
- *Arts and crafts*: Bidri; Chitragars' wood chiselling; specialised card game Ganjifa.
- *Languages*: Kannada, Kodava, Tulu
- *Size*: 191,791 sq. km
- *Population*: 61,095,297
- *Rivers:* Krishna, Tungabhadra, Cauvery, Kabini
- *Forests and wildlife sanctuaries:* Bandipur WS, Nagarhole NP, Mudumalai NP
- *State animal:* Elephant
- *State bird*: Indian roller
- *State flower:* Lotus
- *State tree:* Sandal
- *Major crops*: Rice, jowar, coffee

Factoids

- Another name for Karnataka is Karunadu.
- The central dome of Muhammad Adil Shah's tomb, the Gol Gumbaz of Bijapur, is the second largest in the world.

Kerala

- *Capital*: Thiruvananthapuram
- *Date of formation*: November 1, 1956
- *Governor*: P Sathasivam
- *Chief Minister*: Oommen Chandy
- *Tourist attractions:* Kovalam, Wayanad, Kannur
- *Festivals*: Snake Boat Races, Chinakathoor, Dharani Dance Festival
- *Major dance and music forms*: Mohiniyattam, Kathakali, Kalaripayattu
- *Arts and crafts*: Kalamezhuthu paintings; Murals in temples using 'pure' colours such as white, red, black, green and ochre; Bell metal idols, lamps etc.
- *Languages*: Malayalam
- *Size*: 38,863 sq. km
- *Population*: 33,406,061
- *Rivers:* Periyar, Bharathapuzha
- *Forests and wildlife sanctuaries:* Periyar NP, Wayanad NP, Silent Valley NP
- *State animal:* Elephant
- *State bird*: Great Indian hornbill
- *State flower:* Kanikonna or Indian laburnum or amaltas
- *State tree:* Coconut
- *Major crops*: Coconut, rubber, tea, coffee

Factoids

- Edakkal caves in Ammukutty Mountain have petroglyphs or rock carvings and are believed to have been made by Neolithic men.
- Believed to be the oldest of all martial art forms, Kalaripayattu gets its name from 'kalari' or school and 'payattu' or practice.

Madhya Pradesh

- *Capital*: Bhopal
- *Date of formation*: November 1, 1956
- *Governor*: Ram Naresh Yadav
- *Chief Minister*: Shivraj Singh Chouhan
- *Tourist attractions:* Sanchi Stupa, Gwalior Fort, Orchha Fort, Khajuraho, Ujjain
- *Festivals*: Gana-Gour, Ganga, Dashami, Hareli
- *Major dance and music forms*: Gaur Dance, Muria Dance, Relo Songs
- *Arts and crafts*: Wall paintings or bhittichitras; Chippas or hand-block printers; battubai dolls.
- *Languages*: Hindi
- *Size*: 308,144 sq. km
- *Population*: 72, 626,809
- *Rivers:* Narmada, Tapti, Betwa, Son, Chambal
- *Forests and wildlife sanctuaries:* Bandhavgarh NP, Kanha NP, Pench NP, Indrawati Tiger Reserve, Kheoni WS
- *State animal:* Swamp Deer
- *State bird*: Paradise fly-catcher
- *Major crops*: Rice, wheat, soybeans, spices

Factoids

- One half of Bhawani Mandi station on the Mumbai-Delhi railway line lies in Madhya Pradesh and the other half lies in Rajasthan.
- Pench and Kanha forests in the Satpura ranges, and Bandhavgarh in the Vindhyas, are all tiger reserves.

Maharashtra

- *Capital*: Mumbai
- *Date of formation*: May 1, 1960
- *Governor*: Chennamaneni Vidyasagar Rao
- *Chief Minister*: Devendra Fadnavis
- *Tourist attractions:* Gateway of India, Murud-Janjira Fort, Elephanta Island, Aurangabad Caves
- *Festivals*: Makar Sankranti, Ganesh Chaturthi
- *Major dance and music forms*: Vasudev Dance, Lavni Dance, Dhangari Gaja
- *Arts and crafts*: People of the Warli tribe create ritualistic paintings on cowdung-plastered walls; Paithani saris; Mashru and Himroo fabrics
- *Languages*: Marathi
- *Size*: 307,713 sq. km
- *Population*: 1,12,374,333
- *Rivers:* Godavari, Penganga, Bhima, Varna, Parvara, Mula
- *Forests and wildlife sanctuaries:* Pench NP, Tadoba NP, Nagzira National Park, Nawegoan NP, Devlagaon NP, Gugamal NP.
- *State animal:* Giant squirrel
- *State bird*: Green imperial pigeon
- *State flower:* Jarul
- *State tree:* Mango
- *Major crops*: Paddy, wheat, sugarcane, oranges

Factoids

- Gharapuri, just outside Mumbai, has seven beautiful rock-cut caves carved between the 6th and 7th centuries AD.
- Kolis were among the first residents of the archipelago or arc of seven islands that later became Mumbai.

Manipur

- *Capital*: Imphal
- *Date of formation*: January 21, 1972
- *Governor*: V. Shanmuganathan
- *Chief Minister*: Okram Ibobi Singh
- *Tourist attractions*: Loktak Lake, Sendra Island
- *Festivals*: Heikru Hitongba Boat Races, Baruni
- *Major dance and music forms*: Ras Lila, Lai Haroba, Nongdai Jagoi
- *Arts and crafts*: Bamboo baskets, fish traps, mats, umbrellas, musical instruments etc.
- *Languages*: Manipuri, Thado, Tankhul
- *Size*: 22,327 sq. km
- *Population*: 2,570,390
- *Rivers:* Manipur, Barak
- *Forests and wildlife sanctuaries:* Keibul Lamjao NP, Khonghampat Orchidarium
- *State animal:* Sangai deer
- *State bird*: Nongyeen
- *State flower:* Siroi lily
- *State tree*: Uningthou
- *Major crops*: Paddy, wheat, maize, pulses

Factoids

- The Pung is the Manipuri version of the Mridanga, an ancient drum and is played during the Ras Lila.
- Imphal has an all-women's market or Ima Keithel.

Meghalaya

- *Capital*: Shillong
- *Date of formation*: April 2, 1970
- *Governor*: V Shanmuganathan
- *Chief Minister*: Mukul Sangma
- *Tourist attractions:* Cherrapunji Garo Hills, Tura, Butterfly Museum, Central Museum
- *Festivals*: Wangala (Harvest Festival), Shad Nongkrem
- *Major dance and music forms*: Shad Sukmynsiem, Shad Nongkrem and Doregata dances
- *Arts and crafts*: Endi silk is used to make colourful wraps and shawls; baskets known as khok and thugis are commonly woven; cone shaped bamboo rain shields known as knup are also popular.
- *Languages*: Khasi, Garo, Jaintia, Bengali, Assamese, English
- *Size*: 22,429 sq. km
- *Population*: 2,964,007
- *Rivers:* Simsang, Manda, Darming, Ringge, Gamol, Bugi
- *Forests and wildlife sanctuaries:* Nokrek NP, Balpakram NP, Nongkhyllem WS, Nokrek Biosphere Reserve, Siju Bird Sanctuary
- *State animal:* Clouded leopard
- *State bird*: Hill myna
- *State flower:* Lady slipper orchid
- *State tree:* Gamhar
- *Major crops*: Potato, cotton, pineapple, orange

Mizoram

- *Capital*: Aizawl
- *Date of formation*: February 20, 1987
- *Governor*: Lt. Gen. Nirbhay Sharma
- *Chief Minister*: Lal Thanhawla
- *Tourist attractions:* Phawngpui, Sibuta Lung, Philpui Grave, Pangzawl
- *Festivals*: Chapchar Kut, Mim Kut, Pawl Kut
- *Major dance and music forms*: Khal Lam, Chai, Chhilam, Sawlkin
- *Arts and crafts*: Puan; cane and bamboo baskets, pipes, toys that utilise the natural elasticity of bamboo
- *Languages*: Lushai, Mizo, Bengali, Lakher
- *Size*: 21,081 sq. km
- *Population*: 1,097,206
- *Rivers:* Tlwang, Tlau, Chhimtuipui, Tuichang, Tuirial,
- *Forests and wildlife sanctuaries:* Lengteng WS, Murlen NP, Phawngpui NP, Thorangtlang WS
- *State animal:* Serow
- *State bird*: Hume's bartailed pheasant
- *State flower:* Dancing Girl orchid
- *State tree:* Nag Kesar
- *Major crops*: Paddy, wheat, bamboo, oil palm

Factoids

- Nartiang in Jaintia Hills has a cluster of megaliths and monoliths.
- Garos celebrate a good harvest with Wangala, or the dance of Hundred Drums, in November.

Factoids

- Cheraw or the bamboo dance is a popular form of dancing.
- Pukzing cave, near Aizawl stands at 25 m. Legends say that Mualzavata, a very strong man, carved it out with a hair pin.

Nagaland

- *Capital*: Kohima
- *Date of formation*: Dec. 1, 1963
- *Governor*: P B Acharya
- *Chief Minister*: T. R. Zeliang
- *Tourist attractions:* World War II Cemetery, Kohima Village (Bara Basti), State Museum
- *Festivals*: Moatsu harvest festival, Sekrenyi, Sankarni
- *Major dance and music forms*: Nruirolians (Cock dance), Temangnetin (Fly dance)
- *Arts and crafts*: Naga baskets; cup violin made using bamboo and a gourd; bamboo trumpet
- *Languages*: Ao, Sema, Konyak, Angami, Chakhesang, Chang, Khiamniungan, Kuki
- *Size*: 16,579 sq. km
- *Population*: 1,978,502
- *Rivers:* Milak, Barak, Dhansiri, Doyang, Dikhu, Zungki, Tizu
- *Forests and wildlife sanctuaries:* Intanki NP
- *State animal:* Mithun
- *State bird*: Blyth's tragopan
- *State flower:* Rhododendron
- *State tree:* Alder
- *Major crops*: Rice, maize, millet, rubber

Factoids

- 360 orchid species are found on peaks like Saramati and in low-lying areas.
- The Angami festival of Sekrenyi is celebrated after harvest.

Odisha

- *Capital*: Bhubhaneshwar
- *Date of formation*: August 15, 1947
- *Governor*: S.C. Jamir
- *Chief Minister*: Naveen Patnaik
- *Tourist attractions:* Sun Temple, Konark, Puri, Taptapani
- *Festivals*: Rathyatra, Dol Jatra, Patua Jatra, Chandak Puja
- *Major dance and music forms*: Oddissi, Chitrapada, Dhrubapada, Panchal
- *Arts and crafts*: Pattachitras or palm-leaf ganjifa cards; intricate combs made using bamboo, lac and fabric; Sambalpuri double ikat.
- *Languages*: Oriya
- *Size*: 1,55,707 sq. km
- *Population*: 41,974,218
- *Rivers*: Mahanadi, Baitarni, Brahmani, Tel, Pushkulyam Sabari
- *Forests and wildlife sanctuaries:* Chilka Lake Sanctuary, Simlipal NP, Bhitarkanika WS
- *State animal:* Sambhar
- *State bird*: Blue jay
- *State flower:* Ashoka
- *State tree:* Ashwatha or peepal
- *Major crops*: Paddy, wheat, ragi, maize

Factoids

- The 33 sandstone caves on the Udaygiri and Khandagiri hills in Bhubaneshwar were probably carved under King Kharavela.
- Odisha has 62 tribes including the Santhals, Savaras, Juangs, Gonds, Bondas etc.

PUNJAB

- *Capital*: Chandigarh
- *Date of formation*: January 26, 1950
- *Governor*: Kaptan Singh Solanki
- *Chief Minister*: Parkash Singh Badal
- *Tourist attractions:* Golden Temple, Jallianwalla Bagh, Rock Garden, Leisure Valley

- *Festivals*: Lohri, Baisakhi, Gurpurab
- *Major dance and music forms*: Bhangra dance and music
- *Arts and crafts*: Phulkari or flower embroidery; wood inlay of Hoshiarpur on black shisham wood.

- *Languages*: Punjabi
- *Size*: 50,362 sq. km
- *Population*: 27,743, 338
- *Rivers:* Beas, Sutlej, Ravi
- *Forests and wildlife sanctuaries:* Bir Moti Bagh, Bir Bhunderhari, Bir Dosanjh
- *State animal:* Blackbuck
- *State bird*: Eastern goshawk
- *State tree:* Shisham
- *Major crops*: Wheat, gram, barley, oil seeds

Factoids

- Sikhism, founded by Guru Nanak, is a dominant religion in Punjab. The word 'Sikh' means a 'learner'.
- The first person to give Punjab its independence was Banda Singh Bahadur.

RAJASTHAN

- *Capital*: Jaipur
- *Date of formation*: November 1, 1956
- *Governor*: Kalyan Singh
- *Chief Minister*: Vasundhara Raje

- *Tourist attractions:* Mount Abu, Jaipur Palace, Hawa Mahal, Jaisalmer Fort, Ranthambore, Pushkar
- *Festivals*: Teej, Gangaur festival, Bikaner festival, Marwar festival
- *Major dance and music forms*: Ghoomar and Kalbeliya dances; Kathputali puppet theatre; Bhopa
- *Arts and crafts*: Rajasthani miniature paintings such as Kangra, Jodhpur, Jaipur etc; Pichhvai paintings; hand-block printing; Panihari music
- *Languages*: Rajasthani, Hindi
- *Size*: 3,42,239 sq. km
- *Population*: 68,548,437
- *Rivers:* Luni, Banas, Kali Sindh, Chambal
- *Forests and wildlife sanctuaries:* Sariska Tiger Reserve, Keoladeo Ghana NP, Ranthambore NP, Dhawa WS
- *State animal:* Chinkara
- *State bird*: Great Indian bustard
- *State flower:* Rohira
- *State tree:* Khejri
- *Major crops*: Jowar, pulses, maize, gram

Factoids

- Jaipur's Elephant Festival has a tug-of-war between humans and elephants.
- Bikaner has a Karni Mata temple in which rats are worshipped.

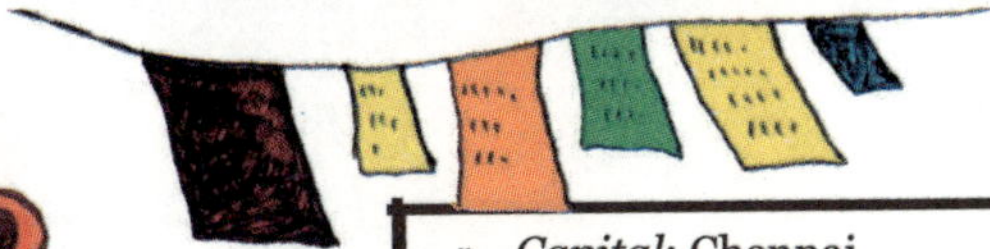

SIKKIM

- *Capital*: Gangtok
- *Date of formation*: May 16, 1975
- *Governor*: Shriniwas Dadasaheb Patil
- *Chief Minister*: Pawan Chamling
- *Tourist attractions:* Tusklakhang, Namgyal, Deer Park, Orchid Sanctuary, Khabelstok
- *Festivals*: Kanchendzonga, Lossong
- *Major dance and music forms*: Khanchendzonga, Kali Topi
- *Arts and crafts*: Thangkas or religious scroll paintings depict scenes from Buddha's life; sand mandala; hand-knotted carpets.
- *Languages*: Lepcha, Bhutia, Limbu, Nepali, Hindi
- *Size*: 7,096 sq. km
- *Population*: 610,577
- *Rivers:* Teesta, Rangit
- *Forests and wildlife sanctuaries:* Kanchendzonga NP, Fambong La WS
- *State animal:* Red panda
- *State bird*: Blood pheasant
- *State flower:* Rhododendron
- *State tree:* Nobile orchid
- *Major crops*: Maize, paddy, wheat, barley

Factoids

- The highly endangered red panda is found in Sikkim.
- Sikkim has around 200 monasteries or Gompas where red-robed lamas chant to drums, horns and trumpets.

TAMIL NADU

- *Capital*: Chennai
- *Date of formation*: August 15, 1947
- *Governor*: Konijeti Rosaiah
- *Chief Minister*: J. Jayalalithaa
- *Tourist attractions:* Marina Beach, Mahabalipuram Beach, Ooty
- *Festivals*: Pongal, Vaikasi, Visakam, Avani Moolam
- *Major dance and music forms*: Bharatnatyam, Paravi Attam, Neyyandi Melam
- *Arts and crafts*: Tanjore style of painting; Kanchipuram silk; Toda women embroider geometrical patterns on shawls called poothkuli
- *Language*: Tamil
- *Size*: 1,30,058 sq. km
- *Population*: 72,147, 030
- *Rivers:* Kaveri, Palar, Periyar, Bhavani
- *Forests and wildlife sanctuaries:* Mudumalai NP, Mukurthi NP, Annamalai NP, Periyar TR
- *State animal:* Nilgiri tahr
- *State bird*: Emerald dove
- *State flower:* Glory lily or Kandhal
- *State tree:* Palmera palm
- *Major crops*: Paddy, jowar, ragi, tea

Factoids

- Mamallapuram is a group of rock cut monuments and temples carved between 7th and 8th centuries AD in Mahabalipuram.
- The magnificent Meenakshi temple at Madurai was built by the Pandyas.

TELANGANA

- *Capital:* Hyderabad
- *Date of formation:* June 2, 2014
- *Governor:* E.S.L. Narasimhan
- *Chief Minister: K. Chandrashekar Rao*
- *Tourist attractions:* Charminar, Golconda Fort, Qutb Shahi Tombs, Chowmahalla Palace, Falaknuma Palace and Bhongir Fort
- *Festivals:* Sivaratri, Pongal, Vinayak Chaviti
- *Major dance and music forms:* Kuchipudi, Bhamakalpam, Dappu
- *Arts and crafts:* Kalamkari cotton, the Nakashis of Cheriyal village paint vibrantly coloured scrolls.
- *Languages:* Telegu, Urdu
- *Size:* 114,840 km
- *Population:* 35,193,978
- *Rivers:* Godavari, Krishna, Wainganga, Tungabhadra, Chitravati, Musi, Banda, Papagni
- *Forests and wildlife sanctuaries:* Shivaram WS, Manjira WS, Nagarjunasagar-Srisailam, WS Etunagaram
- *State animal:* Indian Bison
- *State bird:* Indian roller
- *State flower:* Palash
- *State tree:* Mahua
- *Major crops:* Jowar, rice, bajra

Factoids

- Some of the traditional Telangana dance forms include Golatalu, Sannai Vaidam, Gondola Nrityam and Dhimsa.

Factoids

- The name Telangana is said to have been derived from the word Trilinga, as in the Trilinga Desa, which translates to "the country of the three lingas". Shiva descended in the lingam form on three mountains, Kaleshwaram, Srisailam and Draksharama, which marked the boundaries of the Trilingadesa, later called Telinga, Telunga or Telugu, according to a Hindu legend.

Factoids

- Telangana culture has predominantly South Indian traditions and customs but also follows certain cultural customs from Persian traditions imbibed during the rule of Moghuls and Nizams rule.

Factoids

- The economy of Telangana is mainly driven by agriculture. Two important rivers of India, the Godavari and the Krishna, irrigate the state.

Factoids

- Telangana has abundant wildlife. The state has four tiger reserves at Kawal, Jannaram, Tadavai and Mannanur. Telangana has three National Parks-Kasu Brahmananda Reddy National Park in Hyderabad district, and Mahavir Harina Vanasthali National Park and Mrugavani National Park in Ranga Reddy district.

Tripura

- *Capital*: Agartala
- *Date of formation*: January 21, 1972
- *Governor*: Tathagata Roy
- *Chief Minister*: Manik Sarkar
- *Tourist attractions:* Ujjayant Palace, Chaturdas Devata Temple, Neer Mahal, Sipahijala
- *Festivals*: Kharchi Puja, Jer and Garia Puja, Ganga Puja
- *Major dance and music forms*: Bihu dance, Sarinda, Sumui music
- *Arts and crafts*: Bamboo mats; clothes with snakeskin designs known as Ponmongvom; garments called the risa and the rignai
- *Languages*: Kok-borok, Bengali, Manipuri
- *Size*: 10,491.69 sq. km
- *Population*: 3,673,917
- *Rivers:* Gomti
- *Forests and wildlife sanctuaries:* Shepahijala WS, Trishna WS, Rowa WS
- *State animal:* Phayre's langur or spectacled langur
- *State bird*: Green imperial pigeon
- *State flower:* Nageshwar
- *State tree:* Agar
- *Major crops*: Paddy, wheat, sugarcane, potato

Factoids

- Singers are usually accompanied by instruments like the sarinda, chongpreng, bamboo flute or sumui.
- Lake Rudrsagar is the only lake in eastern India with a palace in it; Neermahal was built by Maharaja Bir Bikram Kishore Manikya Bahadur as a summer resort.

Uttar Pradesh

- *Capital*: Lucknow
- *Date of formation*: January 26, 1950
- *Governor*: Ram Naik
- *Chief Minister*: Akhilesh Yadav
- *Tourist attractions:* Taj Mahal, Sangam, Varanasi, Mussoorie
- *Festivals*: Karva Chauth, Annakoot, Shitala Ashtami, Eid
- *Major dance and music forms*: Kathak, Lucknow and Benares Gharanas of music
- *Arts and crafts*: Chikankari or shadow-work embroidery; Baranasi brocades which include the zari, amru and abrawan; Sanjhi or the art of cutting paper stencils.
- *Languages*: Hindi, Urdu
- *Size*: 2,40,928 sq. km
- *Population*: 199,812,341
- *Rivers:* Ganga, Yamuna, Gomti, Ghaghra, Ramganga, Betwa
- *Forests and wildlife sanctuaries:* Dudhwa NP, Ranipur WS
- *State animal:* Swamp Deer
- *State bird*: Sarus crane
- *State flower:* Brahm kamal
- *State tree:* Ashok
- *Major crops*: Wheat, rice, pulses, apples

Factoids

- The ancient Dhamek Stupa marks the spot where Buddha gave his first sermon in Sarnath.
- Mughal emperor Shah Jahan built the Taj Mahal for his dead wife Mumtaz Mahal; the tomb took 22 years to build.

UTTARAKHAND

- *Capital*: Dehradun
- *Date of formation*: November 9, 2000
- *Governor*: Dr Krishan Kant Paul
- *Chief Minister*: Harish Rawat
- *Tourist attractions:* Corbett NP, Nainital, Almora Valley of Flowers, Nanda Devi Park
- *Festivals*: Devidhura Mela, Nanda Devi Mela, Purnagiri Mela
- *Major dance and music forms*: Garhwali folk dance and music
- *Arts and crafts*: Kholi woodcarving; Aipan or rangoli
- *Languages*: Hindi, Garhwali, Kumaoni
- *Size*: 53,483 sq. km
- *Population*: 10,086,292
- *Rivers:* Ganga, Yamuna, Ramganga, Kali
- *Forests and wildlife sanctuaries:* Nanda Devi NP, Rajaji NP, Corbett Tiger Reserve.
- *State animal:* Himalayan musk deer
- *State bird*: Himalayan monal
- *State flower:* Brahm kamal
- *State tree:* Burans
- *Major crops*: Rice, wheat, barley, jowar, oilseed

Factoids

- Kedarnath temple, at a height of 3584 m, is devoted to Shiva.
- The Kol-Munds, a Dravidian people, were probably the first to live here.

WEST BENGAL

- *Capital*: Kolkata
- *Date of formation*: January 26, 1950
- *Governor*: Keshari Nath Tripathi
- *Chief Minister*: Mamata Banerjee
- *Tourist attractions:* Victoria Memorial, Vidyasagar Setu, Shantiniketan, Darjeeling
- *Festivals*: Durga Puja, Rabindra Jayanti
- *Major dance and music forms*: Jatra theatre; Baul; Rabindrasangeet
- *Arts and crafts*: Terracotta Bankura horses; Kalighat style of painting; hand-woven Baluchari silk textiles
- *Languages*: Bengali, Hindi, Urdu
- *Size*: 88,752 sq. km
- *Population*: 91,276,115
- *Rivers:* Hooghly, Teesta, Torsa, Subarnarekha, Joldhara
- *Forests and wildlife sanctuaries:* Sunderbans Tiger Reserve, Jaldapara WS
- *State animal:* Fishing cat
- *State bird*: White-throated kingfisher
- *State flower:* Shephali
- *State tree:* Devil tree or chatian
- *Major crops*: Rice, maize, oil seeds, sugarcane

Factoids

- Bengali literature developed early thanks to the cultural awakening brought about by the Brahmo Samaj.
- Rabindranath Tagore, the first Asian to win the Nobel Prize for Literature, was from Bengal.

UNION TERRITORIES

Andaman and Nicobar Islands

- *Capital*: Port Blair
- *Date of formation*: November 1, 1956
- *Lt. Governor:* Lt Gen A K Singh
- *Tourist attractions:* Cellular Jail, Ross Island, Havelock Island, Marine Museum
- *Festivals*: Andaman and Nicobar Tourism Festival, ethnic tribal festivals
- *Languages*: Hindi, Nicobarese, Bengali, Tamil, Malayalam, Telugu
- *Size*: 8,249 sq. km
- *Population*: 380,581
- *State animal:* Dugong (Sea Cow)
- *State bird*: Andaman Wood Pigeon
- *State tree:* Andaman Padauk
- *Major crops*: Paddy, coconuts, nuts, banana, mango

Factoids

- It is located in the Bay of Bengal.
- It is composed of 572 Islands.

Chandigarh

- *Capital*: Chandigarh
- *Date of formation*: 1966
- *Administrator:* Kaptan Singh Solanki
- *Tourist attractions:* Rock gardens, Sukhna Lake, Capitol Complex, Open-Hand monument, Rose garden.
- *Festivals*: Festival of Gardens, Mango Festival, Maha Moorkh Sammelan (April Fool's Day)
- *Languages*: Hindi, Punjabi, English
- *Size*: 114 sq. km
- *Population*: 1,055,450
- *Major crops*: wheat, maize, paddy

Factoids

- Chandigarh gets its name from the Goddess Chandi.
- French architect Le Corbusier (Charles Edouard Jeanneret) planned the city.

Delhi

- *Capital*: Delhi
- *Date of formation*: December 1991
- *Lt. Governor:* Najeeb Jung
- *Chief Minister*: Arvind Kejriwal
- *Tourist attractions:* Qutub Minar, Humayun's Tomb, Jantar Mantar, Red Fort, India Gate, Birla Mandir
- *Festivals*: Diwali, Holi, Eid
- *Languages*: Hindi, English, Urdu, Punjabi
- *Size*: 1,483 sq. km
- *Population*: 16,787,941
- *Rivers:* Yamuna
- *Major crops*: rice, maize

Factoids

- The National Capital Region or NCR is one of the world's biggest urban clusters.
- It is believed that Delhi was destroyed and rebuilt at least seven times.

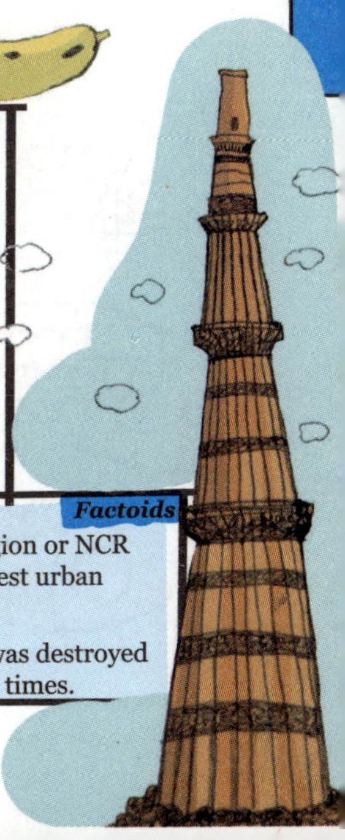

Daman and Diu

- *Capital*: Daman
- *Date of formation*: May 30, 1987
- *Administrator*: Ashish Kundra
- *Tourist attractions:* Somnath Mahadev Temple, Devka Beach, Diu Fort, Panikotha, Nagoa Beach
- *Festivals*: Gangaji Fair, Holi, Diwali
- *Languages*: Gujarati, Marathi
- *Size*: 112 sq. km
- *Population*: 243,247
- *Rivers:* Damanganga, Kolak, Kalai
- *Major crops*: Paddy, ragi, groundnut, pulses

Factoids

- Daman was once a part of the Kushana Empire.
- The ancient river Damanganga lends its name to the region of Daman.

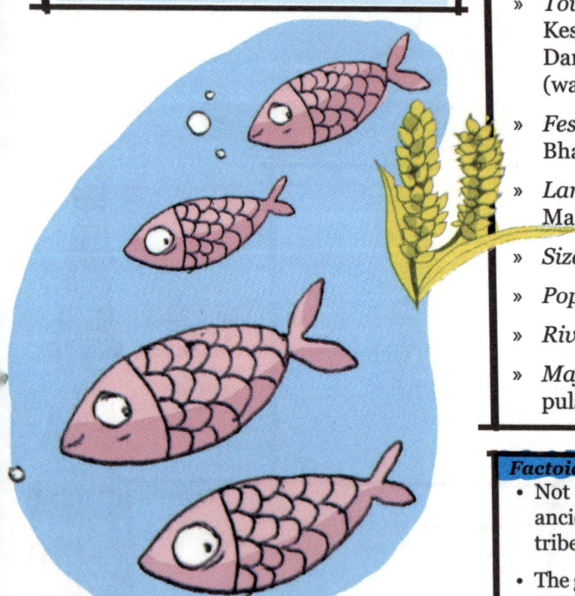

Dadra and Nagar Haveli

- *Capital*: Silvassa
- *Date of formation*: August 11, 1961
- *Administrator*: Ashish Kundra
- *Tourist attractions:* Tad Keshwara Temple, Van Vihar, Damanganga River, Dudhani (water sports)
- *Festivals*: Barash (Diwali), Ivaso, Bhawada
- *Languages*: Gujarati, Hindi, Marathi, Konkani
- *Size*: 491 sq. km
- *Population*: 343,709
- *Rivers:* Silvassa, Khanvel
- *Major crops*: Paddy, ragi, millet, pulses, oilseeds

Factoids

- Not much is known about this region's ancient history which contains many tribes.
- The ghangal, a musical instrument made with a gourd, bamboo and iron strings, is a part of Warli religious rituals.

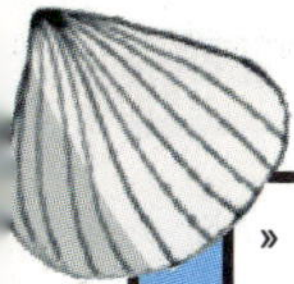

LAKSHADWEEP

- *Capital*: Kavaratti
- *Date of formation*: November 1, 1956
- *Administrator*: H. Rajesh Prasad
- *Tourist attractions:* Kavaratti Kadamat, Kalpeni, Minicoy Lighthouse, Bangaram
- *Festivals*: Sufi Festivals, Eid
- *Languages*: Malayalam, Mahi, Hindi, Tamil
- *Size*: 32 sq. km
- *Population*: 64,473
- *State animal:* Butterfly Fish
- *State bird*: Sooty Tern
- *State tree:* Bread fruit
- *Major crops*: Coconut

Factoids

- Lakshadweep was ruled by Kerala dynasties like the Kuladekharas and the Chirakkal Rajahs.
- Only on the island of Minicoy do they speak Mahi, a dialect of Dhivehi, the national language of Maldives.

PUDUCHERRY

- *Capital*: Puducherry
- *Date of formation*: January 7, 1963
- *Lt. Governor*: Lt. General Ajay Kumar Singh (Retd.)
- *Chief Minister:* N. Rangasamy
- *Tourist attractions:* Serenity Beach, Plage Paradiso, Karaikal Beach, Place du Government, Aurobindo Ashram
- *Festivals*: Fire-Walk Festival, Sedal, Mascarade Festival
- *Languages*: Tamil, Telugu, Malayalam, English and French
- *Size*: 480 sq. km
- *Population*: 1,247,953
- *Major crops*: Paddy, pulses, coconuts, arcanuts, spices

Factoids

- Mahe, a small town in Puducherry, is also known as Mayyazhi or the 'sea's eyebrow'.
- The ancient town of Arikamedu traded pottery, beads, precious stones and textiles with the Romans in exchange for wine, olive oil and fish sauce.

Presidents (past and present)

Dr. Rajendra Prasad: 1950-1962
Dr. Sarvepalli Radhakrishnan: 1962-1967
Dr. Zakir Hussain: 1967-1969
Varahagiri Venkata Giri:
May-July, 1969 (Acting)
Justice Mohammed Hidayatullah:
July-Aug, 1969 (Acting)
Varahagiri Venkata Giri: 1969-1974
Fakhruddin Ali Ahmed: 1974-1977
B.D. Jatti: Feb-July 1977 (Acting)
Neelam Sanjiva Reddy: 1977-1982
Giani Zail Singh: 1982-1987
R. Venkataraman: 1987-1992
Dr. Shankar Dayal Sharma: 1992-1997
K.R. Narayanan: 1997-2002
A.P.J. Abdul Kalam: 2002-2007
Pratibha Patil: 2007-2012
Pranab Mukherjee: 2012-Present

Prime Ministers (past and present)

Jawaharlal Nehru: 1947-1964
Gulzari Lal Nanda: May-June, 1964 (Acting)
Lal Bahadur Shastri: 1964-1966
Gulzari Lal Nanda: 11-24 Jan, 1966 (Acting)
Indira Gandhi: 1966-1977
Morarji Desai: 1977-1979
Charan Singh: 1979-1980
Indira Gandhi: 1980-1984
Rajiv Gandhi: 1984- 1989
Vishwanath Pratap Singh: 1989-1990
Chandrasekhar: 1990-1991
P.V. Narasimha Rao: 1991-1996
Atal Bihari Vajpayee: May 1996
H.D. Deve Gowda: June 1996- April 1997
Inder Kumar Gujral: April 1997-March 1998
Atal Bihari Vajpayee: 1998-2004
Dr. Manmohan Singh: 2004-2014
Narendra Modi: May 2014-Present

Important office-holders

Chief Justice of India: HL Dattu
Chief of the Army Staff: General. Dalbir Singh
Chief of the Naval Staff: Admiral RK Dhowan
Chief of the Air Staff: Air Chief Marshal Arup Raha
Attorney General: Mukul Rohatgi
Chief Election Commissioner: Nasim Zaidi
Comptroller and Auditor General: Shashi Kant Sharma
Foreign Secretary: Dr. Subrahmanyam Jaishankar
Speaker of the Lok Sabha: Sumitra Mahajan
RBI Governor: Dr. Raghuram G. Rajan
Solicitor General: Ranjit Kumar
Finance Secretary: Ratan Watal
R&AW Chief: Rajinder Khanna
Children's Film Society of India Chairman: Mukesh Khanna
NCC Director General: Lt Gen Aniruddha Chakravarty

Important Industrialists

Mukesh D. Ambani *(Reliance Industries Limited)*
Dilip Shangvi *(Sun Pharmaceuticals)*
Azim H. Premji *(Wipro Limited)*
Cyrus Pallonji Mistry *(Tata Group)*
Lakshmi N. Mittal *(Arcelor Mittal)*
Srichand, Gopichand, Prakash and Ashok Hinduja *(Hinduja Group)*
Shiv Nadar *(HCL Technologies)*
Adi Godrej *(Godrej Group)*
Kumar Mangalam Birla *(Aditya Birla Group)*
Sunil Mittal *(Bharti Enterprises)*
Cyrus Poonawalla *(Poonawalla Group)*
Anil D. Ambani *(Reliance Communications, Reliance Capital, Reliance Energy and Reliance Natural Resources Limited)*
Rahul Bajaj *(Bajaj Group)*
Vishal Sikka *(Infosys Technologies)*

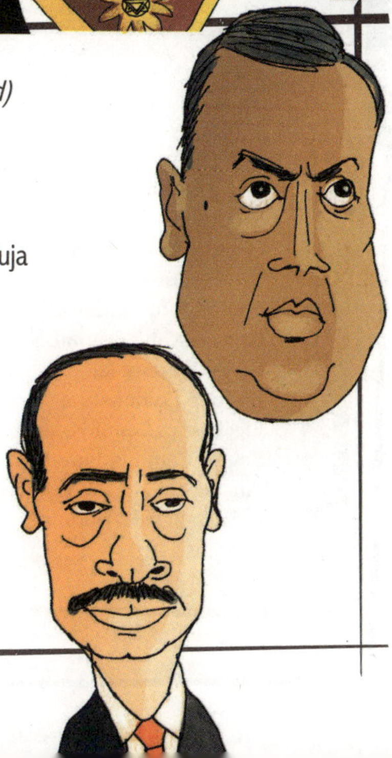

Important Organisations

- Anthropological Survey of India
- Bureau of Public Enterprises
- Central Board of Film Certification
- Comptroller and Auditor-General
- Council of Scientific and Industrial Research
- Defence Research and Development Organisation
- Dental Council of India
- Film and Television Institute of India
- Forest Survey of India
- Geological Survey of India
- Indian Council of Agricultural Research
- Indian Council for Cultural Relations
- Indian Council of Historical Research
- Indian Council of Medical Research
- Indian Council of Philosophical Research
- Indian Council of Social Science Research
- Indian Farmers Fertilisers Cooperative Ltd.
- Indian Institute of Advanced Study
- Indian Institute of Forest Management
- Indian Institute of Mass Communication
- Indira Gandhi National Centre for the Arts
- Indira Gandhi National Open University
- Industrial Development Bank of India
- Industrial Reconstruction Bank of India
- National Archives of India
- National Bank for Agriculture and Rural Development
- National Book Trust
- National Council of Educational Research and Training
- National Development Council
- National Film Festival
- National Informatics Centre
- National Sample Survey Organisation
- National School of Drama
- Press Council of India
- Press Information Bureau
- Reserve Bank of India
- Zoological Survey of India

Important Commissions

- Atomic Energy Commission
- Commission for Agricultural Costs and Prices
- Census Commission
- Central Forestry Commission
- Central Information Commission
- Central Water Commission
- Earth Commission
- Election Commission
- Electronics Commission
- Energy Commission
- Finance Commission
- Indo-Bangladesh Joint Rivers Commission
- Khadi and Village Industries Commission
- Law Commission
- Mandal Commission
- National Commission of Farmers
- National Commission to Review the Working of the Constitution
- National Knowledge Commission
- National Statistical Commission
- Planning Commission
- Staff Selection Commission
- Union Public Service Commission
- University Grants Commission
- Venkataswami Commission

The year 2015 began on a positive note for the ruling BJP-led National Democratic Alliance (NDA) government headed by Prime Minister Narendra Modi. Fresh from its victory in the 2014 parliamentary election, the NDA swept the Assembly elections in Maharashtra and Haryana and gave its best ever performance till date in Jammu and Kashmir, where it surprised many by forming a government in alliance with the People's Democratic Party (PDP).

NEW INITIATIVES

The government initiated a slew of new programmes and policies aimed at improving the quality of life and the economy. While the 'Swachh Bharat' programme was publicised by the Prime Minister wielding the broom himself, the 'Make in India' campaign aims at inviting foreign investments to help revive Indian manufacturing, generate jobs and give Indian economy a boost. The government also announced new schemes such as Smart Cities and Housing for All to make some of the existing cities more livable, with world-class infrastructure and to alleviate a shortfall of affordable housing in urban areas.

MIXED BAG

The government rode a wave of popularity, which also manifested itself in the manner in which the Prime Minister was welcomed when he travelled abroad. There were some difficult moments for the government though; it faced an electoral defeat in the Delhi Assembly election. During the monsoon session of Parliament, it had to contend with an Opposition which did not allow business to be transacted as the latter differed with the government on certain issues, including, but not limited to, acquisition of land by private and government entities.

HOW 2015 SHAPED THE POLITICS OF INDIA

After winning the 2014 Lok Sabha election and some Assembly elections, the first shocker for the Modi Government came in the form of the Delhi Assembly election. The fledgling Aam Aadmi Party (AAP), led by Arvind Kejriwal, took on the might of the established political parties such as the BJP and the Congress and came up triumphant. The AAP's victory shocked many as they had not expected a newly formed political party to win in the face of stiff competition.

The AAP grabbed a record 67 seats, leaving the BJP, which had emerged as the single largest party in the 2013 Assembly election, with just three seats and handing the Congress—which had ruled Delhi for 15 years from 1998—its worst defeat in the Capital as the party failed to even open its account.

THE GRAND OLD PARTY

For the main Opposition party, the Congress, the year has not been smooth sailing, too. The Grand Old Party has not only had to ponder over its defeat and decimation in Delhi but has also had to undertake a rejig of the party organisation at the national level. There is a possibility that the party's vice-president, Rahul Gandhi, will be elevated to the post of president, which is currently held by his mother and UPA chairperson Sonia Gandhi.

LAND OVER MATTERS

The Congress has been at the forefront of attacks on the Modi Government on the Land Acquisition Bill, which, it alleges, had been made anti-farmer on account of the amendments to the bill, pushed for by the government.

Some of the other issues for which the Modi Government was roundly criticised were: loss to agricultural crop due to unseasonal rains in parts of northern India and delay in providing compensation to farmers in the affected states; ban on slaughter of animals and consumption of beef in Maharashtra and elsewhere; the controversy over net neutrality or equality of access to websites.

YOGA DAY

Another hullabaloo erupted when Prime Minister Modi succeeded in getting the United Nations to declare June 21 as International Yoga Day. A debate ensued whether the government was imposing a Hindu tradition or practice on the religious minorities in India. The controversy was also around the practice of Surya Namaskar, which some said went against the tenets of Islam.

BEEF BAN

The Maharashtra Government's ban on the sale of beef impacted the livelihood of some members of the Muslim community, who are involved in the slaughter trade and the leather industry. The ban was also imposed in some of the other BJP-ruled states of Rajasthan, Haryana, Chhattisgarh and Jharkhand, giving rise to a debate whether these bans impinge on individual freedom.

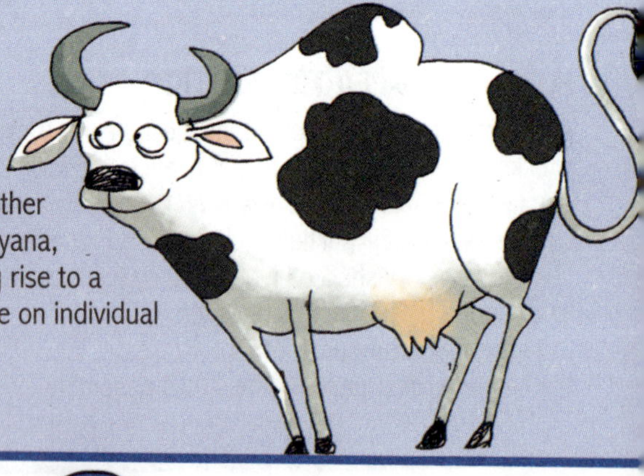

MODIGATE SCANDAL

In June, the BJP found itself in the midst of another unpleasant debate when it was revealed that the External Affairs Minister Sushma Swaraj had facilitated the travel of former Indian Premier League chief Lalit Modi from the United Kingdom to Portugal for his wife's cancer treatment despite his being wanted by the Enforcement Directorate for alleged financial irregularities. The Opposition demanded Sushma Swaraj's resignation alleging that there was a quid pro quo as her husband Swaraj Kaushal and daughter Bansuri had been Modi's lawyers.

The issue snowballed when Lalit Modi's advocate told the media that Rajasthan Chief Minister Vasundhara Raje had supported Modi's immigration plea in the UK. This immediately drew more fire from the Opposition, which now also demanded Vasundhara Raja's resignation. The protests spilled onto the streets and then into Parliament where the Opposition stalled the monsoon session demanding that Sushma Swaraj and Vasundhara Raje resign over "Lalitgate".

The Centre did not yield to this demand and BJP and NDA leaders came out in support of Sushma Swaraj. Swaraj, on her part, in a reply to a debate on the issue on August 12, 2015, tore into the Congress accusing it of allowing the Bhopal gas tragedy accused Warren Anderson, former Union Carbide CEO, to leave India as a quid pro quo for the release of Adil Shahryar, son of Mohammad Yunus, a former bureaucrat and a friend of the Gandhis. Similarly, she claimed that allowing Bofors scam accused Ottavio Quattrochi to flee the country was a quid pro quo, too.

SESSION WASHOUT

The exchange of barbs led to a complete washout of the monsoon session of Parliament, thus preventing the government from reaching a consensus on getting either the amended Land Acquisition Bill or the much-awaited Goods and Services Tax (GST) Bill passed.

With the stock markets tanking in July-August in the wake of the slowdown in China and depreciation of the Yuan, the business community was eagerly expecting development on these two Bills. Though the government delayed proroguing Parliament in the hope that it would be able to reach a middle ground on at least the GST Bill, the Congress stood firm on its demand for the resignations of Sushma Swaraj and Vasundhara Raje. Eventually, the monsoon session was prorogued in September.

WOOING INVESTORS

Even as Prime Minister Narendra Modi paid his second visit to the United States after assuming office, Finance Minister Arun Jaitley assured the international community that India with its amended taxation laws remains the best place to invest. The past year, Jaitley said, has seen a 27 per cent increase in Foreign Direct Investment (FDI) but the recent flight of capital from the stock markets and the fall in the Rupee indicate a sense of unease.

THE BIHAR SAGA

Now all eyes are on the Bihar Assembly election, due in October-November. With political parties drawing up new alliances, old friends turning foes and vice-versa, the election is poised for an interesting finale. The ruling Janata Dal (United) party of Chief Minister Nitish Kumar has for the first time tied up with old foe Lalu Yadav's Rashtriya Janata Dal (RJD). While the Congress has aligned itself with the JD(U)-RJD coalition, the BJP under the stewardship of president Amit Shah has been equally careful in choosing partners as it seeks to social engineer its way to power in the state.

The BJP had come to power along with JD(U) in the last two Assembly elections in Bihar but they parted ways over Nitish's opposition to Modi as the BJP's prime ministerial candidate. Jitan Ram Manjhi, a former chief minister and a leader of the backward classes, has joined hands with the BJP. Manjhi has floated his own outfit, Hindustani Awam Morcha, which, along with Ram Vilas Paswan's Lok Janshakti Party (LJP) and Upendra Kushwaha's Rashtriya Lok Samta Party (RLSP), has aligned with the BJP for the 2015 Bihar Assembly election.

By **RAMESH RAMACHANDRAN**

India, has been showcased as the promised land for 2014-2015—with its high growth phase outshining the Chinese growth story. According to a India Brand Equity Foundation (IBEF) report 'India is set to emerge as the world's fastest-growing major economy by 2015, ahead of China ... The improvement in India's economic fundamentals has accelerated in the year 2015 with the combined impact of strong government reforms.'

NEW GOVERNMENT, NEW FOCUS

The sharp fall in crude oil prices in the last one year helped the BJP-led NDA government control fiscal deficit and inflation. The repo rate cuts by RBI helped in reduction of interest rates. The key hurdle for the government is lack of majority in Rajya Sabha (Upper House of Parliament). While the government managed to get key bills like GST and the Land Acquisition Bill passed in the Lok Sabha, these bills faced serious opposition in the Rajya Sabha.

RESERVE BANK OF INDIA (RBI) CUTS POLICY INTEREST RATES

RBI cut the repo rate thrice in 2015 (January, March and June) as the inflation was trending down. The repo rate, which is a key policy interest rate was reduced by 0.75 per cent to 7.25 per cent in January-June 2015, which helped banks reduce lending rates charged to borrowers.

DISAPPOINTING MONSOONS

The Southwest monsoons, which are crucial for agriculture and farming in India, were below normal this year. Out of 36 meteorological sub-divisions, 18 sub-divisions in India received deficient rainfall in 2015. Even the water storage levels in dams (reservoirs) is lower compared to 2014. This deficit rainfall can lead to lower production of grains, vegetables, pulses and cereals and higher food inflation. Many industries like consumer durables, two-wheelers, tractors and fertilisers are likely to see slowdown in demand.

BANK ACCOUNTS FOR ALL

In August 2014, India had more than 10 crore households without a bank account. The financial inclusion scheme, Pradhan Mantri Jan-Dhan Yojana (PMJDY) that was rolled out to provide a bank account to every

Great start in 2014 ... many challenges in 2015

- Financial markets and global investors were a tad disappointed with the delay in the implementation of GST and Land Acquisition bills, the key promises of the Modi regime when they won elections, early in 2015.
- Steep correction in China's stock market and slower growth in the economy also impacted India. Russia, Brazil and Mexico also saw weak economies.
- The key benchmark CNX Nifty, which appreciated by 31 per cent in the calendar year 2014 (January-December 2014) declined by 5 per cent in January-September 2015. The muted returns from equity/stock markets in this year (January-September 2015) mirror the poor investor sentiment.
- While the various legislative hurdles delayed key reforms, the new government completed auction of coal blocks and telecom spectrum which helped raise revenues for the central and state governments.
- Initiatives like 'Make in India' and 'Digital India' attracted investments into India across sectors like automobiles, electronics, financial services and technology. The former aims to raise manufacturing share in India's GDP (gross domestic product) from 21 per cent to 25 per cent in the next few years.

household, has seen strong traction since its August 2014 launch, with the opening of around 17.9 crore bank accounts. Such financial inclusion can, over a period of time, help reduce the parallel black money economy, increase the government's tax revenue and provide more structure to the unorganised sectors of the economy.

RBI ISSUES LICENSES FOR PAYMENT BANKS AND SMALL FINANCE BANKS

The Indian government plans to set up differentiated banks for specific activities to increase financial inclusion in India. As part of this plan, the Reserve Bank of India (RBI) issued licenses in August 2015 to set up Payment banks. These banks will help people of lower income strata, who use cash for all transactions, to come into the fold of the banking system. The traditional banking system relies on branches with 10-25 employees in each branch to deliver banking services and have high working costs which make them financially unviable and loss making for rural areas and low income customers. However, payment banks which can even be accessed through mobile phones is a low cost yet effective platform to provide basic banking services to these sectors. These banks can slowly translate India into a cashless economy.

Payment banks are also expected to be used by the government to remit subsidies on healthcare, education and gas directly to beneficiaries' accounts. Some of the firms who received approval to set up payment banks are Aditya Birla Nuvo, Airtel

M Commerce, Department of Posts, National Securities Depository (NSDL), Tech Mahindra and Vodafone mPesa. RBI also granted approval to 10 entities for setting up small finance banks which will fund small businesses and entrepreneurs.

PARLIAMENT LOGJAM

The Monsoon session of parliament (July 21 to August 13, 2015) failed to pass the key GST (Goods & Services Tax) bill and Land Acquisition bill due to frequent disruptions and adjournments in the Rajya Sabha. The passage of these bills was important to set the pace for key economic reforms and to drive economic growth and investments in India. These developments had negative impact on investor sentiment and corporates.

CRUDE OIL AND COMMODITY PRICES FALL SHARPLY

Crude oil prices fell by around 50 per cent since the beginning of October 2014 (Brent Crude price fell from USD 97 per barrel to USD 48 per barrel). India is a major importer of crude oil which is used to produce fuels like petrol, diesel, kerosene and cooking gas. The fall in crude oil prices helped the government reduce prices of diesel and petrol. Diesel and Petrol prices were reduced by around 22 per cent and 15 per cent respectively by the government between October 2014 and September 2015.

Commodity prices were sharply down since September-October 2014 due to the prolonged economic slowdown in developed nations and China. Prices of metals like steel, zinc, aluminium and copper fell sharply due to a slowdown in global economic growth and commensurate decline in demand for these industrial commodities.

ECONOMIC INDICATORS

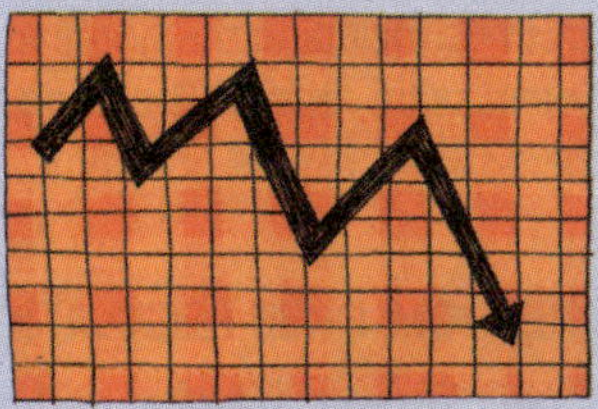

The Wholesale Price Index (WPI)-based inflation declined from 2.38 per cent in September 2014 to 4.95 per cent in August 2015 on account of sharp fall in prices of commodities, manufactured products and fuels. Consumer Price inflation (based on consumer price index) also decreased from 6.46 per cent in September 2014 to 3.66 per cent in August 2015.

Consumer price inflation is below RBI's inflation target of 6 per cent providing scope for further reduction in interest rates.

Fiscal deficit for April-July 2015 was at Rs. 3.85 lakh crores, which is 69.3 per cent of Budget estimates for 2015-16 as government increased plan expenditure in the first half of this financial year. Fiscal deficit is the gap between the government's expenditure and revenue.

India's GDP for the first quarter (April-June 2015) in fiscal year 2015-16 decreased to 7 per cent from 7.5 per cent in the previous quarter (January-March 2015). The data on inflation, GDP growth, interest rates and fiscal deficit point towards gradual improvement in the health of the economy. However, faster implementation of reforms and pick up in GDP growth is expected to take longer than anticipated.

By **YAMINI DHALL**

HANGED BY THE NOOSE

Case: Yakub Memon vs State of Maharashtra and Anr.

Following his conviction, the TADA court in Maharashtra issued a death warrant against the 1993 bomb blast accused Yakub Memon. The court set July 30, 2015, as the date for the hanging of the bomb-blast mastermind Tiger Memon's younger brother. What followed was a flurry of activity—petitions, mercy pleas, re-appeal and so on.

The Supreme Court finally rejected the curative plea. Memon's mercy petition to the Maharashtra Governor and a re-appeal to the President of India, were also turned down. The Supreme Court also dismissed a writ petition, subsequently.

Yakub Memon was finally hanged at the Nagpur jail at 7 am on July 30. Memon's hanging however was strongly criticised by several eminent people on various grounds including the non-implementation of the Srikrishna Commission report. The hanging also sparked off a debate on the issue of capital punishment and death penalty.

FREEDOM OVER REGULATION

Case: Shreya Singhal vs Union of India

The apex court of India passed a landmark judgement on March 24, 2015, striking down Section 66A of the Information Technology Act. This was done to uphold the right to freedom of speech and expression online.

The judgement is seen as an effort to thwart the misuse of the law by the police and the ruling party and to restore freedom of speech online. An often misinterpreted law, Section 66A came into being in the year 2000 after morphed photos of a prominent actress were circulated online. It was meant to deter offensive content online.

The law was challenged in the Supreme Court by law student Shreya Singhal and supported by many rights groups, individuals and even political parties. Singhal filed a petition in 2012 after two Mumbai girls were arrested for their Facebook post which questioned the shutdown of Mumbai following Shiv Sena supremo Bal Thackerey's death.

However, ironically despite repealing the act, people continue to be booked under the act. The latest victim being Uday Sirsat of Nashik who was booked for sending a message on WhatsApp to his estranged wife, who happens to be a police inspector posted in Mumbai.

PLAYING GAMES

Case: Board of Control for Cricket in India vs Cricket Association of Bihar & Others

The Supreme Court in its verdict on the IPL match-fixing and betting scandal came down heavily on BCCI's controversial head N Srinivasan. While Srinivasan was cleared of covering up charges against his son-in-law Gurunath Meiyappan, he was asked to step down as the President of BCCI till he had a stake in any IPL team.

The landmark judgement, forbids anyone with commercial interest in an individual IPL team to contest BCCI elections, citing conflict of interest. Also dismissing BCCI's defense of being a private body, the court declared that the board's public functions are 'amenable to judicial law'. The court also appointed a committee that will punish certain team officials who violated IPL rules.

JUSTICE DELAYED OR DENIED?

Case: Sushil Ansal vs State

The Supreme court dismissed the appeals of industrialists Sushil and Gopal Ansal, against their conviction in the Uphaar Tragedy case bringing an end to almost a two decade-long trial. In his judgement, Justice TS Thakur noted, 'Callous indifference and apathy, extraneous influence or considerations and a cynical "Chalta Hai" attitude more often than not costs the society dearly in man-made tragedies whether in the form of fire incidents, collapse of buildings and bridges, poisonous gas leaks or the like.'

According to the verdict, the two real estate barons stand convicted and sentenced to a two years' jail term. However, due to their advanced age and circumstances the Ansal brothers are expected to pay a fine of rupees 30 crore each to escape the sentence. The two were convicted in Delhi's Uphaar cinema hall tragedy of 1997, which claimed 59 lives.

3000 BC
The Indus Valley Civilisation is established.

543 BC
Bimbisara, follower of Gautama Budhha, conquers and becomes the king of Magadha (modern Bihar).

600 BC
The Upanishads, cornerstone philosophical texts of Hinduism, composed around this time.

200 BC
Mahabharata, famous Sanskrit epic, composed.

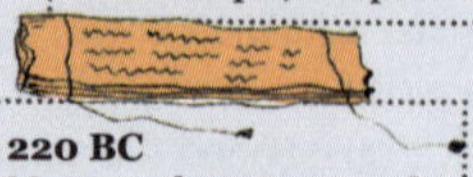

220 BC
Mauryan dynasty expands to almost all of India.

265 BC
After the bloodbath at the battle of Kalinga, Emperor Ashoka embraces Buddhism.

1500 BC
The Aryans arrive from Europe and a unique Indo-Aryan culture develops.

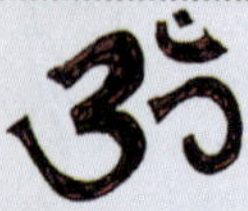

273 BC
Ashoka is the new Mauryan Emperor.

2000 BC
The Indus Valley Civilisation declines.

1100 BC
Indo-Aryans start using iron tools. This is dubbed the Iron Age.

500 BC
Prince Mahavira establishes Jainism in northern India.

000 BC – 1500 BC – 500 BC – 0 BC

1000 BC
One of the oldest books in Sanskrit or any Indo-Eurpoean language, the Rig Veda, is composed.

327 BC
Alexander the Great of Macedonia loses the famous battle with Porus, a ruler in Eastern Punjab.

78 BC
Sunga dynasty declines.

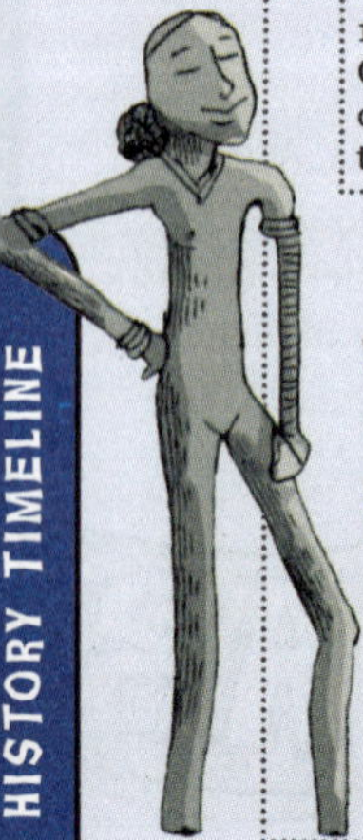

527 BC
Prince Siddhartha Gautama establishes Buddhism and is known as the Buddha.

322 BC
Mauryan Empire founded by Chandragupta Maurya.

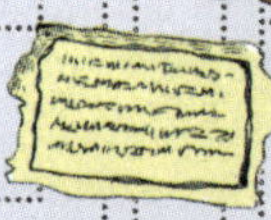

100 BC
Bhagavad Gita is composed.

304 BC
Ramayana, the famous Sanskrit epic, is composed.

184 BC
Mauryan dynasty collapses; Sunga dynasty established.

2500 BC
Cities of Harappa and Mohenjo-Daro in the Indus Valley start flourishing.

300 BC
Chola dynasty establishes the earliest South Indian kingdom with its capital at Thanjavur.

50 AD
First Buddha stupa constructed at Sanchi.

300 AD
Pallava dynasty established in Kanchi.

350AD
Sangam compiled in Tamil in the kingdom of Madurai, and the Puranas composed.

390 AD
Chandra Gupta II extends Gupta kingdom to Gujarat.

650 AD
Pallavas of Kanchipuram are defeated by the Chalukyas.

985 AD
Rajaraja Chola extends the Chola Empire to all of South India and constructs the temple of Thanjavur.

888 AD
Cholas put an end to the Pallava dynasty.

846 AD
Cholas get back their independence from the Pallavas.

753 AD
Rashtrakutas overthrow the Chalukyas.

0 AD ---- 500 AD ---- 750 AD ---- 1000 AD

399 -414 AD
Chinese scholar Fa-Hien travels to India.

450 AD
Monastic university of Nalanda is built.

499 AD
Aryabhatta writes the Aryabhattiyam, a compendium of mathematics and astronomy.

500 AD
Beginning of Bhakti cult in Tamil Nadu.

528 AD
Downfall of Gupta Empire due to continuous barbaric invasions.

606 AD
Harshavardhana, a Buddhist king, unites the kingdoms of Thanesar and Kanauj.

600 AD
Pallavan dynasty governs southern India from Kanchi.

800 AD
Birth of Shankaracharya.

550 AD
Chalukyan kingdom established in central India with Badami as the capital.

997 AD
Mahmud of Ghazni raids northern India.

1000 AD
Chola king Rajaraja builds the Brihadeshvara Temple in Thanjavur.

Not to scale.

1017 AD
Al-Biruni, Persian mathematician, travels to India.

1556 AD
Humayun dies and his son Akbar becomes one of the greatest rulers of India.

1555 AD
Humayun fights Sher Shah and regains India.

1100 AD
Chandelas, Cholas, Kadambas and Rashtrakutas reign in different parts of India.

1540 AD
Humayun loses the empire to Afghan leader Sher Shah and goes into exile.

1190 AD
Chalukya Empire is split among Hoysalas, Yadavas and Kakatiyas.

1530 AD
Babur dies and his son Humayun is the next Mughal Emperor.

1192 AD
Mohammad of Ghori captures Delhi and establishes a Muslim Sultanate at Delhi.

1526 AD
Babur, a Afghan ruler, establishes the Mughal dynasty in India.

1490 AD
Guru Nanak Dev Ji establishes Sikhism.

1010 AD — 1250 AD — 1450 AD — 1600 AD

1190 AD
Chalukya Empire is split among Hoysalas, Yadavas and Kakatiyas.

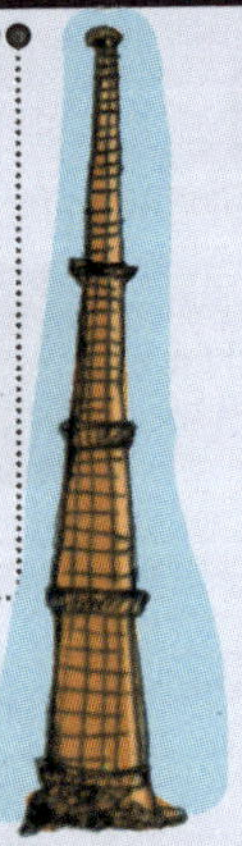

1336 -1565
Vijayanagar Empire is established.

1370 AD
Vijayanagar kingdom takes over the Muslim Sultanate of Madura in Tamil Nadu.

1206 AD
Qutub-ud-din Aibak becomes the first Sultan of Delhi.

1345 AD
Bahmani kingdom established in the Deccan.

1250 AD
Chola dynasty comes to an end.

1325 AD
Turks invade and Muhammad bin Tughlaq becomes Sultan of Delhi.

1300 AD
Establishment of the Khilji Sultanate at Delhi.

1288 AD
Marco Polo comes to India.

1605 AD
Jahangir succeeds his father Akbar.

1611 AD
East India Company is established in India by the British.

1631 AD
Shah Jahan succeeds Jahangir.

1658 AD
Shah Jahan's son Aurangzeb seizes power.

1658 AD
Shah Jahan builds Taj Mahal, Jama Masjid and Red Fort.

1674 AD
Shivaji's coronation takes place and Maratha Empire established.

1707 AD
Aurangzeb dies, Mughal Empire destabilised, Bahadur Shah I comes to the throne.

1757 AD
British defeat Siraj-ud-daulah at the Battle of Plassey in Bengal.

1761 AD
Marathas rule over most of northern India.

1769 AD
A famine kills ten million people in Bengal and the East India Company is ineffectual.

1773 AD
Warren Hastings, Governor of Bengal, establishes a monopoly on the sale of opium.

1793 AD
Permanent Settlement of Bengal—reorganisation of the tax laws by the British.

1799 AD
British defeat Tipu Sultan.

1818 AD
End of the Maratha Empire—British control extends over most of India.

1829 AD
Prohibition of Sati by law.

1831 AD
Administration of Mysore is taken over by East India Company.

1848 AD
Lord Dalhousie becomes the Governor-General of India.

1853 AD
Railway, postal services and telegraph line introduced in India.

1857 AD
First War of Indian Independence also known as Revolt of 1857 or Sepoy Mutiny.

1877 AD
Queen of England is proclaimed the Empress of India.

1885 AD
Formation of the Indian National Congress.

1899 AD
Lord Curzon becomes Governor-General and Viceroy of India.

1650 AD — 1700 AD — 1800 AD — 1899 AD

1919 AD
The Jallianwalla Bagh massacre takes place due to protests against the Rowlatt Act.

1920 AD
Non-cooperation Movement formally launched.

1928 AD
Lala Lajpat Rai killed by the British during a peaceful protest.

1928 AD
Simon Commission comes to India and is boycotted by all parties.

1912 AD
The Imperial capital shifts from Calcutta to Delhi.

1930 AD
Salt Satyagraha is launched as an agitation against salt tax.

1900 AD — 1920 AD — 1935 AD

1906 AD
Muslim League is formed.

1931 AD
Second Round Table Conference takes place and Irwin-Gandhi Pact is signed.

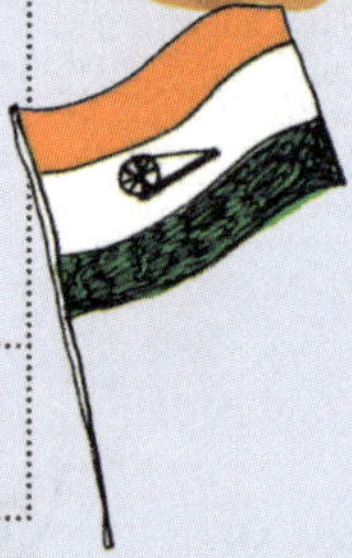

1934 AD
Civil Disobedience Movement is called off.

1905 AD
The Partition of Bengal takes place.

1939 AD
First Round Table Conference in London to discuss constitutional reforms for India.

1942
Quit India Movement is launched.

1942 AD
Cripps Mission deputed by British Parliament to contain political crisis in India.

1942
Indian National Army is formed with Netaji Subhash Chandra Bose spearheading the movement.

1947 AD
Partition of India and Independence from British rule.

1947-48
Widespread communal riots during and after the Partition into two nations: India and Pakistan.

1948
First war over Kashmir with Pakistan.

1948
Mahatma Gandhi assassinated by Nathuram Godse.

1951
First General Elections and Jawaharlal Nehru of the Congress Party elected Prime Minister.

1962
The main pretext for the India-China War is a disputed Himalayan border.

1964
Lal Bahadur Shastri becomes Prime Minister after Nehru's death.

1965
Second war with Pakistan over Kashmir.

1966
Indira Gandhi, Nehru's daughter, elected Prime Minister.

1971
Third war with Pakistan over creation of Bangladesh.

1971
Soviet Union and India sign 20-year treaty of friendship.

1974
India's first underground nuclear test is carried out.

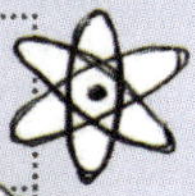

1975
Indira Gandhi declares Emergency—considered the darkest hour of Indian democracy.

1940 AD — 1960 AD — 1975 AD

1977
Indira Gandhi loses the General Elections.

1980
Indira Gandhi returns to power.

1991
Rajiv Gandhi assassinated by suicide bomber.

1991
Economic reform begun by Prime Minister PV Narasimha Rao and Finance Minister Manmohan Singh.

1992
Hindu extremists demolish Babri mosque in Ayodhya, triggering widespread Hindu-Muslim violence.

1989
Congress defeated in General Elections. VP Singh is Prime Minister.

1987
India sends troops for peacekeeping operations in Sri Lanka's civil conflict with the LTTE.

1998
India conducts five nuclear tests, closely followed by Pakistan.

1980 AD — 1990 AD — 1998 AD

1984
Gas leak at Union Carbide pesticides plant in Bhopal. Thousands are killed.

1984
Indira Gandhi assassinated by bodyguards, sparking off anti-Sikh riots in Delhi.

1984
Troops storm Golden Temple in Amritsar, the hide-out of Sikh militants demanding self rule.

1983
India win the cricket Prudential World Cup under the captaincy of Kapil Dev.

1996
Congress suffers worst ever electoral defeat as the BJP emerges as largest single party.

2001
Massive earthquakes hit Gujarat, leaving at least 30,000 dead.

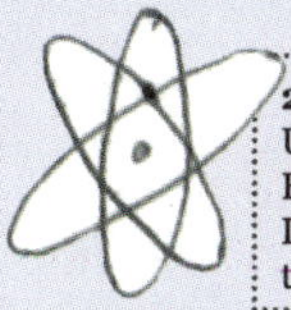

2006
US President George W Bush signs agreement with Indian PM for sharing nuclear technology with India.

2001
US lifts sanctions imposed on India and Pakistan after they staged nuclear tests in 1998.

2000
The billionth Indian citizen is born.

2002
Retired scientist and architect of India's nuclear programme APJ Abdul Kalam is elected President of India.

2003
India and Pakistan agree to resume air links, banned for years.

2007
Pratibha Patil becomes India's first woman President.

2008
Terrorists of Pakistani origin execute large-scale attack on various busy spots in Mumbai.

2010
The first international multi-sport event to be staged in India, the 2010 Commonwealth Games, are held in New Delhi from October 3-14.

2011
India wins the Cricket World Cup again after 28 years, beating Sri Lanka by six wickets. The last World Cup victory came in 1983.

2000 AD — 2005 AD — 2011 AD

1999
Cyclone devastates Odisha, leaving at least 10,000 dead.

1999
War with Pakistan-backed forces in the Kargil region of India-held Kashmir.

1999
Prime Minister Vajpayee takes the bus to Pakistan to sign bilateral Lahore peace declaration.

2004
Whole islands and tribes in the Andaman and Nicobar Islands disappear due to tsunami.

2004
Manmohan Singh becomes Prime Minister.

2009
India's lunar mission Chandrayaan-I discovers traces of water on the moon. This is India's greatest space discovery so far, opening the possibility of setting up future lunar colonies.

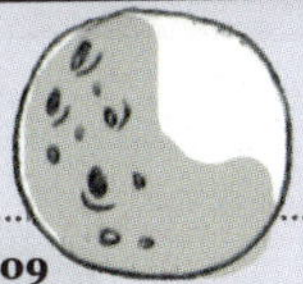

2009
The world's cheapest car, Nano, manufactured in India, hits the roads.

2005
At least 1,000 people are killed in floods and mudslides in Maharashtra.

2004
A huge earthquake in Indonesia triggers a tsunami. India's southern coast severely affected.

2012
Former Finance Minister Pranab Mukherjee becomes new President of India.

2013
The 163-year-old telegram service breathed its last, marking the end of an era.

2014
India's low-cost Mars Mission, *Mangalyaan*, successfully entered the Mars orbit on its maiden attempt.

2012 AD — 2013 AD — 2015 AD

2011-2012
Widespread corruption in government exposed in 2G scam and Coalgate.

2013
India's cricketing god Sachin Tendulkar announced retirement from all forms of cricket.

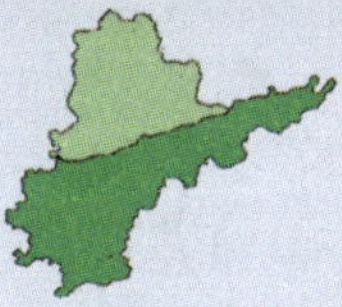

2014
The 29th Indian state—Telangana—came into being, with the division of Andhra Pradesh.

2015
The People's president, A.P.J. Abdul Kalam, also called the Missile Man of India died on July 27.

WORLD

- ☑ WORLD
  - ☑ COUNTRIES OF THE WORLD
  - ☑ INTERNATIONAL ORGANISATIONS
  - ☑ IMPORTANT OFFICE-HOLDERS
  - ☑ WORLD ROUNDUP
  - ☑ SAARC ROUNDUP
  - ☑ WORLD HISTORY TIMELINE
  - ☑ TOP TEN

ALGERIA

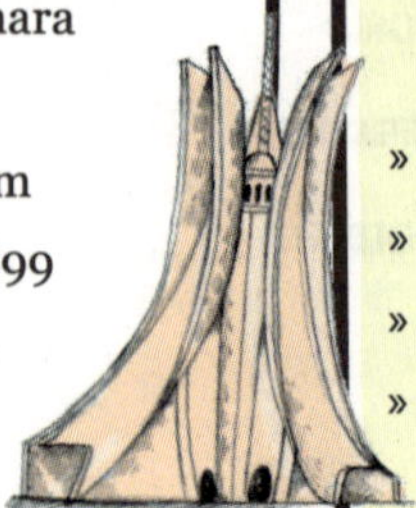

- Location: North Africa
- Neighbours: Libya, Mali, Mauritania, Morocco, Niger, Tunisia, Western Sahara
- Capital: Algiers
- Area: 2,381,741 sq. km
- Population: 40,198,899
- Language(s): Arabic, French
- Dominant religion: Islam
- Time zone: +1
- Currency: Algerian Dinar
- Current head of state: Abdelaziz Bouteflika
- Type of government: Presidential Republic
- Literacy rate: 86%
- GDP: $187.166 billion
- HDI ranking: 93

ANGOLA

- Location: South-central Africa
- Neighbours: D.R. Congo, Republic of Congo, Namibia, Zambia
- Capital: Luanda
- Area: 1,246,699 sq. km
- Population: 22,441,824
- Language(s): Portuguese, Bantu
- Dominant religions: Christianity, Indigenous faiths
- Time zone: +1
- Currency: Kwanza
- Current head of state: José Eduardo dos Santos
- Type of government: Presidential Republic
- Literacy rate: 71.1%
- GDP: $106.149 billion
- HDI ranking: 149

BENIN

- Location: Western Africa
- Neighbours: Burkina Faso, Niger, Nigeria, Togo
- Capital: Porto-Novo
- Area: 110,619 sq. km
- Population: 11,179,193
- Language(s): French, Fon, Yoruba
- Dominant religions: Christianity, Islam, Vodoun
- Time zone: +1
- Currency: CFA Franc
- Current head of state: Yayi Boni
- Type of government: Presidential Republic
- Literacy rate: 42.4%
- GDP: $8.332 billion
- HDI ranking: 165

BOTSWANA

- Location: Southern Africa
- Neighbours: Namibia, South Africa, Zambia, Zimbabwe
- Capital: Gaborone
- Area: 600,370 sq. km
- Population: 2,130,638
- Language(s): English, Setswana, Kalanga
- Dominant religion: Christianity
- Time zone: +2
- Currency: Pula
- Current head of state: Ian Khama
- Type of government: Parliamentary Republic
- Literacy rate: 88.5%
- GDP: $15.768 billion
- HDI ranking: 109

BURUNDI

- Location: East Africa
- Neighbours: Rwanda, Tanzania, D.R. Congo
- Capital: Bujumbura
- Area: 27,830 sq. km
- Population: 11,170,562
- Language(s): Kirundi, French
- Dominant religion: Christianity
- Time zone: +2
- Currency: Burundi Franc
- Current head of state: Pierre Nkurunziza
- Type of government: Republic
- Literacy rate: 85.6%
- GDP: $3.388 billion
- HDI ranking: 180

BURKINA FASO

- Location: West Africa
- Neighbours: Benin, Cote d'Ivoire, Ghana, Mali, Niger, Togo
- Capital: Ouagadougou
- Area: 274,200 sq. km
- Population: 18,421,471
- Language(s): French, Sudanese
- Dominant religion: Islam, Catholicism, Animist
- Time zone: GMT
- Currency: CFA Franc
- Current head of state: Gilbert Diendéré
- Type of government: Military
- Literacy rate: 36%
- GDP: $11.323 billion
- HDI ranking: 181

CAMEROON

- Location: West Africa
- Neighbours: Central African Republic, Chad, Republic of the Congo, Equatorial Guinea, Gabon, Nigeria
- Capital: Yaounde
- Area: 475,440 sq. km
- Population: 23,463,782
- Language(s): French, English, African languages
- Dominant religions: Indigenous beliefs, Christianity, Islam
- Time zone: +1
- Currency: Central African Franc
- Current head of state: Paul Biya
- Type of government: Presidential Republic
- Literacy rate: 75%
- GDP: $28.826 billion
- HDI ranking: 152

CENTRAL AFRICAN REPUBLIC

- Location: Central Africa
- Neighbours: Cameroon, Chad, D.R. of the Congo, Republic of the Congo, South Sudan, Sudan
- Capital: Bangui
- Area: 622,980 sq. km
- Population: 4,897,337
- Language(s): French, Sangho
- Dominant religions: Indigenous beliefs, Christianity, Islam
- Time zone: +1
- Currency: CFA Franc
- Current head of state: Catherine Samba-Panza
- Type of government: Republic
- Literacy rate: 56.6%
- GDP: $1.801 billion
- HDI ranking: 185

CAPE VERDE

- Location: Off the western coast of Africa
- Capital: Praia
- Area: 4,030 sq. km
- Population: 521,677
- Language(s): Portuguese, Crioulo
- Dominant religion: Roman Catholicism
- Time zone: -1
- Currency: Cape Verdean Escudo
- Current head of state: Jorge Carlos Fonseca
- Type of government: Presidential Republic
- Literacy rate: 87.6%
- GDP: $1.802 billion
- HDI ranking: 123

CHAD

- Location: East Africa
- Capital: N'Djamena
- Neighbours: Cameroon, Central African Republic, Libya, Niger, Nigeria, Sudan
- Area: 1,284,000 sq. km
- Population: 13,405,905
- Language(s): Arabic, French,
- Dominant religion: Islam, Christianity
- Time zone: +1
- Currency: Central African Franc
- Current head of state: Idriss Déby
- Type of government: Republic
- Literacy rate: 35.4%
- GDP: $12.016 billion
- HDI ranking: 184

COMOROS

- Location: Off the coast of Southern Africa
- Capital: Moroni
- Area: 2,170 sq. km
- Population: 791,988
- Language(s): Arabic, French, Shikomoro
- Dominant religion: Islam
- Time zone: +3
- Currency: Comorian Franc
- Head of state: Ikililou Dhoinine
- Type of government: Federal Presidential Republic
- Literacy rate: 75.5%
- GDP: $0.677 billion
- HDI ranking: 159

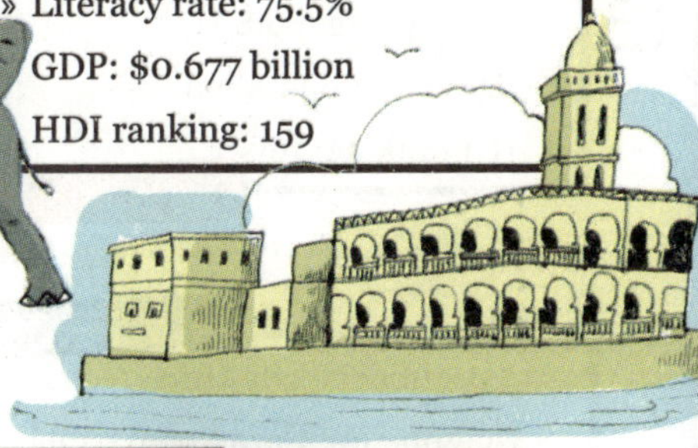

REPUBLIC OF THE CONGO

- Location: Central Africa
- Neighbours: Angola, Cameroon, Central African Republic, D.R. Congo, Gabon
- Capital: Brazzaville
- Area: 342,000 sq. km
- Population: 4,811,022
- Language(s): French
- Dominant religion: Christianity
- Time zone: +2
- Currency: Central African Franc
- Current head of state: Denis Sassou Nguesso
- Type of government: Presidential Republic
- Literacy rate: 83.8%
- GDP: $10.175 billion
- HDI ranking: 140

DEMOCRATIC REPUBLIC OF CONGO

- Location: Southern Africa
- Neighbours: Angola, Burundi, Central African Republic, Congo, Rwanda, South Sudan, Tanzania, Uganda, Zambia
- Capital: Kinshasa
- Area: 2,345,410 sq. km
- Population: 72,314,283
- Language(s): French, Lingala
- Dominant religion: Christianity
- Time zone: +1, +2
- Currency: Congolese Franc
- Current head of state: Joseph Kabila
- Type of government: Presidential Republic
- Literacy rate: 66.8%
- GDP: $39.064 billion
- HDI ranking: 186

EGYPT

- Location: North Africa
- Neighbours: Gaza Strip, Israel, Libya, Sudan
- Capital: Cairo
- Area: 1,001,450 sq. km
- Population: 86,778,592
- Language(s): Arabic, English
- Dominant religion: Islam
- Time zone: +2
- Currency: Egyptian Pound
- Current head of state: Abdel Fattah el-Sisi
- Type of government: Semi-Presidential Republic
- Literacy rate: 73.8%
- GDP: $548.100 billion
- HDI ranking: 110

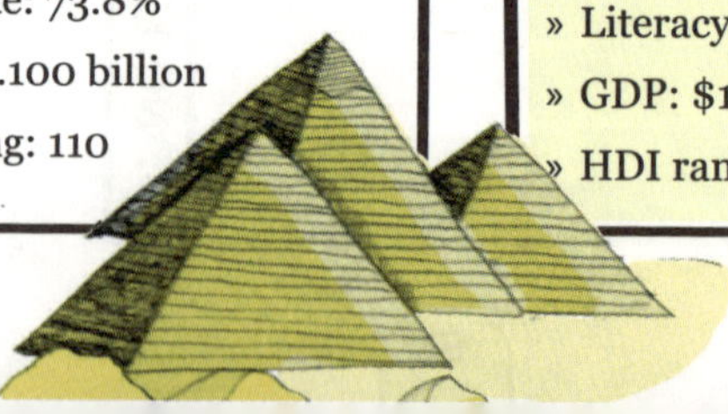

DJIBOUTI

- Location: East Africa
- Neighbours: Eritrea, Somalia, Ethiopia
- Capital: Djibouti
- Area: 23,000 sq. km
- Population: 933,430
- Language(s): French, Arabic
- Dominant religion: Islam
- Time zone: +3
- Currency: Djiboutian Franc
- Current head of state: Ismaïl Omar Guelleh
- Type of government: Semi-Presidential Republic
- Literacy rate: 70%
- GDP: $1.743 billion
- HDI ranking: 170

EQUATORIAL GUINEA

- Location: Central Africa
- Neighbours: Cameroon, Gabon
- Capital: Malabo
- Area: 28,050 sq. km
- Population: 811,111
- Language(s): Spanish, French
- Dominant religion: Roman Catholicism
- Time zone: +1
- Currency: Central African Franc
- Current head of state: Teodoro Obiang Nguemea Mbasogo
- Type of government: Semi-Presidential Republic
- Literacy rate: 95.3%
- GDP: $8.506 billion
- HDI ranking: 144

ERITREA

- Location: East Africa
- Neighbours: Djibouti, Ethiopia, Sudan
- Capital: Asmara
- Area: 121,320 sq. km
- Population: 6,713,467
- Language(s): Afar, Arabic
- Dominant religion: Islam
- Time zone: +3
- Currency: Nakfa
- Current head of state: Isaias Afwerki
- Type of government: Presidential Republic
- Literacy rate: 80%
- GDP: $4.253 billion
- HDI ranking: 182

ETHIOPIA

- Location: East Africa
- Neighbours: Djibouti, Eritrea , Kenya, Somalia, South Sudan, Sudan
- Capital: Addis Ababa
- Area: 1,127,127 sq. km
- Population: 103,055,012
- Language(s): Oromo, Amharic, Somali, Tigrigna, Afar, English
- Dominant religion: Christianity
- Time zone: +3
- Currency: Birr
- Current head of state: Mulatu Teshome
- Type of government: Federal Parliamentary Republic
- Literacy rate: 49.1%
- GDP: $57.557 billion
- HDI ranking: 173

GABON

- Location: West Africa
- Neighbour(s): Cameroon, Congo, Equatorial Guinea
- Capital: Libreville
- Area: 267,667 sq. km
- Population: 1,757,543
- Language(s): French, Fang
- Dominant religions: Christianity, Animist
- Time zone: +1
- Currency: Central African Franc
- Current head of state: Ali Bongo Ondimba
- Type of government: Presidential Republic
- Literacy rate: 88.4%
- GDP: $15.027 billion
- HDI ranking: 112

GHANA

- Location: West Africa
- Neighbours: Cote d'Ivoire, Burkina Faso, Togo
- Capital: Accra
- Area: 239,460 sq. km
- Population: 27,133,818
- Language(s): English, indigenous languages
- Dominant religion: Christianity
- Time zone: GMT
- Currency: Cedi
- Current head of state: John Dramani Mahama
- Type of government: Presidential Constitutional Republic
- Literacy rate: 76.6%
- GDP: $39.219 billion
- HDI ranking: 138

THE GAMBIA

- Location: Western Africa
- Neighbour(s): Senegal
- Capital: Banjul
- Area: 11,300 sq. km
- Population: 1,956,091
- Language(s): English, Indigenous languages
- Dominant religion: Islam
- Time zone: GMT
- Currency: Dalasi
- Current head of state: Yahya Jammeh
- Type of government: Presidential Republic
- Literacy rate: 50%
- GDP: $0.781 billion
- HDI ranking: 172

GUINEA

- Location: West Africa
- Neighbours: Cote d'Ivoire, Guinea-Bissau, Liberia, Mali, Senegal, Sierra Leone
- Capital: Conakry
- Area: 245,861 sq. km
- Population: 12,617,095
- Language(s): French
- Dominant religion: Islam
- Time zone: GMT
- Currency: Guinean Franc
- Current head of state: Alpha Condé
- Type of government: Republic
- Literacy rate: 30.4%
- GDP: $7.155 billion
- HDI ranking: 179

GUINEA-BISSAU

- Location: West Africa
- Neighbour(s): Guinea, Senegal
- Capital: Bissau
- Area: 36,120 sq. km
- Population: 1,790,191
- Language(s): Portuguese
- Dominant religions: Islam and indigenous faiths only
- Time zone: GMT
- Currency: West African Franc
- Current head of state: José Mário Vaz
- Type of government: Presidential Republic
- Literacy rate: 59.9%
- GDP: $0.982 billion
- HDI ranking: 177

CÔTE D'IVOIRE

- Location: Western Africa
- Neighbour(s): Burkina Faso, Ghana, Guinea, Liberia, Mali
- Capital: Yamoussoukro
- Area: 322,460 sq. km
- Population: 21,420,247
- Language(s): French, Dioula
- Dominant religions: Islam, Christianity, indigenous beliefs
- Time zone: GMT
- Currency: CFA Franc
- Current head of state: Alassane Ouattara
- Type of government: Presidential Republic
- Literacy rate: 56.9%
- GDP: $31.753 billion
- HDI ranking: 171

KENYA

- Location: East Africa
- Neighbours: Sudan, Uganda, Ethiopia, Somalia, Tanzania
- Capital: Nairobi
- Area: 582,650 sq. km
- Population: 47,262,232
- Language(s): English, Kiswahili
- Dominant religion: Christianity
- Time zone: +3
- Currency: Kenytaan Shilling
- Current head of state: Uhuru Kenyatta
- Type of government: Presidential Republic
- Literacy rate: 87.4%
- GDP: $65.899 billion
- HDI ranking: 147

LIBERIA

- Location: West Africa
- Neighbours: Sierra Leone, Guinea, Cote d'Ivoire
- Capital: Monrovia
- Area: 111,370 sq. km
- Population: 4,704,859
- Language(s): English, ethnic languages
- Dominant religions: Christianity, Islam, Indigenous beliefs
- Time zone: GMT
- Currency: Liberian Dollar
- Current head of state: Ellen Johnson Sirleaf
- Type of government: Presidential Constitutional Republic
- Literacy rate: 60.8%
- GDP: $2.056 billion
- HDI ranking: 175

LESOTHO

- Location: Southern Africa
- Neighbours: South Africa
- Capital: Maseru
- Area: 30,350 sq. km
- Population: 2,077,284
- Language(s): Sesotho, English
- Dominant religion: Christianity
- Time zone: +2
- Currency: Loti
- Current head of state: King Letsie III
- Type of government: Constitutional Monarchy
- Literacy rate: 89.6%
- GDP: $2.114 billion
- HDI ranking: 158

LIBYA

- Location: North Africa
- Neighbours: Algeria, Chad, Egypt, Niger, Sudan, Tunisia
- Capital: Tripoli
- Area: 1,759,540 sq. km
- Population: 6,641,324
- Language(s): Arabic, Italian, English
- Dominant religion: Islam
- Time zone: +1
- Currency: Libyan Dollar
- Current head of state: Abdullah al-Thani
- Type of government: Disputed
- Literacy rate: 94.2%
- GDP: $34.239 billion
- HDI ranking: 55

MADAGASCAR

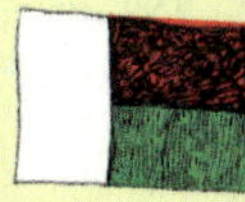

- Location: Southern African coast
- Capital: Antanarivo
- Area: 587,040 sq. km
- Population: 24,850,830
- Language(s): Malagasy, English, French
- Dominant religions: Indigenous faiths, Christianity
- Time zone: +3
- Currency: Madagascar Ariary
- Current head of state: Hery Martial Rakotoarimanana Rajaonarimampianina
- Type of government: Republic
- Literacy rate: 64.7%
- GDP: $10.750 billion
- HDI ranking: 155

MALAWI

- Location: Southern Africa
- Neighbour(s) : Mozambique, Tanzania, Zambia
- Capital: Lilongwe
- Area: 118,480 sq. km
- Population: 24,850,830
- Language(s): English, Chinchewa
- Dominant religion: Christianity
- Time zone: +2
- Currency: Malawian Kwach
- Current head of state: Peter Mutharika
- Type of government: Democratic Republic
- Literacy rate: 74.8%
- GDP: $4.943 billion
- HDI ranking: 174

MALI

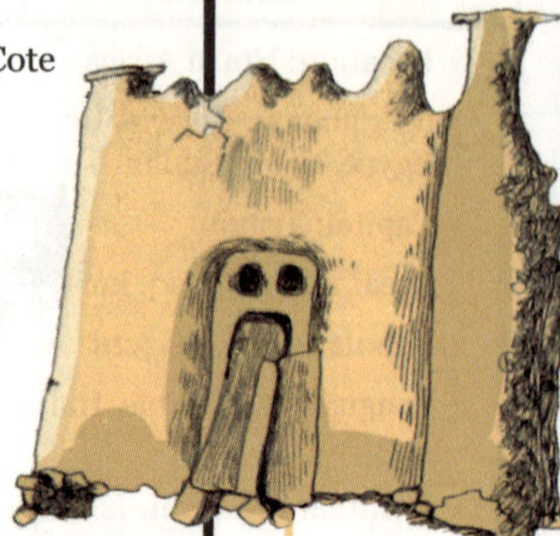

- Location: West Africa
- Neighbours: Algeria , Burkina Faso, Guinea, Cote d'Ivoire, Mauritania, Niger, Senegal
- Capital: Barnako
- Area: 1,240,000 sq. km
- Population: 16,335,528
- Language(s): Bambara, French
- Dominant religion: Islam
- Time zone: GMT
- Currency: Central African Franc
- Current head of state: Ibrahim Boubacar Keita
- Type of government: Republic
- Literacy rate: 27.7%
- GDP: $10.968 billion
- HDI ranking: 176

MAURITANIA

- Location: Northern Africa
- Neighbours: Algeria, Mali, Senegal, Western Sahara
- Capital: Nouakchott
- Area: 1,030,700 sq. km
- Population: 4,136,303
- Language(s): Arabic, Pulaar, Soninke, Wolof
- Dominant religion: Islam
- Time zone: GMT
- Currency: Ouguyia
- Current head of state: Mohamed Ould Abdel Aziz
- Type of government: Republic
- Literacy rate: 52.1%
- GDP: $4.994 billion
- HDI ranking: 161

MAURITIUS

- Location: Off the coast of Southern Africa
- Capital: Port Louis
- Area: 2,040 sq. km
- Population: 1,326,908
- Language(s): Creole, French, Bhojpuri, English
- Dominant religions: Hinduism, Christianity
- Time zone: +4
- Currency: Mauritian Rupee
- Current head of state: Ameenah Gurib
- Type of government: Parliamentary Democracy
- Literacy rate: 89.8%
- GDP: $13.358 billion
- HDI ranking: 63

MOROCCO

- Location: North Africa
- Neighbour(s): Algeria, Spain, Western Sahara
- Capital: Rabat
- Area: 446,550 sq. km
- Population: 33,831,352
- Language(s): Arabic
- Dominant religion: Islam
- Time zone: WET
- Currency: Moroccan Dirham
- Current head of state: Mohammed VI
- Type of government: Constitutional Monarchy
- Literacy rate: 72%
- GDP: $102.044 billion
- HDI ranking: 129

MOZAMBIQUE

- Location: Southeast Africa
- Neighbours: Zimbabwe, South Africa
- Capital: Maputo
- Area: 801,590 sq. km
- Population: 27,554,932
- Language(s): Emakhuwa, Xichagana, Portuguese
- Dominant religions: Christianity, Islam
- Time zone: +2
- Currency: Metical
- Current head of state: Armando Guebuza
- Type of government: Republic
- Literacy rate: 58.8%
- GDP: $16.921 billion
- HDI ranking: 178

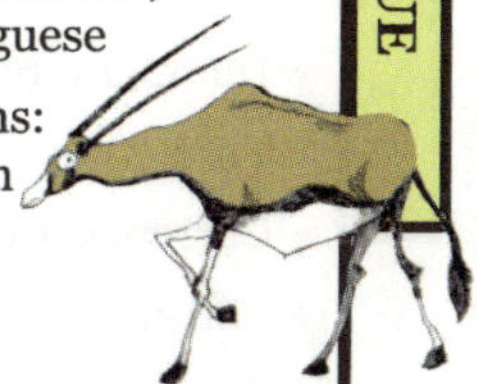

NAMIBIA

- Location: Southern Africa
- Neighbours: Angola, Botswana, South Africa, Zambia
- Capital: Windhoek
- Area: 825,418 sq. km
- Population: 2,333,754
- Language(s): English, Oshiwambo languages
- Dominant religion: Christianity
- Time zone: +1
- Currency: Namibian Dollar
- Current head of state: Hage Geingob
- Type of government: Republic
- Literacy rate: 88.8%
- GDP: $12.571 billion
- HDI ranking: 127

NIGER

- Location: West Africa
- Neighbours: Algeria, Benin, Burkina Faso, Chad, Libya, Mali, Nigeria
- Capital: Niamey
- Area: 1,267,000 sq. km
- Population: 19,566,121
- Language(s): French, Hausa, Djerma
- Dominant religion: Islam
- Time zone: +1
- Currency: Central African Franc
- Current head of state: Mahamadou Issoufou
- Type of government: Semi-presidential Republic
- Literacy rate: 28.7%
- GDP: $7.270 billion
- HDI ranking: 187

NIGERIA

- Location: West Africa
- Neighbours: Benin, Cameroon, Chad, Niger
- Capital: Abuja
- Area: 923,768 sq. km
- Population: 181,274,699
- Language(s): English, Hausa
- Dominant religions: Islam, Christianity
- Time zone: +1
- Currency: Naira
- Current head of state: Muhammadu Buhari
- Type of government: Federal Republic
- Literacy rate: 78.6%
- GDP: $515.431 billion
- HDI ranking: 152

RWANDA

- Location: Central Africa
- Neighbours: Burundi, D.R. Congo, Tanzania, Uganda
- Capital: Kigali
- Area: 26,338 sq. km
- Population: 12,682,470
- Language(s): Kinyarwanda, French, English
- Dominant religion: Christianity
- Time zone: +2
- Currency: Rwandan Franc
- Current head of state: Paul Kagame
- Type of government: Presidential Republic
- Literacy rate: 71.1%
- GDP: $8.763 billion
- HDI ranking: 151

SÃO TOMÉ AND PRÍNCIPE

- Location: Off the coast of West Africa
- Capital: Sao Tome
- Area: 1,001 sq. km
- Population: 202,788
- Language(s): Portuguese
- Dominant religion: Christianity
- Time zone: GMT
- Currency: Dobra
- Current head of state: Manuel Pinto da Costa
- Type of government: Republic
- Literacy rate: 84.9%
- GDP: $0.388 billion
- HDI ranking: 142

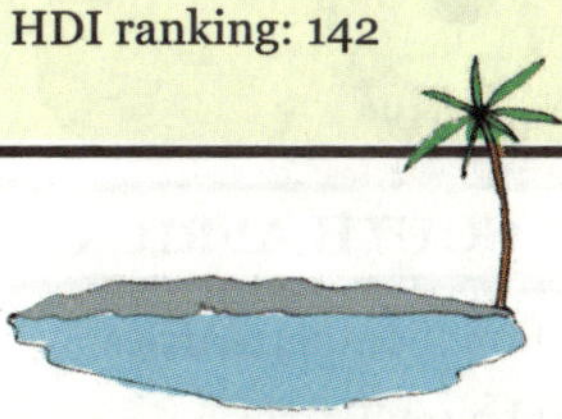

SENEGAL

- Location: West Africa
- Neighbours: Gambia, Guinea, Guinea-Bissau, Mali, Mauritania
- Capital: Dakar
- Area: 196,190 sq. km
- Population: 15,067,130
- Language(s): French, Wolof
- Dominant religion: Islam
- Time zone: GMT
- Currency: Central African Franc
- Current head of state: Macky Sall
- Type of government: Republic
- Literacy rate: 39.3%
- GDP: $15.051 billion
- HDI ranking: 163

SEYCHELLES

- Location: Eastern African Coast
- Capital: Victoria
- Area: 456 sq. km
- Population: 91,450
- Language(s): Creole, English, French
- Dominant religion: Christianity
- Time zone: +4
- Currency: Seychellois Rupee
- Current head of state: James Michel
- Type of government: Republic
- Literacy rate: 91.8%
- GDP: $1.378 billion
- HDI ranking: 71

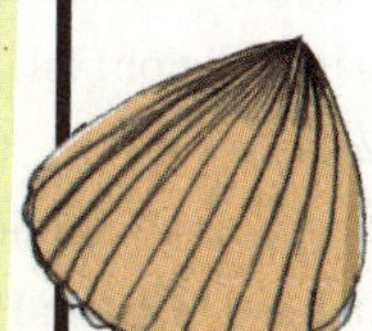

SIERRA LEONE

- Location: West Africa
- Neighbour(s): Guinea, Liberia
- Capital: Freetown
- Area: 71,740 sq. km
- Population: 6,491,025
- Language(s): English, Mende, Temne
- Dominant religion: Islam, Indigenous faiths
- Time zone: GMT
- Currency: Leone
- Current head of state: Ernest Bai Koroma
- Type of government: Constitutional Democracy
- Literacy rate: 35.1%
- GDP: $4.401 billion
- HDI ranking: 183

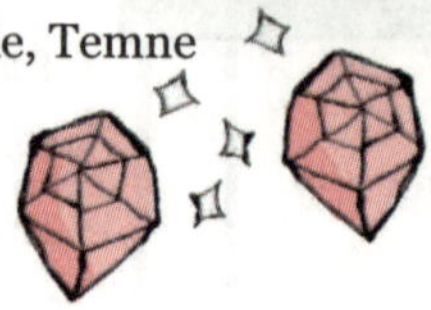

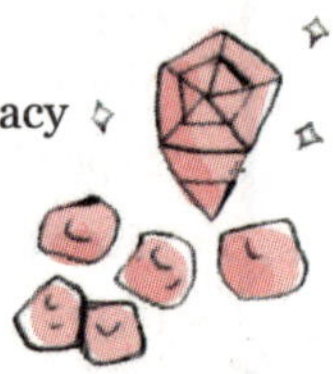

SOMALIA

- Location: East Africa
- Neighbours: Djibouti, Ethiopia, Kenya
- Capital: Mogadishu
- Area: 637,657 sq. km
- Population: 10,814,869
- Language(s): Somali, Arabic
- Dominant religion: Islam
- Time zone: +3
- Currency: Somali Shilling
- Current head of state: Hassan Sheikh Mohamud
- Type of government: Federal Republic
- Literacy rate: N/A
- GDP: $5.896 billion
- HDI ranking: 193

SOUTH AFRICA

- Location: Southern Africa
- Neighbours: Botswana, Lesotho, Mozambique, Namibia, Swaziland, Zimbabwe
- Capital: Pretoria
- Area: 1,219,912 sq. km
- Population: 48,601,098
- Language(s): English, Afrikaans
- Dominant religion: Christianity
- Time zone: +2
- Currency: Rand
- Current head of state: Jacob Zuma
- Type of government: Republic
- Literacy rate: 93%
- GDP: $323.809 billion
- HDI ranking: 118

SUDAN

- Location: Northeastern Africa
- Neighbours: Egypt, Libya, Chad, Ethiopia, Eritrea, Congo, South Sudan, Uganda, Central African Republic
- Capital: Khartoum
- Area: 2,505,810 sq. km
- Population: 40,722,321
- Language(s): Arabic, English
- Dominant religions: Islam, Christianity
- Time zone: +3
- Currency: Sudanese Pound
- Current head of state: Lt. Gen. Omar Hassan Ahmad al-Bashir
- Type of government: Republic
- Literacy rate: 75.9%
- GDP: $64.495 billion
- HDI ranking: 166

SOUTH SUDAN

- Location: Northeastern Africa
- Neighbours: Ethiopia, Kenya, Uganda, Central African Republic, Democratic Republic of the Congo, Sudan
- Capital: Juba
- Area: 619,745 sq. km
- Population: 11,865,174
- Language(s): English, Arabic, indigenous languages
- Dominant religions: Christianity, indigenous religions
- Time zone: +3
- Currency: South Sudanese Pound
- Current head of state: Salva Kiir Mayardit
- Type of government: Republic
- Literacy rate: 27%
- GDP: $76.204 billion

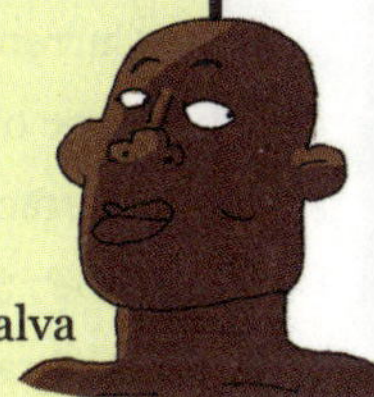

TANZANIA

- Location: Eastern Africa
- Neighbours: Burundi, D.R. Congo, Kenya, Malawi, Mozambique, Rwanda, Uganda, Zambia
- Capital: Dodoma
- Area: 945,087 sq. km
- Population: 51,422,316
- Language(s): Swahili, English, Arabic
- Dominant religions: Islam, Indigenous beliefs, Christianity
- Time zone: +3
- Currency: Tanzanian Shilling
- Current head of state: Jakaya Kikwete
- Type of government: Republic
- Literacy rate: 70.6%
- GDP: $49.966 billion
- HDI ranking: 159

SWAZILAND

- Location: Southern Africa
- Neighbour(s): Mozambique, South Africa
- Capital: Mbabane
- Area: 17,363 sq. km
- Population: 1,286,963
- Language(s): English, SiSwati
- Dominant religions: Zionism, Roman Catholicism
- Time zone: +2
- Currency: Lilageni
- Current head of state: King Mswati III
- Type of government: Monarchy
- Literacy rate: 87.5%
- GDP: $3.634 billion
- HDI ranking: 148

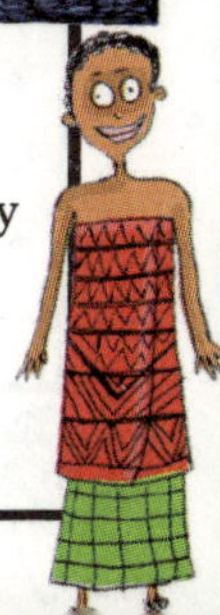

TOGO

- Location: West Africa
- Neighbours: Benin, Burkina Faso, Ghana
- Capital: Lome
- Area: 56,785 sq. km
- Population: 7,345,173
- Language(s): French, Ewe, Mina, Kabye, Dogombo
- Dominant religions: Indigenous beliefs, Christianity, Islam
- Time zone: GMT
- Currency: West African Franc
- Current head of state: Faure Gnassingbé
- Type of government: Republic
- Literacy rate: 60.9%
- GDP: $4.514 billion
- HDI ranking: 166

TUNISIA

- Location: North Africa
- Neighbours: Libya, Algeria
- Capital: Tunis
- Area: 163,610 sq. km
- Population: 11,175,214
- Language(s): Arabic, French, Berber
- Dominant religion: Islam
- Time zone: +1
- Currency: Tunisian Dollar
- Current head of state: Beji Caid Essebsi
- Type of government: Republic
- Literacy rate: 88.3%
- GDP: $45.276 billion
- HDI ranking: 90

UGANDA

- Location: East Africa
- Neighbours: D.R. Congo, Kenya, Rwanda , South Sudan, Tanzania
- Capital: Kampala
- Area: 236,040 sq. km
- Population: 41,352,879
- Language(s): English, Ganda
- Dominant religions: Christianity, Islam
- Time zone: +3
- Currency: Ugandan Shilling
- Current head of state: Yoweri Museveni
- Type of government: Republic
- Literacy rate: 78.4%
- GDP: $26.814 billion
- HDI ranking: 164

ZAMBIA

- Location: Southern Africa
- Neighbours: Angola, Botswana, D.R.Congo, Malawi, Mozambique, Namibia, Tanzania , Zimbabwe
- Capital: Lusaka
- Area: 740,724 sq. km
- Population: 15,729,148
- Language(s): English, various dialects
- Dominant religions: Christianity, Islam
- Time zone: +2
- Currency: Kwacha
- Current head of state: Edgar Lungu
- Type of government: Republic
- Literacy rate: 80.6%
- GDP: $28.445 billion
- HDI ranking: 141

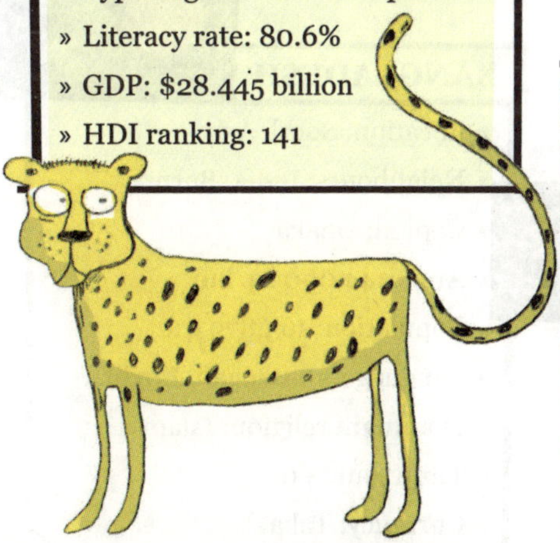

ZIMBABWE

- Location: Southern Africa
- Neighbours: Zambia, Botswana, Mozambique, South Africa
- Capital: Harare
- Area: 386,669 sq. km
- Population: 16,016,984
- Language(s): English, Shona
- Dominant religions: Christianity, indigenous faiths
- Time zone: +2
- Currency: Zimbabwean dollar formerly
- Current head of state: Robert Mugabe
- Type of government: Presidential Republic
- Literacy rate: 90.7%
- GDP: $13.966 billion
- HDI ranking: 156

AFGHANISTAN

- Location: Southcentral Asia
- Neighbours: China, Iran, Pakistan, Tajikistan, Turkmenistan, Uzbekistan
- Capital: Kabul
- Area: 647,500 sq. km
- Population: 32,992,580
- Language(s): Pashto, Dari
- Dominant religion: Islam
- Time zone: +4:30
- Currency: Afghan
- Current head of state: Ashraf Ghani
- Type of government: Islamic Republic
- Literacy rate: 28.1%
- GDP: $21.526 billion
- HDI ranking: 169

BAHRAIN

- Location: Southcentral Asia
- Neighbours: Saudi Arabia, Qatar
- Capital: Manama
- Area: 665 sq. km
- Population: 1,459,770
- Language(s): Arabic, English, Farsi
- Dominant religion: Islam
- Time zone: +3
- Currency: Bahraini Dinar
- Current head of state: Hamad bin Isa Al Khalifa
- Type of government: Constitutional Monarchy
- Literacy rate: 94.6%
- GDP: $31.315 billion
- HDI ranking: 44

BANGLADESH

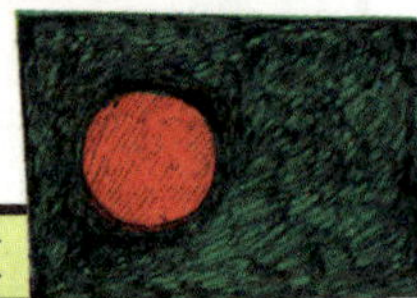

- Location: South Asia
- Neighbours: India, Burma
- Capital: Dhaka
- Area: 144,000 sq. km
- Population: 163,879,412
- Language(s): Bengali, English
- Dominant religion: Islam
- Time zone: +6
- Currency: Taka
- Current head of state: Abdul Hamid
- Type of government: Parliamentary democracy
- Literacy rate: 57.7%
- GDP: $205.327 billion
- HDI ranking: 142

BHUTAN

- Location: South Asia
- Neighbours: Nepal, Bangladesh, China
- Capital: Thimpu
- Area: 47,000 sq. km
- Population: 775,499
- Language(s): Dzongka, Nepali
- Dominant religion: Buddhism
- Time zone: +6
- Currency: Ngultrum
- Current head of state: Jigme Khesar Namgyal Wangchuck
- Type of government: Constitutional Monarchy
- Literacy rate: 64.9%
- GDP: $2.246 billion
- HDI ranking: 136

BRUNEI

- Location: Southeast Asia
- Neighbour(s): Malaysia
- Capital: Bandar Seri Begawan
- Area: 5,770 sq. km
- Population: 439,025
- Language(s): Malay, English, Chinese
- Dominant religion: Islam
- Time zone: +8
- Currency: Brunei Dollar
- Current head of state: Hassanal Bolkiah
- Type of government: Constitutional Monarchy
- Literacy rate: 95.4%
- GDP: $17.536 billion
- HDI ranking: 30

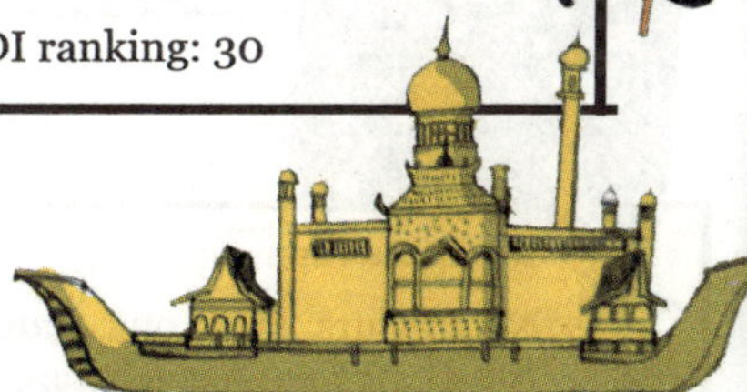

BURMA (MYANMAR)

- Location: Southeast Asia
- Neighbours: India, Bangladesh, China, Laos, Thailand
- Capital: Nai Pyi Taw
- Area: 678,500 sq. km
- Population: 54,958,709
- Language(s): Burmese
- Dominant religion: Buddhism
- Time zone: +6:30
- Currency: Kyat
- Current head of state: Thein Sein
- Type of government: Unitary Presidential Republic
- Literacy rate: 93.1%
- GDP: $69.143 billion
- HDI ranking: 150

CAMBODIA

- Location: East Asia
- Neighbours: Vietnam, Thailand, Laos
- Capital: Phnom Penh
- Area: 181,040 sq. km
- Population: 15,823,111
- Language(s): Khmer
- Dominant religion: Theravada Buddhism
- Time zone: +7
- Currency: Riel
- Current head of state: Norodom Sihamoni
- Type of government: Constitutional Monarchy
- Literacy rate: 77.2%
- GDP: $17.814 billion
- HDI ranking: 136

PEOPLE'S REPUBLIC OF CHINA

- Location: Asia
- Neighbours: Mongolia, India, Nepal, Burma, Kazakhstan, Kyrgyzstan, Afghanistan, Pakistan
- Capital: Beijing
- Area: 9,596,960 sq. km
- Population: 1,375,774,929
- Language(s): Mandarin, various Chinese dialects
- Dominant religions: Atheism (official), Taoism
- Time zone: +8
- Currency: Yuan/Renminbi
- Current head of state: Xi Jinping
- Type of government: Communist
- Literacy rate: 95.1%
- GDP: $11,211.928 billion
- HDI ranking: 91

EAST TIMOR

- Location: Southeast Asia
- Neighbour(s): Indonesia, Australia
- Capital: Dili
- Area: 14,609 sq. km
- Population: 1,301,427
- Language(s): Tetum, Portuguese, English, Indonesian
- Dominant religion: Roman Catholicism
- Time zone: +9
- Currency: US Dollar
- Current head of state: Taur Matan Ruak
- Type of government: Republic
- Literacy rate: 67.5%
- GDP: $4.912 billion
- HDI ranking: 128

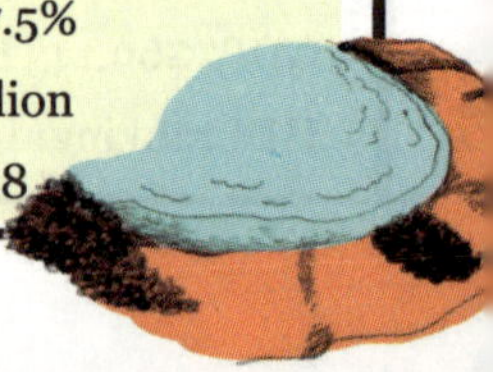

INDIA

- Location: South Asia
- Neighbours: Pakistan, China, Bangladesh, Myanmar, Nepal, Bhutan
- Capital: New Delhi
- Area: 3,287,590 sq. km
- Population: 1,299,256,504
- Language(s): Hindi, English and 21 other official languages
- Dominant religions: Hinduism, Islam, Sikhism, Christianity
- Time zone: +5.30
- Currency: Rupee
- Current head of state: Pranab Mukherjee
- Type of government: Federal Republic and Parliamentary Democracy
- Literacy rate: 74.4%
- GDP: $2,308.018 billion
- HDI ranking: 135

INDONESIA

- Location: Southeast Asia
- Neighbours: Malaysia, Australia, Papua New Guinea
- Capital: Jakarta
- Area: 1,919,440 sq. km
- Population: 256,960,858
- Language(s): Bahasa Indonesia
- Dominant religion: Islam
- Time zone: +9
- Currency: Indonesian Rupaiah
- Current head of state: Joko Widodo
- Type of government: Republic
- Literacy rate: 92.8%
- GDP: $895.677 billion
- HDI ranking: 108

IRAN

- Location: Middle East
- Neighbours: Iraq, Turkmenistan, Pakistan, Afghanistan
- Capital: Tehran
- Area: 1,648,000 sq. km
- Population: 80,031,158
- Language(s): Farsi, Turkish
- Dominant religion: Islam
- Time zone: +4
- Currency: Iranian Rial
- Current head of state: Hassan Rouhani
- Type of government: Islamic Republic
- Literacy rate: 86.8%
- GDP: $393.495 billion
- HDI ranking: 75

IRAQ

- Location: Middle East
- Neighbours: IIran, Syria, Saudi Arabia, Jordan, Kuwait
- Capital: Baghdad
- Area: 433,970 sq. km
- Population: 35,560,969
- Language(s): Arabic, Kurdish
- Dominant religion: Islam
- Time zone: +3
- Currency: New Iraqi Dinar
- Current head of state: Fuad Masum
- Type of government: Parliamentary Democracy
- Literacy rate: 80.2%
- GDP: $173.819 billion
- HDI ranking: 120

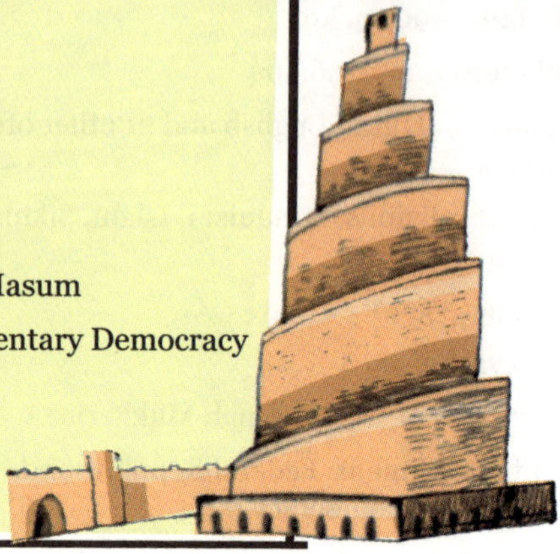

ISRAEL

- Location: Middle East
- Neighbours: Egypt, Jordan, Lebanon, Gaza Strip and West Bank
- Capital: Jerusalem
- Area: 20,770 sq. km
- Population: 8,385,912
- Language(s): Hebrew, Arabic, English
- Dominant religion: Judaism
- Time zone: +2
- Currency: New Israeli Shekel
- Current head of state: Reuven Rivlin
- Type of government: Parliamentary Democracy
- Literacy rate: 97.8%
- GDP: $306.873 billion
- HDI ranking: 19

JAPAN

- Location: East Asia
- Capital: Tokyo
- Neighbours: Korea, Russia
- Area: 377,835 sq. km
- Population: 126,236,770
- Language(s): Japanese
- Dominant religions: Shinto, Buddhism
- Time zone: +9
- Currency: Yen
- Current head of State: Akihito
- Type of government: Constitutional Monarchy
- Literacy rate: 99%
- GDP: $4,210.363 billion
- HDI ranking: 17

JORDAN

- Location: Middle East
- Neighbours: Iraq, Israel, Saudi Arabia, Syria, West Bank
- Capital: Amman
- Area: 92,300 sq. km
- Population: 6,843,714
- Language(s): Arabic, English
- Dominant religion: Islam
- Time zone: +2
- Currency: Jordanian Dinar
- Current head of state: Abdullah II
- Type of government: Constitutional Monarchy
- Literacy rate: 93.4%
- GDP: $38.145 billion
- HDI ranking: 77

KAZAKHSTAN

- Location: Central Asia
- Neighbours: China, Kyrgyzstan, Russia, Turkmenistan, Uzbekistan
- Capital: Astana
- Area: 2,717,300 sq. km
- Population: 17,043,696
- Language(s): Kazakh, Russian
- Dominant religions: Islam, Christianity
- Time zone: +4
- Currency: Tenge
- Current head of state: Nursultan Nazarbayev
- Type of government: Presidential Republic
- Literacy rate: 99.5%
- GDP: $203.140 billion
- HDI ranking: 70

KOREA (NORTH)

- Location: Eastern Asia
- Neighbours: South Korea, China
- Capital: Pyongyang
- Area: 120,540 sq. km
- Population: 25,265,068
- Language(s): Korean
- Dominant religions: Buddhism, Chondogyo
- Time zone: +1
- Currency: North Korean Won
- Current head of state: Kim Jong-un
- Type of government: Democratic Republic
- Literacy rate: 100%
- GDP: $40 billion
- HDI ranking: NA

KOREA (SOUTH)

- Location: Eastern Asia
- Neighbour(s): North Korea
- Capital: Seoul
- Area: 98,189 sq. km
- Population: 50,433,949
- Language(s): Korean
- Dominant religions: Christianity, Buddhism
- Time zone: +9
- Currency: South Korean Won
- Current head of state: Park Geun-hye
- Type of government: Republic
- Literacy rate: 97.9%
- GDP: $1,435.076 billion
- HDI ranking: 15

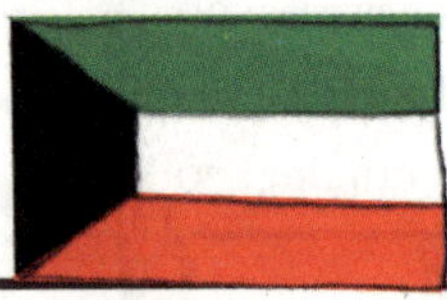

KUWAIT

- Location: Middle East
- Neighbours: Iraq, Saudi Arabia
- Capital: Kuwait City
- Area: 17,819 sq. km
- Population: 3,511,156
- Language(s): Arabic, English
- Dominant religion: Islam
- Time zone: +3
- Currency: Kuwaiti Dinar
- Current head of state: Sabah Al-Ahmad Al-Jaber Al-Sabah
- Type of government: Constitutional Monarchy
- Literacy rate: 94%
- GDP: $134.478 billion
- HDI ranking: 46

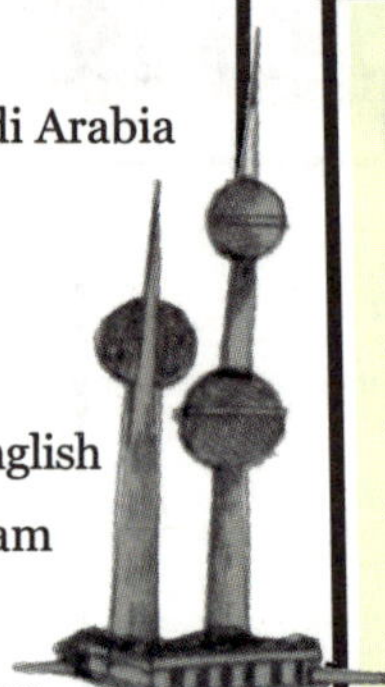

KYRGYZSTAN

- Location: Central Asia
- Neighbours: Kazakhstan, Tajikistan, China, Uzbekistan
- Capital: Bishkek
- Area: 191,300 sq. km
- Population: 5,910,227
- Language(s): Kyrgyz, Russian, Uzbek
- Dominant religion: Islam, Russian Orthodox
- Time zone: +6
- Currency: Som
- Current head of state: Almazbek Atambayev
- Type of government: Republic
- Literacy rate: 98.7%
- GDP: $7.368 billion
- HDI ranking: 125

LAOS

- Location: Southeast Asia
- Neighbours: Cambodia, China, Thailand, Vietnam, Myanmar
- Capital: Vientiane
- Area: 236,800 sq. km
- Population: 7,070,539
- Language(s): Lao, French
- Dominant religion: Buddhism
- Time zone: +7
- Currency: Kip
- Current head of state: Choummaly Sayasone
- Type of government: Communist
- Literacy rate: 79.9%
- GDP: $12.764 billion
- HDI ranking: 139

LEBANON

- Location: Middle East
- Neighbour(s): Israel, Syria
- Capital: Beirut
- Area: 10,400 sq. km
- Population: 4,465,391
- Language(s): Arabic, French
- Dominant religions: Islam, Christianity
- Time zone: +2
- Currency: Lebanese Pound
- Current head of state: Tammam Salam
- Type of government: Republic
- Literacy rate: 93.9%
- GDP: $54.671 billion
- HDI ranking: 65

MALAYSIA

- Location: Southeast Asia
- Neighbour(s): Indonesia, Singapore, Thailand
- Capital: Kuala Lumpur
- Area: 329,750 sq. km
- Population: 30,987,202
- Language(s): Bahasa Malay, English, Tamil, Cantonese
- Dominant religions: Islam, Buddhism
- Time zone: +8
- Currency: Ringgit
- Current head of state: Najib Razak
- Type of government: Constitutional Monarchy
- Literacy rate: 93.1%
- GDP: $327.890 billion
- HDI ranking: 62

MALDIVES

- Location: Southeast Asia
- Capital: Male
- Area: 300 sq. km
- Population: 336,543
- Language(s): Maldivian Dhivehi, English
- Dominant religion: Islam
- Time zone: +5
- Currency: Rufiyaa
- Current head of state: Abdulla Yameen
- Type of government: Republic
- Literacy rate: 99%
- GDP: $3.032 billion
- HDI ranking: 103

MONGOLIA

- Location: North Asia
- Neighbours: Russia, China
- Capital: Ulan Bator
- Area: 1,565,000 sq. km
- Population: 2,954,258
- Language(s): Khalkha Mongol
- Dominant religion: Buddhism
- Time zone: +7, +8
- Currency: Togrog
- Current head of state: Tsakhiagiin Elbegdorj
- Type of government: Republic
- Literacy rate: 97.4%
- GDP: $12.455 billion
- HDI ranking: 103

NEPAL

- Location: South Asia
- Neighbours: China, India
- Capital: Kathmandu
- Area: 140,800 sq. km
- Population: 29,138,308
- Language(s): Nepali
- Dominant religion: Hinduism
- Time zone: +6
- Currency: Nepali Rupee
- Current head of state: Ram Baran Yadav
- Type of government: Federal Democratic Republic
- Literacy rate: 66%
- GDP: $21.688 billion
- HDI ranking: 145

OMAN

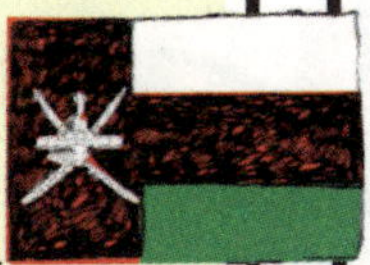

- Location: Middle East
- Neighbours: Saudi Arabia, UAE, Yemen
- Capital: Muscat
- Area: 212,460 sq. km
- Population: 3,568,984
- Language(s): Arabic
- Dominant religion: Islam
- Time zone: +4
- Currency: Omani Rial
- Current head of State: Qaboos bin Said Al Said
- Type of government: Monarchy
- Literacy rate: 81.4%
- GDP: $62.935 billion
- HDI ranking: 56

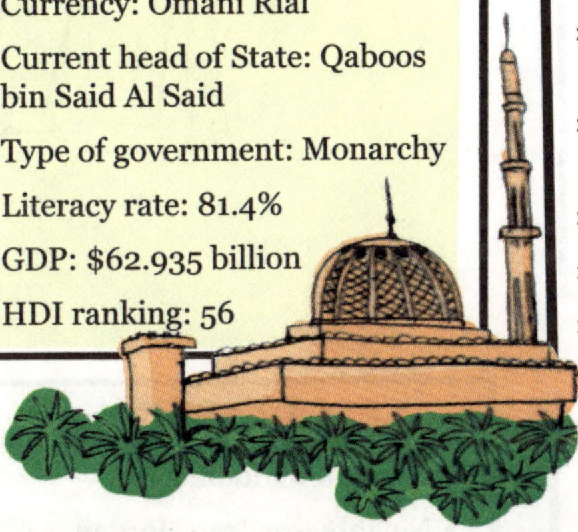

PAKISTAN

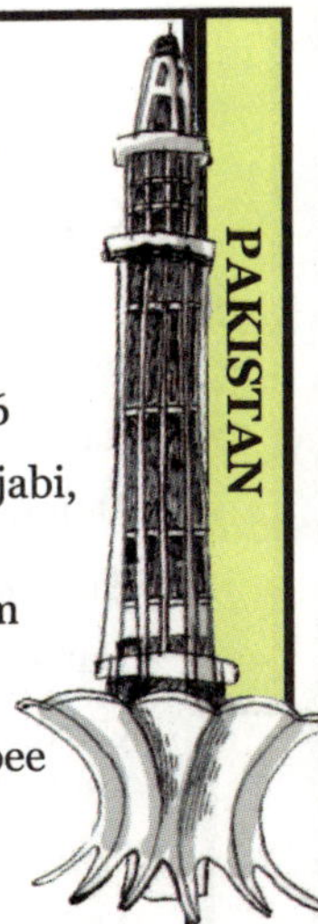

- Location: South Asia
- Neighbours: India, Iran, Afghanistan
- Capital: Islamabad
- Area: 212,460 sq. km
- Population: 189,948,686
- Language(s): Urdu, Punjabi, English
- Dominant religion: Islam
- Time zone: +5
- Currency: Pakistani Rupee
- Current head of state: Mamnoon Hussain
- Type of government: Federal Republic
- Literacy rate: 55%
- GDP: $464.9 billion
- HDI ranking: 146

PHILIPPINES

- Location: Southeast Asia
- Capital: Manila
- Area: 300,000 sq. km
- Population: 103,702,963
- Language(s): Filipino, English
- Dominant religion: Catholicism
- Time zone: +8
- Currency: Philippines Peso
- Current head of state: Benigno Aquino III
- Type of government: Republic
- Literacy rate: 96.3%
- GDP: $308.033 billion
- HDI ranking: 117

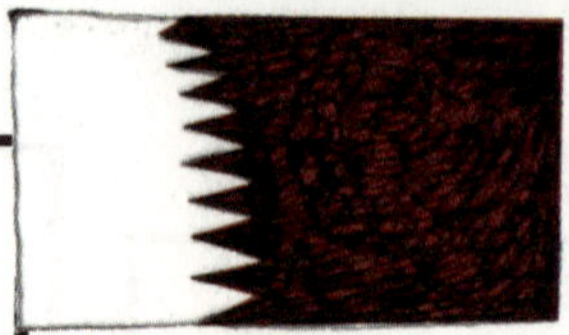

QATAR

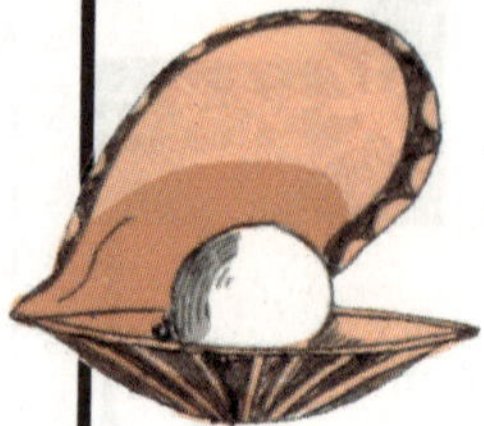

- Location: Middle East
- Neighbours: Saudi Arabia, UAE
- Capital: Doha
- Area: 11,437 sq. km
- Population: 2,113,185
- Language(s): Arabic, English
- Dominant religion: Islam
- Time zone: +3
- Currency: Qatari Rial
- Current head of state: Tamim bin Hamad Al Thani
- Type of government: Monarchy
- Literacy rate: 96.3%
- GDP: $196.964 billion
- HDI ranking: 31

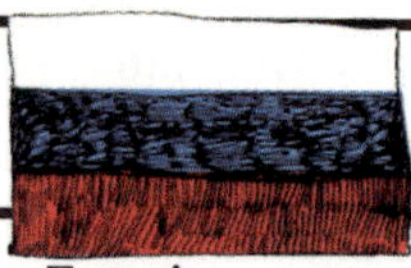

RUSSIAN FEDERATION

- Location: Eurasia
- Neighbours: Mongolia, China, Kazakhstan, Ukraine, Finland
- Capital: Moscow
- Area: 7,075,400 sq. km
- Population: 146,345,138
- Language(s): Russian
- Dominant religion: Russian Orthodox, Islam
- Time zone: + 3 to + 12
- Currency: Rouble
- Current head of state: Vladimir Putin
- Type of government: Federal Semi-presidential Republic
- Literacy rate: 99.7%
- GDP: $1,175.996 billion
- HDI ranking: 57

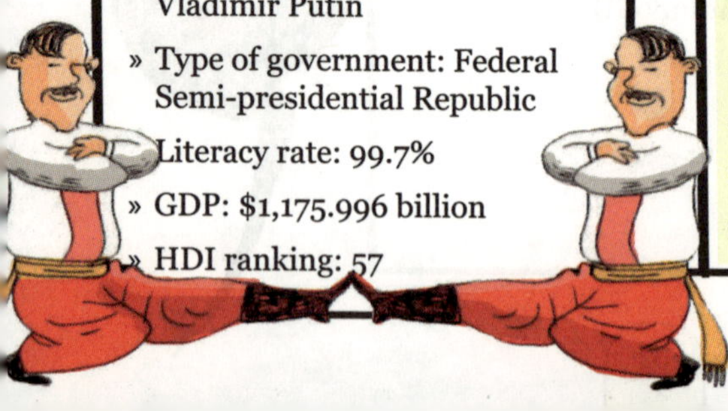

SAUDI ARABIA

- Location: Middle East
- Neighbours: Iraq, Jordan, Kuwait, Oman, Qatar, UAE , Yemen
- Capital: Riyadh
- Area: 2,149,690 sq. km
- Population: 29,935,908
- Language(s): Arabic
- Dominant religion: Islam
- Time zone: +3
- Currency: Saudi Rial
- Current head of state: Salman bin Abdulaziz Al Saud
- Type of government: Monarchy
- Literacy rate: 86.6%
- GDP: $648.971 billion
- HDI ranking: 34

SINGAPORE

- Location: Southeast Asia
- Neighbour(s): Malaysia, Indonesia
- Capital: City of Singapore
- Area: 624 sq. km
- Population: 5,476,174
- Language(s): English, Malay, Mandarin, Tamil
- Dominant religions: Buddhism, Islam, Christianity
- Time zone: +8
- Currency: Singapore Dollar
- Current head of state: Tony Tan
- Type of government: Parliamentary Republic
- Literacy rate: 95.9%
- GDP: $296.057 billion
- HDI ranking: 9

SRI LANKA

- Location: South Asia
- Capital: Colombo
- Area: 65,610 sq. km
- Population: 21,044,221
- Language(s): Sinhala, Tamil
- Dominant religions: Buddhism, Christianity
- Time zone: +5:30
- Currency: Sri Lankan Rupee
- Current head of state: Maithripala Sirisena
- Type of government: Republic
- Literacy rate: 98.1%
- GDP: $80.591 billion
- HDI ranking: 73

SYRIA

- Location: Middle East
- Neighbour(s): Iraq, Israel, Jordan, Lebanon, Turkey
- Capital: Damascus
- Area: 85,180 sq. km
- Population: 23,170,577
- Language(s): Arabic
- Dominant religion: Islam
- Time zone: +2
- Currency: Syrian Pound
- Current head of state: Bashar al-Assad
- Type of government: Semi-presidential Republic
- Literacy rate: 79.6%
- GDP: $107.400 billion
- HDI ranking: 118

TAJIKISTAN

» Location: Central Asia
» Neighbours: Afghanistan, China, Uzbekistan, Kyrgyzstan
» Capital: Dushanbe
» Area: 143,100 sq. km
» Population: 8,570,483
» Language(s): Tajik, Russian
» Dominant religion: Islam
» Time zone: +5
» Currency: Somoni
» Current head of state: Emomalii Rahmon
» Type of government: Semi-presidential Republic
» Literacy rate: 99.7%
» GDP: $8.533 billion
» HDI ranking: 133

THAILAND

» Location: Southeast Asia
» Neighbour(s): Cambodia, Vietnam, Malaysia, Myanmar
» Capital: Bangkok
» Area: 514,000 sq. km
» Population: 68,206,754
» Language(s): Thai
» Dominant religion: Buddhism
» Time zone: +7
» Currency: Baht
» Current head of state: King Bhumibol Adulyadej
» Type of government: Constitutional Monarchy
» Literacy rate: 96.7%
» GDP: $386.291 billion
» HDI ranking: 89

TURKEY

» Location: Eurasia
» Neighbour(s): Syria, Iran, Bulgaria
» Capital: Ankara
» Area: 780,580 sq. km
» Population: 77,450,004
» Language(s): Turkish
» Dominant religion: Islam
» Time zone: +2
» Currency: Lira
» Current head of state: Recep Tayyip Erdoğan
» Type of government: Parliamentary Democracy
» Literacy rate: 95.4%
» GDP: $861.079 billion
» HDI ranking: 69

TURKMENISTAN

- Location: Central Asia
- Neighbours: Iran, Uzbekistan, Kazakhstan
- Capital: Ashgabat
- Area: 488,100 sq. km
- Population: 5,395,363
- Language(s): Turkmen
- Dominant religion: Islam
- Time zone: +5
- Currency: Turkmen New Manat
- Current head of state: Gurbanguly Berdimuhamedow
- Type of government: Presidential Republic
- Literacy rate: 98.8%
- GDP: $44.663 billion
- HDI ranking: 103

UNITED ARAB EMIRATES

- Location: Middle East
- Neighbours: Saudi Arabia, Oman, Iran
- Capital: Abu Dhabi
- Area: 83,600 sq. km
- Population: 10,294,094
- Language(s): Arabic
- Dominant religion: Islam
- Time zone: +4
- Currency: Emirati Dirham
- Current head of state: Sheikh Khalifa bin Zayed Al Nahyan
- Type of government: Monarchy
- Literacy rate: 76.9%
- GDP: $363.707 billion
- HDI ranking: 40

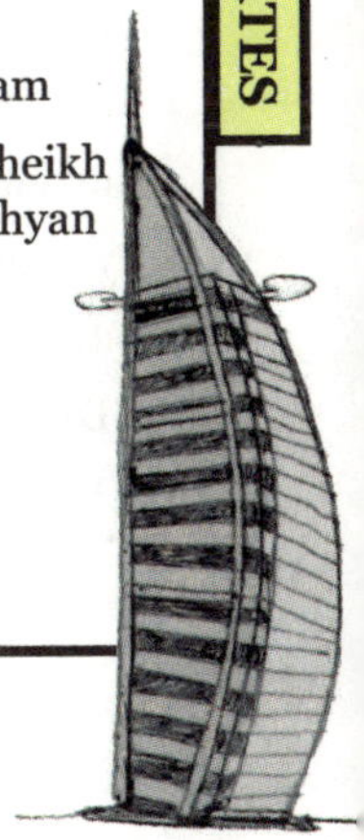

UZBEKISTAN

- Location: Central Asia
- Neighbours: Kazakhstan, Turmkenistan, Tajikistan
- Capital: Tashkent
- Area: 447,400 sq. km
- Population: 30,830,351
- Language(s): Uzbek
- Dominant religion: Islam
- Time zone: +5
- Currency: Uzbekistan Som
- Current head of state: Islam Karimov
- Type of government: Presidential Republic
- Literacy rate: 99.3%
- GDP: $68.190 billion
- HDI ranking: 116

VIETNAM

- Location: Southeast Asia
- Neighbours: Cambodia, Laos, China
- Capital: Hanoi
- Area: 329,560 sq. km
- Population: 92,380,314
- Language(s): Vietnamese, English
- Dominant religions: Buddhism, Christianity
- Time zone: +7
- Currency: Dong
- Current head of state: Truong Tan Sang
- Type of government: Communist
- Literacy rate: 94%
- GDP: $204.493 billion
- HDI ranking: 121

YEMEN

- Location: Southwest Asia
- Neighbours: Saudi Arabia, Oman
- Capital: Sana'a
- Area: 527,969 sq. km
- Population: 26,266,995
- Language(s): Arabic
- Dominant religion: Islam
- Time zone: +3
- Currency: Yemeni Rial
- Current head of state: Abd Rabbuh Mansur Hadi
- Type of government: Republic
- Literacy rate: 63.9%
- GDP: $43.140 billion
- HDI ranking: 154

ALBANIA

- Location: Southeast Europe
- Neighbours: Macedonia, Greece, Montenegro, Kosovo, Italy
- Capital: Tirana
- Area: 28,748 sq. km
- Population: 3,193,644
- Language(s): Albanian
- Dominant religions: Christianity
- Time zone: +1
- Currency: Lek
- Current head of state: Bujar Nishani
- Type of government: Parliamentary Republic
- Literacy rate: 96.8%
- GDP: $12.405 billion
- HDI ranking: 95

ANDORRA

- Location: Western Europe
- Neighbours: France, Spain
- Capital: Andorra la Vella
- Area: 451 sq. km
- Population: 79,333
- Language(s): Catalan
- Dominant religion: Roman Catholic
- Time zone: +1
- Currency: Euro
- Current head of state: Antoni Martí
- Type of government: Diarchy
- Literacy rate: 100%
- GDP: $3.249 billion
- HDI ranking: 37

ARMENIA

- Location: Eurasia
- Neighbours: Azerbaijan, Georgia, Iran, Turkey
- Capital: Yerevan
- Area: 29,800 sq. km
- Population: 2,976,089
- Language(s): Armenian
- Dominant religion: Armenian Apostolic
- Time zone: +4
- Currency: Dram
- Current head of state: Serzh Sargsyan
- Type of government: Presidential Representative Democratic Republic
- Literacy rate: 99.6%
- GDP: $9.301 billion
- HDI ranking: 87

AUSTRIA

- Location: Central Europe
- Neighbours: Czech Republic, Germany, Hungary, Italy, Liechtenstein, Slovakia, Slovenia, Switzerland
- Capital: Vienna
- Area: 83,870 sq. km
- Population: 8,440,725
- Language(s): German
- Dominant religion: Roman Catholicism
- Time zone: +1
- Currency: Euro
- Current head of State: Heinz Fischer
- Type of government: Federal Semi-presidential Republic
- Literacy rate: 98%
- GDP: $380.555 billion
- HDI ranking: 21

AZERBAIJAN

- Location: Eurasia
- Neighbours: Armenia, Georgia, Iran, Russia, Turkey
- Capital: Baku
- Area: 86,600 sq. km
- Population: 9,592,247
- Language(s): Azerbaijani, Russian, Armenian
- Dominant religion: Islam
- Time zone: +4
- Currency: Manat
- Current head of state: Ilham Aliyev
- Type of government: Presidential Republic
- Literacy rate: 99.8%
- GDP: $62.199 billion
- HDI ranking: 76

BELARUS

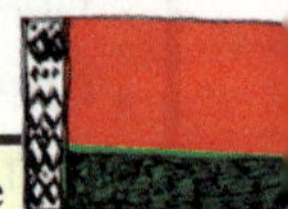

- Location: Eastern Europe
- Neighbours: Ukraine, Russia, Poland, Lithuania, Latvia
- Capital: Minsk
- Area: 207,600 sq. km
- Population: 9,335,741
- Language(s): Belarusian, Russian
- Dominant religion: Eastern Orthodox Church
- Time zone: +3
- Currency: Belarusian Rouble
- Current head of state: Alexander Lukashenko
- Type of government: Presidential Republic
- Literacy rate: 99.6%
- GDP: $60.530 billion
- HDI ranking: 53

BELGIUM

- Location: Northwestern Europe
- Neighbours: Germany, France, Luxembourg, The Netherlands
- Capital: Brussels
- Area: 30,528 sq. km
- Population: 11,157,847
- Language(s): Dutch, French, German
- Dominant religion: Roman Catholicism
- Time zone: +1
- Currency: Euro
- Current head of state: Philippe
- Type of government: Constitutional Monarchy
- Literacy rate: 99%
- GDP: $463.799 billion
- HDI ranking: 21

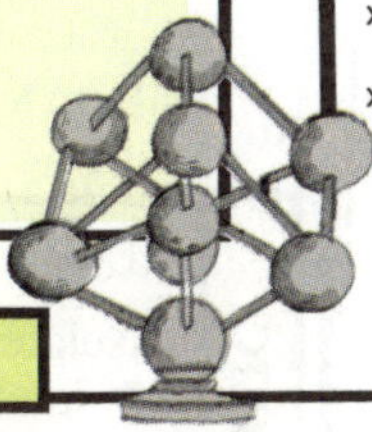

BOSNIA AND HERZEGOVINA

- Location: Southeastern Europe
- Neighbours: Serbia, Croatia, Montenegro
- Capital: Sarajevo
- Area: 51,129 sq. km
- Population: 3,835,208
- Language(s): Serbian, Croatian, Bosnian
- Dominant religions: Christianity, Islam
- Time zone: +1
- Currency: Convertible mark
- Current head of State: Bakir Izetbegović
- Type of government: Federal Democratic Republic
- Literacy rate: 99.4%
- GDP: $16.638 billion
- HDI ranking: 86

BULGARIA

- Location: Southeastern Europe
- Neighbours: Greece, Macedonia, Romania, Serbia, Turkey
- Capital: Sofia
- Area: 110,910 sq. km
- Population: 7,093,304
- Language(s): Bulgarian
- Dominant religion: Christianity
- Time zone: +2
- Currency: Lev
- Current head of state: Rosen Plevneliev
- Type of government: Parliamentary Republic
- Literacy rate: 98.4%
- GDP: $51.551 billion
- HDI ranking: 58

CROATIA

- Location: Southeastern Europe
- Neighbours: Slovenia, Hungary, Yugoslavia, Bosnia and Herzegovina, Montenegro
- Capital: Zagreb
- Area: 56,542 sq. km
- Population: 4,255,464
- Language(s): Croatian
- Dominant religion: Roman Catholicism
- Time zone: +1
- Currency: Kuna
- Current head of state: Kolinda Grabar-Kitarović
- Type of government: Parliamentary Republic
- Literacy rate: 99.2%
- GDP: $48.874 billion
- HDI ranking: 47

CYPRUS

- Location: Eastern Mediterranean
- Capital: Nicosia
- Area: 9,241 sq. km
- Population: 1,198,240
- Language(s): Greek, Turkish
- Dominant religion: Greek Orthodox Church
- Time zone: +2
- Currency: Euro
- Current head of state: Nicos Anastasiades
- Type of government: Republic
- Literacy rate: 98.7%
- GDP: $19.812 billion
- HDI ranking: 32

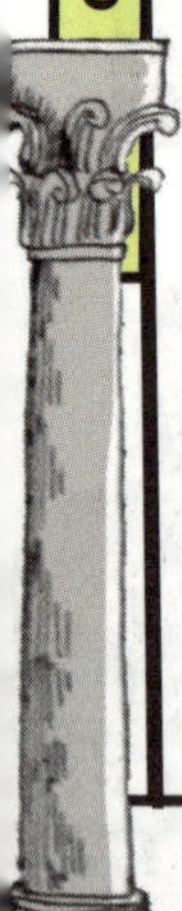

CZECH REPUBLIC

- Location: Central Europe
- Neighbours: Austria, Germany, Poland, Slovakia
- Capital: Prague
- Area: 78,866 sq. km
- Population: 10,463,996
- Language(s): Czech
- Dominant religion: Christianity
- Time zone: +1
- Currency: Czech Koruna
- Current head of state: Miloš Zeman
- Type of government: Parliamentary Republic
- Literacy rate: 99%
- GDP: $180.789 billion
- HDI ranking: 28

DENMARK

- » Location: Northern Europe
- » Capital: Copenhagen
- » Area: 43,094 sq. km
- » Population: 5,644,229
- » Language(s): Danish, English
- » Dominant religion: Evangelical Lutheran Church
- » Time zone: -4 to +1
- » Currency: Danish Krone
- » Current head of state: Queen Margrethe II
- » Type of government: Constitutional Monarchy
- » Literacy rate: 99%
- » GDP: $297.359 billion
- » HDI ranking: 10

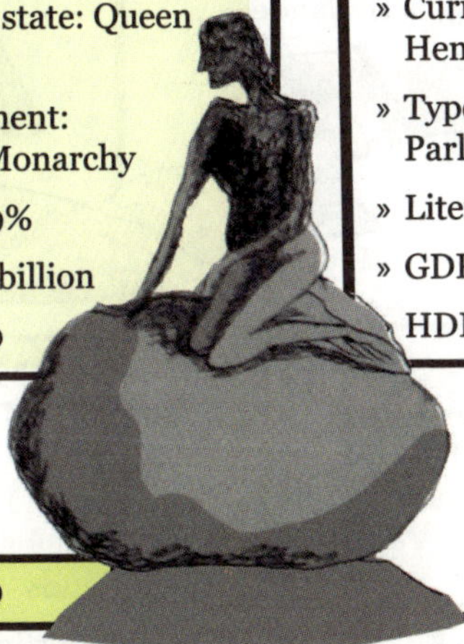

ESTONIA

- » Location: Eastern Europe
- » Neighbours: Latvia, Russia
- » Capital: Tallinn
- » Area: 43,211 sq. km
- » Population: 1,305,238
- » Language(s): Estonian, Russian
- » Dominant religion: Lutheran, Orthodox
- » Time zone: +2
- » Currency: Estonian Kroon
- » Current head of state: Toomas Hendrik Ilves
- » Type of government: Parliamentary Republic
- » Literacy rate: 99.8%
- » GDP: $23.113 billion
- » HDI ranking: 33

FINLAND

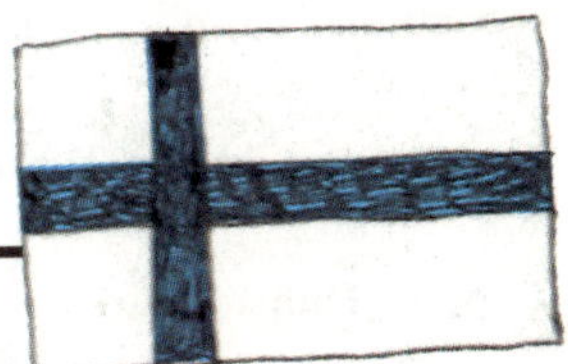

- » Location: Northern Europe
- » Neighbours: Russia, Sweden, Norway
- » Capital: Helsinki
- » Area: 338,145 sq. km
- » Population: 5,429,184
- » Language(s): Finnish, Swedish
- » Dominant religion: Lutheran
- » Time zone: +2
- » Currency: Euro
- » Current head of state: Sauli Niinistö
- » Type of government: Republic
- » Literacy rate: 100%
- » GDP: $235.276 billion
- » HDI ranking: 24

FRANCE

- Location: Western Europe
- Neighbours: Germany, Italy, Spain, Belgium
- Capital: Paris
- Area: 547,030 sq. km
- Population: 66,929,107
- Language(s): French
- Dominant religion: Roman Catholicism
- Time zone: -10 to +12
- Currency: Euro
- Current head of state: François Hollande
- Type of government: Republic
- Literacy rate: 99%
- GDP: $2,469.530 billion
- HDI ranking: 20

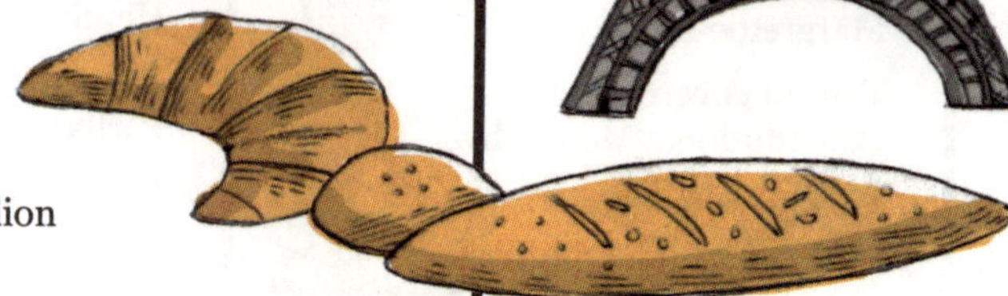

GEORGIA

- Location: Southwest Asia/East Europe
- Neighbours: Russia, Turkey, Azerbaijan
- Capital: Tbilisi
- Area: 69,700 sq. km
- Population: 4,436,194
- Language(s): Georgian, Russian, Armenian, Azerbaijani
- Dominant religion: Orthodox Christian
- Time zone: +4
- Currency: Lari
- Current head of state: Giorgi Margvelashvili
- Type of government: Republic
- Literacy rate: 99.8%
- GDP: $13.758 billion
- HDI ranking: 79

GERMANY

- Location: Western Europe
- Neighbours: France, Austria, Czech Republic, Poland, the Netherlands
- Capital: Berlin
- Area: 357,021 sq. km
- Population: 79,800,484
- Language(s): German
- Dominant religion: Roman Catholic, Protestant
- Time zone: +1
- Currency: Euro
- Current head of state: Joachim Gauck
- Type of government: Federal Republic
- Literacy rate: 99%
- GDP: $3,908.80 billion
- HDI ranking: 6

GREECE

- Location: Southeastern Europe
- Capital: Athens
- Neighbours : Turkey, Bugaria, Macedonia, Albania
- Area: 131,940 sq. km
- Population: 11,127,269
- Language(s): Greek
- Dominant religion: Greek Orthodox Church
- Time zone: +2
- Currency: Euro
- Current head of state: Prokopis Pavlopoulos
- Type of government: Parliamentary Republic
- Literacy rate: 98.9%
- GDP: $207.148 billion
- HDI ranking: 29

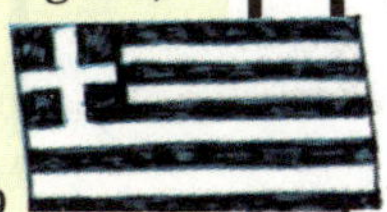

HUNGARY

- Location: Central Europe
- Neighbours: Slovakia, Romania, Croatia, Greece, Serbia, Turkey, Macedonia
- Capital: Budapest
- Area: 93,030 sq. km
- Population: 9,857,671
- Language(s): Hungarian
- Dominant religion: Eastern Orthodox
- Time zone: +1
- Currency: Forint
- Current head of state: János Áder
- Type of government: Parliamentary Republic
- Literacy rate: 99%
- GDP: $126.691 billion
- HDI ranking: 43

ICELAND

- Location: Northern Europe
- Capital: Reykjavik
- Area: 103,000 sq. km
- Population: 328,999
- Language(s): Icelandic, English
- Dominant religion: Evangelical Lutheran Church of Iceland
- Time zone: GMT
- Currency: Icelandic Krona
- Current head of state: Ólafur Ragnar Grímsson
- Type of government: Constitutional Republic
- Literacy rate: 99%
- GDP: $17.807 billion
- HDI ranking: 13

IRELAND

- Location: Western Europe
- Capital: Dublin
- Neighbouring countries: Northern Ireland, England, Scotland (The UK)
- Area: 70,280 sq. km
- Population: 4,823,387
- Language(s): Irish, English
- Dominant religion: Roman Catholicism
- Time zone: WET
- Currency: Euro
- Current head of state: Michael D. Higgins
- Type of government: Republic
- Literacy rate: 99%
- GDP: $220.011 billion
- HDI ranking: 11

ITALY

- Location: Southern Europe
- Neighbour(s): France
- Capital: Rome
- Area: 301,230 sq. km
- Population: 60,479,221
- Language(s): Italian
- Dominant religion: Roman Catholicism
- Time zone: +1
- Currency: Euro
- Current head of state: Sergio Mattarella
- Type of government: Republic
- Literacy rate: 99%
- GDP: $2,152.99 billion
- HDI ranking: 26

LATVIA

- Location: Eastern Europe
- Neighbours: Russia, Belarus
- Capital: Riga
- Area: 64,589 sq. km
- Population: 1,989,061
- Language(s): Latvian
- Dominant religion: Christianity
- Time zone: +2
- Currency: Latvian Lat
- Current head of state: Raimonds Vējonis
- Type of government: Parliamentary Republic
- Literacy rate: 99.9%
- GDP: $28.362 billion
- HDI ranking: 48

LIECHTENSTEIN

- Location: Central Europe
- Neighbours: Switzerland, Germany
- Capital: Vaduz
- Area: 161 sq. km
- Population: 37,556
- Language(s): German
- Dominant religion: Roman Catholicism
- Time zone: +1
- Currency: Swiss Franc
- Current head of state: Hans-Adam II
- Type of government: Constitutional Monarchy
- Literacy rate: 100%
- GDP: $5.488 billion
- HDI ranking: 18

LITHUANIA

- Location: Eastern Europe
- Neighbours: Belarus, Poland, Latvia, Russia
- Capital: Vilnius
- Area: 65,200 sq. km
- Population: 2,956,964
- Language(s): Lithuanian
- Dominant religion: Roman Catholicism
- Time zone: +2
- Currency: Litas
- Current head of state: Dalia Grybauskaitė
- Type of government: Parliamentary Republic
- Literacy rate: 99.8%
- GDP: $42.642 billion
- HDI ranking: 35

LUXEMBOURG

- Location: Western Europe
- Neighbours: Germany, Belgium, France
- Capital: Luxembourg City
- Area: 2,585 sq. km
- Population: 553,919
- Language(s): Luxembourgish, French, German
- Dominant religion: Roman Catholicism
- Time zone: +1
- Currency: Constitutional Monarchy
- Current head of state: Grand Duke Henri
- Type of government: Constitutional Monarchy
- Literacy rate: 100%
- GDP: $54.940 billion
- HDI ranking: 21

MACEDONIA

» Location: Southeastern Europe
» Neighbours: Albania, Bulgaria, Greece, Kosovo, Serbia
» Capital: Skopje
» Area: 25,333 sq. km
» Population: 2,125,167
» Language(s): Macedonian, Albanian
» Dominant religions: Macedonian Orthodox, Islam
» Time zone: +1
» Currency: Macedonian Dimar
» Current head of state: Gjorge Ivanov
» Type of government: Parliamentary Republic
» Literacy rate: 97.3%
» GDP: $10.147 billion
» HDI ranking: 84

MALTA

» Location: Southern Europe
» Capital: Valletta
» Area: 321 sq. km
» Population: 425,378
» Language(s): Maltese, English
» Dominant religion: Roman Catholicism
» Time zone: +1
» Currency: Euro
» Current head of government: Marie Louise Coleiro Preca
» Type of government: Parliamentary Republic
» Literacy rate: 92.8%
» GDP: $9.508 billion
» HDI ranking: 39

MOLDOVA

» Location: Eastern Europe
» Neighbours: Ukraine, Romania
» Capital: Chisinau
» Area: 33,843 sq. km
» Population: 3,550,062
» Language(s): Moldovan, Romanian, Russian
» Dominant religion: Moldovan Orthodox Church
» Time zone: +2
» Currency: Moldovan Leu
» Current head of state: Nicolae Timofti
» Type of government: Parliamentary Republic
» Literacy rate: 98.5%
» GDP: $6.140 billion
» HDI ranking: 113

MONACO

- Location: Western Europe
- Capital: Monaco
- Neighbouring Countries: France
- Area: 1.95 sq. km
- Population: 37,404
- Language(s): French, English
- Dominant religion: Roman Catholicism
- Time zone: +1
- Currency: Euro
- Current head of state: Prince Albert II
- Type of government: Constitutional Monarchy
- Literacy rate: 99%
- GDP: $976.300 billion

MONTENEGRO

- Location: Southeast Europe
- Neighbours: Serbia, Albania, Bosnia and Herzegovinia, Croatia, Kosovo
- Capital: Podgorica
- Area: 14,026 sq. km
- Population: 605,253
- Language(s): Montenegrin, Serbian
- Dominant religions: Christian Orthodox
- Time zone: +1
- Currency: Euro
- Current head of state: Filip Vujanović
- Type of government: Republic
- Literacy rate: 98.4%
- GDP: $4.239 billion
- HDI ranking: 51

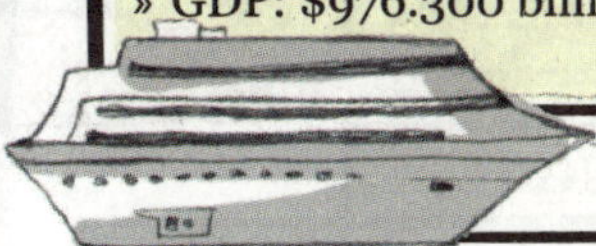

NETHERLANDS

- Location: Western Europe
- Neighbour(s): Belgium, Germany
- Capital: Amsterdam
- Area: 41,526 sq. km
- Population: 16,988,540
- Language(s): Dutch
- Dominant religion: Christianity
- Time zone: +1
- Currency: Euro
- Current head of state: Willem-Alexander
- Type of government: Constitutional Monarchy
- Literacy rate: 99%
- GDP: $749.365 billion
- HDI ranking: 4

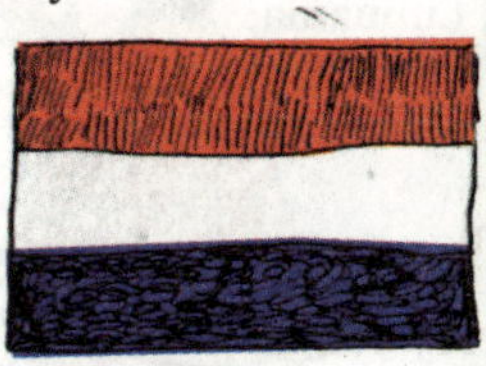

NORWAY

- Location: North Europe
- Neighbour(s): Finland, Sweden, Russia
- Capital: Oslo
- Area: 324,220 sq. km
- Population: 5,080,784
- Language(s): Bokmal Norwegian, Nynorsk Norwegian
- Dominant religion: Evangelical Lutheran
- Time zone: +1
- Currency: Norwegian krone
- Current head of state: Harald V
- Type of government: Constitutional Monarchy
- Literacy rate: 100%
- GDP: $420.958 billion
- HDI ranking: 1

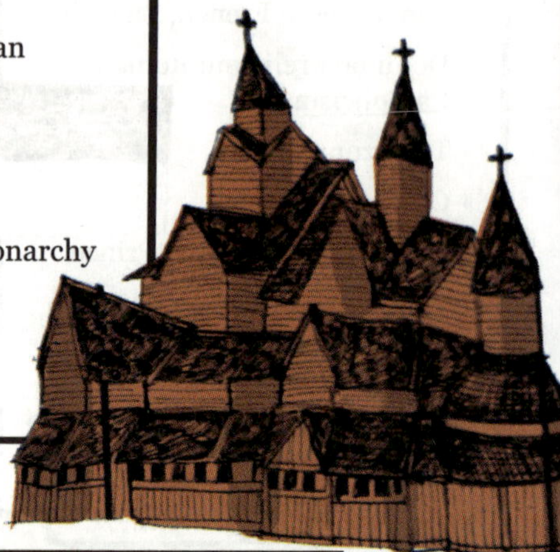

POLAND

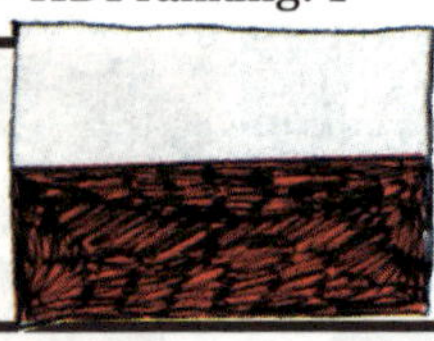

- Location: Central Europe
- Neighbours: Belarus, Czech Republic, Germany, Lithuania, Russia, Slovakia, Ukraine
- Capital: Warsaw
- Area: 312,685 sq. km
- Population: 38,444,962
- Language(s): Polish
- Dominant religion: Catholicism
- Time zone: +1
- Currency: Zloty
- Current head of state: Andrzej Duda
- Type of government: Republic
- Literacy rate: 99.7%
- GDP: $491.239 billion
- HDI ranking: 35

PORTUGAL

- Location: Southwestern Europe
- Neighbour(s): Spain
- Capital: Lisbon
- Area: 92,391 sq. km
- Population: 10,598,502
- Language(s): Portuguese
- Dominant religion: Roman Catholicism
- Time zone: WET
- Currency: Euro
- Current head of government: Aníbal Cavaco Silva
- Type of government: Parliamentary Republic
- Literacy rate: 95.4%
- GDP: $201.036 billion
- HDI ranking: 41

ROMANIA

» Location: Southeastern Europe

» Neighbours: Ukraine, Bulgaria, Hungary, Serbia, Moldova

» Capital: Bucharest

» Area: 237,500 sq. km

» Population: 19,887,559

» Language(s): Romanian, Hungarian

» Dominant religion: Eastern Orthodox

» Time zone: +2

» Currency: New Leu

» Current head of state: Klaus Iohannis

» Type of government: Republic

» Literacy rate: 97.7%

» GDP: $189.747 billion

» HDI ranking: 54

SAN MARINO

» Location: Southern Europe

» Neighbour(s): Italy

» Capital: San Marino

» Area: 60 sq. km

» Population: 32,478

» Language(s): Italian

» Dominant religion: Roman Catholicism

» Time zone: +1

» Currency: Euro

» Current head of state: Andrea Belluzzi and Roberto Venturini

Type of government: Republic

» Literacy rate: 96%

» GDP: $1.543 billion

SERBIA

» Location: Eastern Europe

» Neighbours: Romania, Montenegro, Croatia, Albania, Bulgaria

» Capital: Belgrade

» Area: 77,474 sq. km

» Population: 7,098,236

» Language(s): Serbian

» Dominant religion: Serbian Orthodox

» Time zone: +1

» Currency: Serbian Dinar

» Current head of state: Tomislav Nikolić

» Type of government: Republic

» Literacy rate: 98%

» GDP: $40.665 billion

HDI ranking: 77

SLOVAKIA

- Location: Central Europe
- Neighbours: Austria, Czech Republic, Hungary, Poland, Ukraine
- Capital: Bratislava
- Area: 48,845 sq. km
- Population: 5,431,305
- Language(s): Slovak
- Dominant religion: Roman Catholicism
- Time zone: +1
- Currency: Slovak Koruna
- Current head of state: Andrej Kiska
- Type of government: Parliamentary Republic
- Literacy rate: 99.6%
- GDP: $87.528 billion
- HDI ranking: 37

SLOVENIA

- Location: Central Europe
- Neighbours: Austria, Croatia, Hungary, Italy
- Capital: Ljubljana
- Area: 20,273 sq. km
- Population: 2,044,613
- Language(s): Slovenian
- Dominant religion: Catholicism
- Time zone: +1
- Currency: Euro
- Current head of state: Borut Pahor
- Type of government: Republic
- Literacy rate: 99.7%
- GDP: $43.021 billion
- HDI ranking: 25

SPAIN

- Location: Southwest Europe
- Neighbour(s): Andorra, Gibraltar, Portugal, Morocco
- Capital: Madrid
- Area: 504,782 sq. km
- Population: 47,773,281
- Language(s): Castilian Spanish, Catalan
- Dominant religion: Roman Catholicism
- Time zone: +1
- Currency: Euro
- Current head of state: Felipe VI
- Type of government: Constitutional Monarchy
- Literacy rate: 97.7%
- GDP: $1,421.71 billion
- HDI ranking: 27

SWEDEN

- Location: Northern Europe
- Neighbour(s): Finland, Norway
- Capital: Stockholm
- Area: 449,964 sq. km
- Population: 9,577,584
- Language(s): Swedish
- Dominant religion: Lutheran
- Time zone: +1
- Currency: Swedish Krona
- Current head of state: King Carl XVI Gustaf
- Type of government: Constitutional Monarchy
- Literacy rate: 99%
- GDP: $487.396 billion
- HDI ranking: 12

SWITZERLAND

- Location: Central Europe
- Neighbours: France, Germany, Austria, Italy
- Capital: Berne
- Area: 41,290 sq. km
- Population: 8,059,885
- Language(s): German, French, Italian
- Dominant religion: Christianity
- Time zone: +1
- Currency: Swiss Franc
- Current head of state: Didier Burkhalter
- Type of government: Confederation
- Literacy rate: 99%
- GDP: $688.434 billion
- HDI ranking: 3

UKRAINE

- Location: Eastern Europe
- Neighbours: Belarus, Hungary, Moldova, Poland, Romania , Russia, Slovakia
- Capital: Kiev
- Area: 603,700 sq. km
- Population: 42,602,820
- Language(s): Ukranian, Russian
- Dominant religion: Ukranian Orthodox Church
- Time zone: +2
- Currency: Hryvnia
- Current head of state: Petro Poroshenko
- Type of government: Republic
- Literacy rate: 99.7%
- GDP: $85.440 billion
- HDI ranking: 83

VATICAN CITY

- Location: South Europe (a city-state in Rome, Italy)
- Neighbour(s): Italy
- Capital: Vatican City
- Area: 0.44 sq. km
- Population: 842
- Language(s): Italian, Latin
- Dominant religion: Roman Catholicism
- Time zone: +1
- Currency: Euro
- Current head of state: Pope Francis
- Type of government: Monarchy
- Literacy rate: 99%
- GDP: $3.333 billion

UNITED KINGDOM

- Location: Western Europe
- Neighbours: Ireland, France
- Capital: London
- Area: 244,820 sq. km
- Population: 64,943,792
- Language(s): English
- Dominant religion: Christianity
- Time zone: GMT
- Currency: British Pound
- Current head of state: Queen Elizabeth II
- Type of government: Constitutional Monarchy & Parliamentary system
- Literacy rate: 99%
- GDP: $2,853.357 billion
- HDI ranking: 14

BARBADOS

- Location: Caribbean Sea
- Capital: Bridgetown
- Area: 431 sq. km
- Population: 287,116
- Language(s): English, Bajan
- Dominant religion: Protestant
- Time zone: -4
- Currency: Barbados Dollar
- Current head of state: Queen Elizabeth II
- Type of government: Constitutional Monarchy and Parliamentary system
- Literacy rate: 99.7%
- GDP: $4.442 billion
- HDI ranking: 59

ANTIGUA AND BARBUDA

- Location: Central America
- Capital: Saint John's
- Area: 440 sq. km
- Population: 93,419
- Language(s): English
- Dominant religion: Protestant
- Time zone: -4
- Currency: East Caribbean Dollar
- Current head of state: Queen Elizabeth II
- Type of government: Parliamentary Democracy under a Constitutional Monarchy
- Literacy rate: 99%
- GDP: $1.281 billion
- HDI ranking: 61

BAHAMAS

- Location: Central America
- Capital: Nassau
- Area: 10,070 sq. km
- Population: 384,905
- Language(s): English, Creole
- Dominant religion: Protestantism
- Time zone: -5
- Currency: Bahamian Dollar
- Current head of state: Queen Elizabeth II
- Type of government: Parliamentary Democracy and Constitutional Monarchy
- Literacy rate: 95.6%
- GDP: $9.185 billion
- HDI ranking: 51

BELIZE

- Location: Central America
- Neighbour(s): Guatemala, Mexico
- Capital: Belmopan
- Area: 22,966 sq. km
- Population: 349,439
- Language(s): English, Creole, Spanish
- Dominant religion: Christianity
- Time zone: -6
- Currency: Belizean Dollar
- Current head of state: Queen Elizabeth II
- Type of government: Parliamentary Democracy and Constitutional Monarchy
- Literacy rate: 79.7%
- GDP: $1.759 billion
- HDI ranking: 84

CANADA

- Location: North America
- Neighbours: US, Greenland
- Capital: Ottawa
- Area: 9,984,670 sq. km
- Population: 35,796,185
- Language(s): English, French
- Dominant religion: Christianity
- Time zone: -3:30 to -8
- Currency: Canadian Dollar
- Current head of state: Queen Elizabeth II
- Type of government: Parliamentary Democracy and Constitutional Monarchy
- Literacy rate: 99%
- GDP: $1,615.471 billion
- HDI ranking: 8

COSTA RICA

- Location: Central America
- Neighbours: Nicaragua, Panama
- Capital: San Jose
- Area: 51,100 sq. km
- Population: 5,043,280
- Language(s): Spanish
- Dominant religion: Roman Catholicism
- Time zone: -6
- Currency: Costa Rican Colon
- Current head of state: Luis Guillermo Solís
- Type of government: Democratic Republic
- Literacy rate: 97.8%
- GDP: $52.800 billion
- HDI ranking: 68

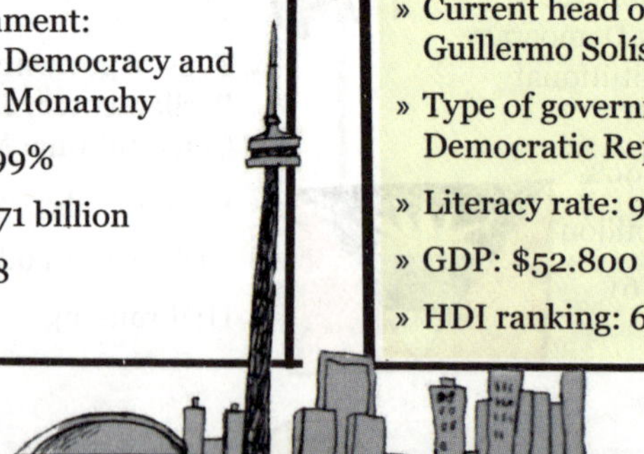

CUBA

- Location: Central America
- Capital: Havana
- Area: 110,860 sq. km
- Population: 11,227,072
- Language(s): Spanish
- Dominant religions: Atheism (official), Christianity
- Time zone: -5
- Currency: Cuban Preso
- Current head(s) of government: Raúl Castro
- Type of government: Communist
- Literacy rate: 99.8%
- GDP: $121 billion
- HDI ranking: 44

DOMINICA

- Location: Central America
- Capital: Roseau
- Area: 751 sq. km
- Population: 72,257
- Language(s): English, French patois
- Dominant religion: Christianity
- Time zone: -4
- Currency: East Caribbean Dollar
- Current head of state: Charles Savarin
- Type of government: Parliamentary Republic
- Literacy rate: 94%
- GDP: $0.534 billion
- HDI ranking: 93

DOMINICAN REPUBLIC

- Location: Central America
- Capital: Santo Domingo
- Area: 48,671 sq. km
- Population: 10,794,631
- Language(s): Spanish
- Dominant religion: Roman Catholicism
- Time zone: -4
- Currency: Dominican Peso
- Current head of state: Danilo Medina
- Type of government: Democratic Republic
- Literacy rate: 91.8%
- GDP: $66.199 billion
- HDI ranking: 102

EL SALVADOR

- Location: South America
- Neighbours: Honduras, Guatemala
- Capital: San Salvador
- Area: 21,040 sq. km
- Population: 6,372,623
- Language(s): Spanish, Nahua
- Dominant religion: Christianity
- Time zone: -6
- Currency: US Dollar
- Current head of state: Salvador Sánchez Cerén
- Type of government: Republic
- Literacy rate: 88%
- GDP: $26.152 billion
- HDI ranking: 115

GRENADA

- Location: Central America
- Capital: St. George's
- Area: 339 sq. km
- Population: 107,670
- Language(s): English
- Dominant religion: Christianity
- Time zone: -4
- Currency: East Caribbean Dollar
- Current head of state: Queen Elizabeth II, Keith Mitchell
- Type of government: Parliamentary Democracy and Constitutional monachy
- Literacy rate: 96%
- GDP: $0.882 billion
- HDI ranking: 79

GUATEMALA

- Location: Central America
- Neighbours: Mexico, Belize, Honduras, El Salvador
- Capital: Guatemala City
- Area: 108,890 sq. km
- Population: 16,223,217
- Language(s): Spanish, indigenous languages
- Dominant religions: Christianity, indigenous faiths
- Time zone: -6
- Currency: Quetzal
- Current head of state: Alejandro Maldonado
- Type of government: Republic
- Literacy rate: 83.4%
- GDP: $66.037 billion
- HDI ranking: 125

HAITI

- Location: Central America
- Capital: Port au-Prince
- Area: 27,750 sq. km
- Population: 10,475,692
- Language(s): French, Creole
- Dominant religion: Christianity
- Time zone: -5
- Currency: Gourde
- Current head of state: Michel Martelly
- Type of government: Republic
- Literacy rate: 60.7%
- GDP: $9.152 billion
- HDI ranking: 168

HONDURAS

- Location: Central America
- Neighbour(s): Guatemala, El Salvador, Nicaragua
- Capital: Tegucigalpa
- Area: 112,090 sq. km
- Population: 8,505,501
- Language(s): Spanish
- Dominant religion: Roman Catholicism
- Time zone: -6
- Currency: Lempira
- Current head of state: Juan Orlando Hernández
- Type of government: Republic
- Literacy rate: 88.5%
- GDP: $19.977 billion
- HDI ranking: 129

JAMAICA

- Location: Central America
- Capital: Kingston
- Area: 10,991 sq. km
- Population: 2,782,513
- Language(s): English, Jamaican Patois
- Dominant religions: Christianity, Hinduism
- Time zone: -5
- Currency: Jamaican Dollar
- Current head of state: Queen Elizabeth II, Portia Simpson-Miller
- Type of government: Constitutional Parliamentary Democracy
- Literacy rate: 88.7%
- GDP: $13.850 billion
- HDI ranking: 96

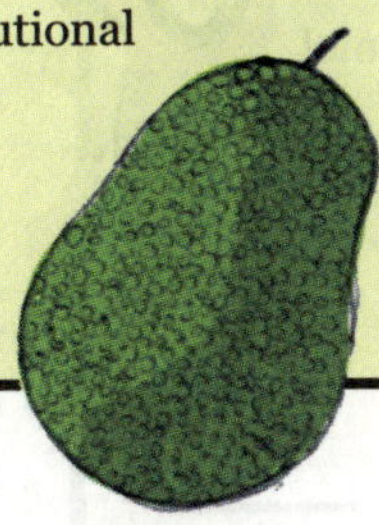

MEXICO

- Location: North America
- Neighbour(s): US, Belize, Guatemala
- Capital: Mexico City
- Area: 1,923,039 sq. km
- Population: 125,886,464
- Language(s): Spanish
- Dominant religion: Roman Catholicism
- Time zone: -6
- Currency: Mexican Peso
- Current head of state: Enrique Peña Nieto
- Type of government: Federal Republic
- Literacy rate: 95.1%
- GDP: $1,231.982 billion
- HDI ranking: 71

NICARAGUA

- Location: Central America
- Neighbour(s): Honduras, Costa Rica
- Capital: Managua
- Area: 129,494 sq. km
- Population: 6,238,376
- Language(s): Spanish
- Dominant religion: Christianity
- Time zone: -6
- Currency: Gold Cordoba
- Current head of state: Daniel Ortega
- Type of government: Republic
- Literacy rate: 82.8%
- GDP: $12.296 billion
- HDI ranking: 132

PANAMA

- Location: Central America
- Neighbours: Costa Rica, Colombia
- Capital: Panama City
- Area: 78,200 sq. km
- Population: 4,009,244
- Language(s): Spanish
- Dominant religion: Roman Catholicism
- Time zone: -5
- Currency: Balboa
- Current head of state: Juan Carlos Varela
- Type of government: Constitutional Republic
- Literacy rate: 95%
- GDP: $47.478 billion
- HDI ranking: 65

ST. KITTS & NEVIS

- Location: Central American Coast
- Capital: Bassetere
- Area: 168 sq. km
- Population: 55,245
- Language(s): English
- Dominant religion: Christianity
- Time zone: -4
- Currency: East Caribbean Dollar
- Current head of state: Queen Elizabeth II and Timothy Harris
- Type of government: Parliamentary Democracy and Constitutional Monarchy
- Literacy rate: 97.8%
- GDP: $0.890 billion
- HDI ranking: 73

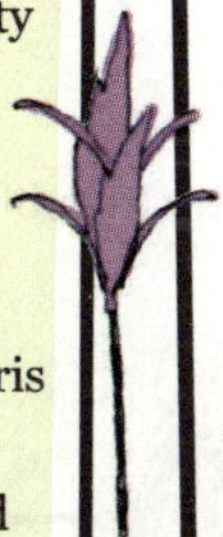

ST. LUCIA

- Location: Central America, Caribbean
- Capital: Castries
- Area: 611 sq. km
- Population: 183,496
- Language(s): English
- Dominant religion: Christianity
- Time zone: -4
- Currency: East Caribbean Dollar
- Current head of state: Queen Elizabeth II and Kenny Anthony
- Type of government: Parliamentary Democracy and Constitutional Monarchy
- Literacy rate: 90.1%
- GDP: $1.410 billion
- HDI ranking: 97

ST. VINCENT & THE GRENADINES

- Location: Central America, Caribbean
- Capital: Kingstown
- Area: 389 sq. km
- Population: 108,031
- Language(s): English
- Dominant religion: Protestantism
- Time zone: -4
- Currency: East Caribbean Dollar
- Current head of state: Queen Elizabeth II and Ralph Gonsalves
- Type of government: Parliamentary Democracy and Constitutional Monarchy
- Literacy rate: 96%
- GDP: $0.758 billion
- HDI ranking: 91

TRINIDAD & TOBAGO

- » Location: Central America
- » Capital: Port of Spain
- » Area: 5,131 sq. km
- » Population: 1,333,078
- » Language(s): English, Caribbean Hindustani
- » Dominant religion: Christianity, Hinduism
- » Time zone: -4
- » Currency: T&T Dollar
- » Current head of state: Anthony Carmona
- » Type of government: Parliamentary Republic
- » Literacy rate: 98.6%
- » GDP: $29.210 billion
- » HDI ranking: 64

UNITED STATES

- » Location: North America
- » Neighbours: Canada, Mexico
- » Capital: Washington D.C.
- » Area: 9,631,420 sq. km
- » Population: 325,622,313
- » Language(s): English
- » Dominant religion: Christianity
- » Time zone: -5 to -9
- » Currency: US Dollar
- » Current head of state: Barack Obama
- » Type of government: Federal Republic
- » Literacy rate: 99%
- » GDP: $18,124.731 billion
- » HDI ranking: 5

AUSTRALIA

- Location: Pacific Ocean
- Capital: Canberra
- Area: 7,686,850 sq. km
- Population: 23,708,989
- Language(s): English
- Dominant religion: Christianity
- Time zone: +8 to +10:30
- Currency: Australian Dollar
- Current head of state: Queen Elizabeth II & Malcolm Turnbull
- Type of government: Federal Parliamentary Democracy and Constitutional Monarchy
- Literacy rate: 96%
- GDP: $1,252.273 billion
- HDI ranking: 2

FIJI

- Location: South Pacific Ocean
- Capital: Suva
- Area: 18,270 sq. km
- Population: 901,047
- Language(s): English, Fijian
- Dominant religion: Christianity
- Time zone: +12
- Currency: Fijian Dollar
- Current head of state: Epeli Nailatikau
- Type of government: Republic
- Literacy rate: 93.7%
- GDP: $4.413 billion
- HDI ranking: 88

KIRIBATI

- Location: Pacific Ocean
- Capital: Tarawa
- Area: 811 sq. km
- Population: 105,549
- Language(s): English, Kiribati
- Dominant religion: Christianity
- Time zone: +12 to +14
- Currency: Australian Dollar
- Current head of state: Anote Tong
- Type of government: Republic
- Literacy rate: 94%
- GDP: $0.168 billion
- HDI ranking: 133

MARSHALL ISLANDS

- Location: Oceania
- Capital: Majuro
- Area: 181 sq. km
- Population: 56,465
- Language(s): Marshallese, English
- Dominant religion: Christianity
- Time zone: +12
- Currency: US Dollar
- Current head of state: Christopher Loeak
- Type of government: Parliamentary Republic
- Literacy rate: 93.7%
- GDP: $0.195 billion

MICRONESIA

- Location: North Pacific Ocean
- Capital: Palikir
- Area: 702 sq. km
- Population: 106,104
- Language(s): English
- Dominant religion: Christianity
- Time zone: +10, +11
- Currency: US Dollar
- Current head of state: Peter M. Christian
- Type of government: Presidential Republic
- Literacy rate: 89%
- GDP: $0.316 billion
- HDI ranking: 124

NAURU

- Location: Pacific Ocean
- Capital: Yaren
- Area: 21 sq. km
- Population: 10,483
- Language(s): Nauruan, English
- Dominant religion: Christianity
- Time zone: +12
- Currency: Australian Dollar
- Current head of state: Baron Waqa
- Type of government: Republic
- GDP: $60 million

NEW ZEALAND

- Location: Oceania
- Capital: Wellington
- Area: 268,680 sq. km
- Population: 4,580,566
- Language(s): English, Maori dialect
- Dominant religion: Christianity
- Time zone: +12
- Currency: New Zealand Dollar
- Current head of state: Queen Elizabeth II and John Phillip Key
- Type of government: Parliamentary Democracy and Constitutional Monarchy
- Literacy rate: 99%
- GDP: $191.730 billion
- HDI ranking: 7

PALAU

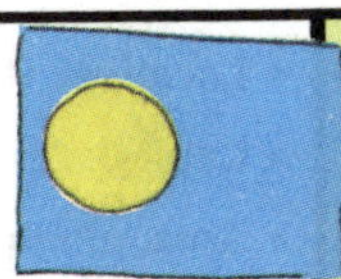

- Location: Oceania
- Capital: Melekeok
- Area: 458 sq. km
- Population: 21,037
- Language(s): Palauan, Filipino
- Dominant religion: Christianity
- Time zone: +9
- Currency: US Dollar
- Current head of state: Tommy Remengesau
- Type of government: Constitutional Republic
- Literacy rate: 92%
- GDP: $0.278 billion
- HDI ranking: 60

PAPUA NEW GUINEA

- Location: Oceania
- Neighbour(s): Indonesia
- Capital: Port Moresby
- Area: 462,840 sq. km
- Population: 7,709,208
- Language(s): Tok Pisin, English, Hiri Motu
- Dominant religion: Christianity
- Time zone: +10
- Currency: Kina
- Current head of state: Queen Elizabeth II and Peter O'Neill
- Type of government: Parliamentary Democracy and Constitutional Monarchy
- Literacy rate: 64.2%
- GDP: $20.042 billion
- HDI ranking: 157

SAMOA

- Location: Oceania
- Capital: Apia
- Area: 2,944 sq. km
- Population: 193,166
- Language(s): Samoan, English
- Dominant religion: Christianity
- Time zone: +13
- Currency: Tala
- Current head of state: Tupua Tamasese Tupuola Tufuga Efi
- Type of government: Parliamentary Republic
- Literacy rate: 99.7%
- GDP: $0.868 billion
- HDI ranking: 106

SOLOMON ISLANDS

- Location: Oceania
- Capital: Honiara
- Area: 28,450 sq. km
- Population: 596,163
- Language(s): Solomons Pidgin
- Dominant religion: Protestantism
- Time zone: +11
- Currency: Solomon Island Dollar
- Current head of state: Queen Elizabeth II & Manasseh Sogavare
- Type of government: Parliamentary Democracy and Constitutional Monarchy
- Literacy rate: 84.1%
- GDP: $1.206 billion
- HDI ranking: 157

TONGA

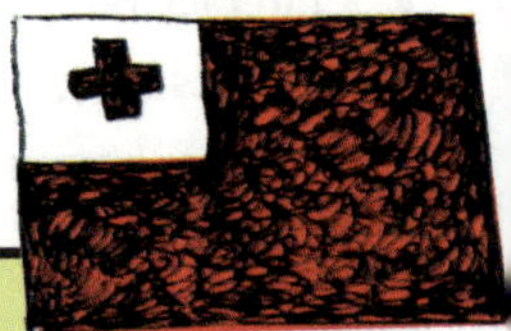

- Location: South Pacific Ocean
- Capital: Nuku'alofa
- Area: 748 sq. km
- Population: 105,899
- Language(s): Tongan, English
- Dominant religion: Protestantism
- Time zone: +13
- Currency: Pa'anga
- Current head of state: King Tupou VI
- Type of government: Constitutional Monarchy
- Literacy rate: 98.9%
- GDP: $0.476 billion
- HDI ranking: 100

TUVALU

- Location: Pacific Ocean
- Capital: Funafuti
- Area: 26 sq. km
- Population: 10,121
- Language(s): Tuvaluan, English
- Dominant religions: Church of Tuvalu
- Time zone: +12
- Currency: Tuvaluan Dollar
- Current head of state: Queen Elizabeth II & Enele Sosene Sopoaga
- Type of government: Parliamentary Democracy and Constitutional Monarchy
- GDP: $0.035 billion

VANUATU

- Location: South Pacific Ocean
- Capital: Port Vila
- Area: 12,200 sq. km
- Population: 259,847
- Language(s): Bislama, English
- Dominant religion: Protestantism
- Time zone: +11
- Currency: Vanuatu Vatu
- Current head of state: Baldwin Lonsdale
- Type of government: Parliamentary Republic
- Literacy rate: 85.2%
- GDP: $0.745 billion
- HDI ranking: 131

ARGENTINA

- Location: South America
- Neighbours: Chile, Paraguay, Uruguay, Bolivia
- Capital: Buenos Aires
- Area: 2,766,890 sq. km
- Population: 42,664,840
- Language(s): Spanish
- Dominant religion: Roman Catholicism
- Time zone: -3
- Currency: Peso
- Current head of state: Cristina Fernández de Kirchner
- Type of government: Federal Presidential Republic
- Literacy rate: 97.9%
- GDP: $563.138 billion
- HDI ranking: 49

BOLIVIA

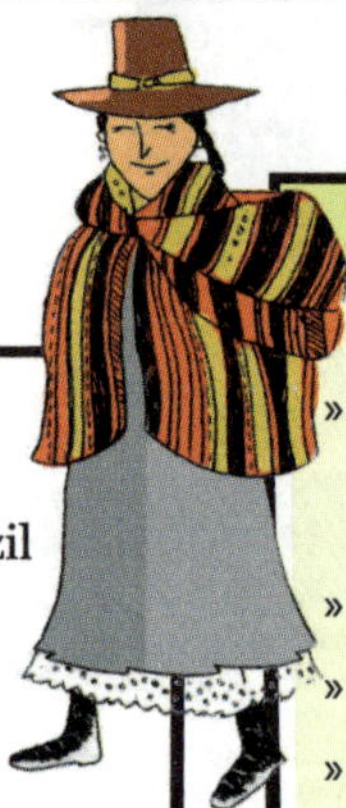

- Location: South America
- Neighbours: Peru, Chile, Argentina, Paraguay, Brazil
- Capital: La Paz
- Area: 1,098,580 sq. km
- Population: 11,172,036
- Language(s): Spanish, Quehcua, Aymara, Guarani
- Dominant religion: Roman Catholicism
- Time zone: -4
- Currency: Boliviano
- Current head of state: Evo Morales
- Type of government: Republic
- Literacy rate: 95.7%
- GDP: $35.027 billion
- HDI ranking: 113

BRAZIL

- Location: South America
- Neighbours: Peru, Bolivia, Ecuador, Paraguay, Colombia, Venezuela, Guyana, Suriname
- Capital: Brasilia
- Area: 8,511,965 sq. km
- Population: 207,194,552
- Language(s): Spanish, Portuguese
- Dominant religion: Christianity
- Time zone: -4
- Currency: Real
- Current head of state: Dilma Rousseff
- Type of government: Presidential Federal Republic
- Literacy rate: 91.33%
- GDP: $1,903.934 billion
- HDI ranking: 79

CHILE

- Location: South America
- Neighbour(s): Argentina, Peru, Bolivia
- Capital: Santiago
- Area: 756,950 sq. km
- Population: 18,015,916
- Language(s): Spanish
- Dominant religion: Christianity
- Time zone: -4
- Currency: Chilean Peso
- Current head of state: Michelle Bachelet
- Type of government: Presidential Republic
- Literacy rate: 98.6%
- GDP: $250.472 billion
- HDI ranking: 41

COLOMBIA

- Location: South America
- Neighbours: Brazil, Ecuador, Panama, Peru, Venezuela
- Capital: Bogota
- Area: 1,138,910 sq. km
- Population: 49,791,271
- Language(s): Spanish
- Dominant religion: Roman Catholicism
- Time zone: -5
- Currency: Columbian Peso
- Current head of state: Juan Manuel Santos
- Type of government: Republic
- Literacy rate: 94.7%
- GDP: $332.384 billion
- HDI ranking: 98

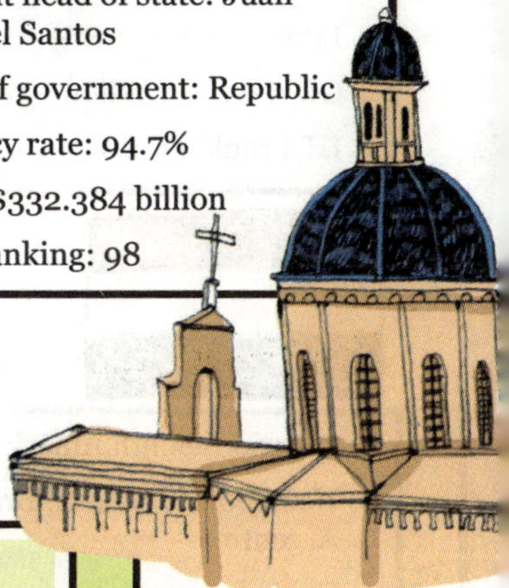

ECUADOR

- Location: Western South America
- Neighbours: Peru, Colombia
- Capital: Quito
- Area: 283,560 sq. km
- Population: 16,340,772
- Language(s): Spanish
- Dominant religion: Roman Catholicism
- Time zone: -5
- Currency: US Dollar
- Current head of state: Rafael Correa
- Type of government: Republic
- Literacy rate: 94.5%
- GDP: $102.663 billion
- HDI ranking: 98

GUYANA

» Location: Central America

» Neighbours: Suriname, Brazil, Venezuela

» Capital: Georgetown

» Area: 214,970 sq. km

» Population: 782,293

» Language(s): English, local dialects

» Dominant religion: Christianity, Hinduism

» Time zone: -4

» Currency: Guyanese Dollar

» Current head of state: David Granger

» Type of government: Republic

» Literacy rate: 91.8%

» GDP: $3.147 billion

» HDI ranking: 121

PARAGUAY

» Location: South America

» Neighbours: Bolivia, Brazil, Argentina

» Capital: Asuncion

» Area: 406,750 sq. km

» Population: 7,012,373

» Language(s): Spanish, Guarani

» Dominant religion: Roman Catholicism

» Time zone: -4

» Currency: Guarani

» Current head of state: Horacio Manuel Cartes Jara

» Type of government: Republic

» Literacy rate: 94%

» GDP: $30.754 billion

» HDI ranking: 111

PERU

» Location: South America

» Neighbours: Peru, Bolivia, Argentina

» Capital: Lima

» Area: 1,285,220 sq. km

» Population: 31,153,186

» Language(s): Spanish, Quechua

» Dominant religion: Christianity

» Time zone: -5

» Currency: Nuevo Sol

» Current head of state: Ollanta Humala

» Type of government: Democratic Republic

» Literacy rate: 94.5%

» GDP: $190.268 billion

» HDI ranking: 82

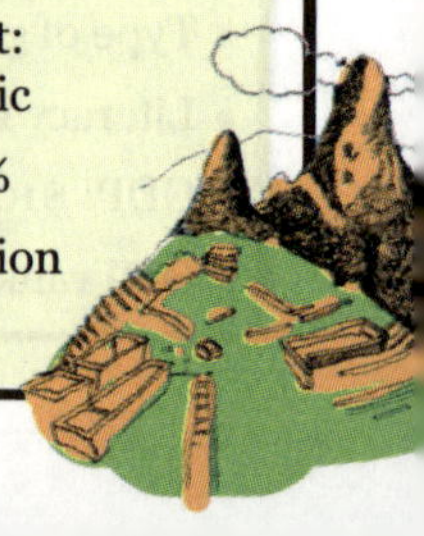

SURINAME

- Location: North South America
- Neighbours: French Guiana, Guyana, Brazil
- Capital: Paramaribo
- Area: 163,270 sq. km
- Population: 556,537
- Language(s): Dutch
- Dominant religion: Hinduism, Protestantism
- Time zone: -3
- Currency: Surinamese Dollar
- Current head of state: Dési Bouterse
- Type of government: Democratic Republic
- Literacy rate: 95.6%
- GDP: $5.552 billion
- HDI ranking: 100

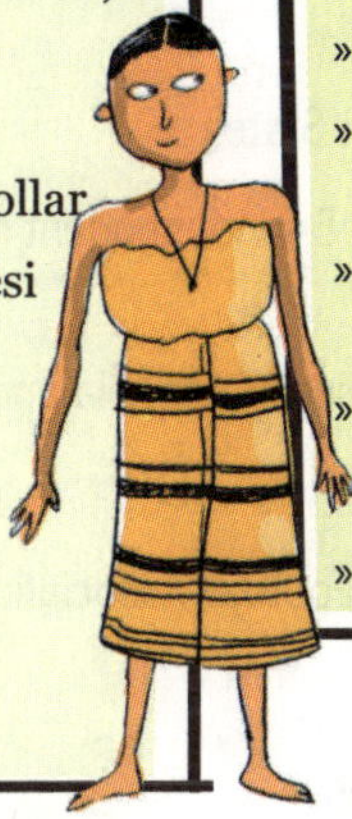

URUGUAY

- Location: South America
- Neighbours: Brazil, Argentina
- Capital: Montevideo
- Area: 176,220 sq. km
- Population: 3,424,714
- Language(s): Spanish, Portunol
- Dominant religion: Roman Catholicism
- Time zone: -3
- Currency: Uruguayan Peso
- Current head of state: Tabaré Vázquez
- Type of government: Presidential Republic
- Literacy rate: 98.5%
- GDP: $56.845 billion
- HDI ranking: 50

VENEZUELA

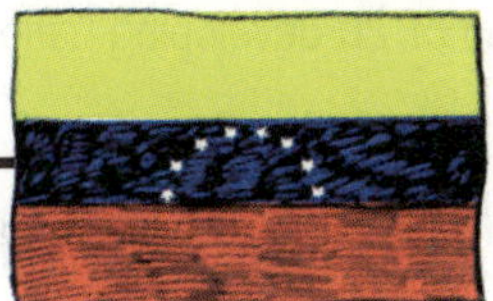

- Location: South America
- Neighbours: Colombia, Brazil, Guyana
- Capital: Caracas
- Area: 912,050 sq. km
- Population: 31,651,744
- Language(s): Spanish, indigenous languages
- Dominant religion: Roman Catholicism
- Time zone: -4:30
- Currency: Bolivar
- Current head of state: Nicolás Maduro
- Type of government: Federal Presidential Republic
- Literacy rate: 95.5%
- GDP: $169.673 billion
- HDI ranking: 67

AL—Arab League

ACP- African, Caribbean, and Pacific countries

APEC—Asia Pacific Economic Cooperation

ASDB—Asian Development Bank

ASEAN—Association of Southeast Asian Nations

AI—Amnesty International

AU—African Union

CIS—Commonwealth of Independent States

The Commonwealth—Association of 54 independent member states, previously known as the British Commonwealth

ESCAP—Economic and Social Commission for Asia and the Pacific

EUC—European Community

FIFA—Federation Internationale de Football Association

G8—Group of 8 countries

G20—Group of 20 developing nations

GCC—Gulf Cooperation Council

IAEA—International Atomic Energy Agency

IBRD—International Bank for Reconstruction and Development

IDA—International Development Association

INTERPOL—International Criminal Police Organisation

IFAD—International Fund for Agricultural Development

IFC—International Finance Corporation

IFRC—International Federation of Red Cross and Red Crescent Societies

IMF—International Monetary Fund

IMO—International Maritime Organisation

INMARSAT—International Maritime Satellite Organisation

IOC—International Olympic Committee

ISO—International Organisation for Standardisation

ITU—International Telecom Union

INTELSAT—International Telecommunications Satellite Organisation

MERCOSUR—Trading bloc in Latin America comprising Brazil, Argentina, Uruguay and Paraguay

NAM—Non-aligned Movement

NATO—North Atlantic Treaty Organisation

OAS—Organisation of American States

OECD—Organisation for Economic Cooperation and Development

OPEC—Organisation of Petroleum Exporting Countries

SAARC—South Asian Association for Regional Cooperation

WIPO—World Intellectual Property Organisation

WMO—World Metereological Organisation

WTO—World Trade Organisation

WWF—World Wide Fund for Nature

UNITED NATIONS

UN—United Nations

UN General Assembly

UN Security Council

Economic and Social Council

UN Trusteeship Council

International Court of Justice

United Nations Secretariat

UN SPECIALISED AGENCIES

WHO—World Health Organisation

UNESCO—United Nations Educational, Scientific and Cultural Organisation

UNICEF—United Nations International Children's Emergency Fund

UNIDO—United Nations Industrial Development Organisation

UNDP—United Nations Development Programme

UNHCR—United Nations High Commissioner for Refugees

FAO—Food and Agriculture Organisation

UNHRC—United Nations Human Rights Council

IMPORTANT OFFICE-HOLDERS

President of the World Bank: Jim Yong Kim

Secretary-General of the United Nations: Ban Ki-moon

Secretary General Amnesty International: Salil Shetty

Director-General of UNESCO: Irina Bokova

Executive Director of UNICEF: Anthony Lake

Director General of WHO: Dr. Margaret Chan

ILO Director General: Guy Ryder

International Court of Justice President: Ronny Abraham

International Olympic Committee President: Thomas Bach

Federation Internationale de Football Association President: Issa Hayatou (acting)

United Nations Human Rights Council (UNHRC) President: Joachim Rücker

SAARC Secretary General: H.E Arjun Bahadur Thapa

President of the European Commission: Jean-Claude Juncker

Director-General of the WTO: Roberto Azevedo

HUMANITY ATTACKED

December 16, 2014 was no ordinary day for Peshawar's Army Public School: it became a target of Taliban's wrath. Terrorists stormed into the school and mercilessly killed scores of students aged between eight and eighteen years. Of the 141 lives lost, 132 were school children! The eight-hour rescue operation ended with all attackers killed and 960 people rescued. The Tehrik-i-Taliban Pakistan claimed responsibility, marking it a revenge for Operation Zarb-e-Azb, the Pakistani army offensive in North Waziristan in the summer of 2014. The annual death toll due to terrorist attacks is on the rise in the country.

THE UN MOVES!

For the first time in 23 years, the UN General assembly adopted a "Decision on UNSC Reforms", in September 2015. This means a set of proposals on Security Council expansion can now be discussed, debated and even opposed. This is significant from the Indian viewpoint. The draft decision contains a negotiating text on how the powerful 15-nation body should be expanded in its permanent and non-permanent categories. India is a leading candidate for a permanent seat in the expanded Security Council and has the support of four of the five permanent members of the Security Council.

A NEW HUMAN

In a dark chamber of a South African cave, six women scientists discovered a previously unidentified species of the early human lineage—*Homo naledi*. The new hominin species was announced on September 10, 2015 by an international team of more than 60 scientists led by Lee R Berger, an American paleoanthropologist. The species name, *H. naledi*, refers to the cave where the bones lay undisturbed for so long; *naledi* means "star" in the local Sesotho language.

LIFELESS WORLD

The world's faith in humanity was shaken when three-year-old Syrian toddler Aylan Kurdi's lifeless body washed up ashore on September 2, 2015 on a beach in western Turkey. Aylan's death sparked international debate and brought instant focus on the migrant crisis besieging Europe that is seeing an increased influx of migrants fleeing Syria in fear of the ISIS.

Aylan drowned along with his brother and mother when the boat they were travelling in from the Greek island of Kos to the Turkish town of Bodrum capsized. The family had fled after Islamic State militants advanced upon their home town.

BRUTALITY UNPARALLELED

A terror group that the world had never heard of prior to 2014, known as the Islamic State of Iraq and Syria (ISIS), took brutality to a new level with graphic beheadings and brutal takeover of entire towns in Syria and Iraq. ISIS traces its roots back to an Iraq-based faction of Al-Qaeda, which has now distanced itself from this new group on account of its brutality.

The group's ultimate goal is to create an Islamic state. It was able to gain power in areas of Syria devastated by the country's civil war. In addition to plundering villages and forcing mass executions, ISIS gained notoriety in the West after beheading captured Western journalists and aid workers and then posting videos of the murders online.

THE GREEK TRAGEDY

The Greek economic crisis deepened with a messy showdown between the country and its creditors. The Greeks voted NO in a referendum rejecting the bailout package drawn up by creditors. However, Prime Minister Alexis Tsipras of Greece, who later won the national elections, went on to accept a new package of budget cuts, tax increases and other economic policy changes in return for an additional aid of 86 billion euros. This aid is essential to reopen banks and avoid default on its loans. The country weighed down under a huge debt, faces several challenges ahead.

GLOBAL HEALTH CRISIS

When a deadly hemorrhagic fever started in West Africa in the spring of 2014 and began to spread rapidly in late summer, no doctor in the world expected it to become a world epidemic. Though contained in three countries (Guinea, Sierra Leone and Liberia), the Ebola epidemic spread rapidly the world over.

According to latest World Health Organisation figures, more than 6,000 people have died from the outbreak, out of a total of over 17,100 cases. The contagious disease created a global epidemic and world researchers are still scrambling to produce a vaccine for it.

THE BIG ONE

In the biggest online sale ever in a single day, Alibaba Group Holding Ltd. reported more than $9 billion in sales on November 11, 2014. This illustrates the growing buying power of the Chinese consumers along with the prowess of the e-commerce giant in the online space.

The sale surged past the earlier record of 57.1 billion Yuan in 2013. The shopping day—24-hours "Singles Day" online shopping festival hosted by Alibaba—was similar to Black Friday in the US, where retailers offered promotional sales.

POWER SHIFT

The focus once again comes on the economic power shift from the west to east. China's rise as a significant global business player has been fast. So much so, that today it is the second largest foreign investor in the US after Canada. And this despite the Chinese economy being in the midst of an economic slowdown.

CUBA RE-VISITED

US President Barack Obama made his promise of December 17, 2014 come good on July 20, 2015 with the opening of the Cuban embassy in Washington and the US embassy in Havana, thus restoring diplomatic relations. The US, however, continues with the commercial, economic and financial embargo. This means that though the two countries have softened travel restrictions, neither allows its citizens to have financial or business dealings with the other.

EARTH SHAKES, AGAIN!

The April 25 Nepal earthquake led to a huge loss of life and property and complete destruction of some of the world's most visited UNESCO heritage sites. With an intensity of 7.8, the quake was the worst natural disaster to strike Nepal in the last 50 years. Geophysicists and other experts had warned for decades that Nepal was vulnerable to a deadly earthquake, particularly because of its geology, increasing urbanisation and architecture. A massive 8.3-magnitude earthquake rocked Chile on September 16, 2015.

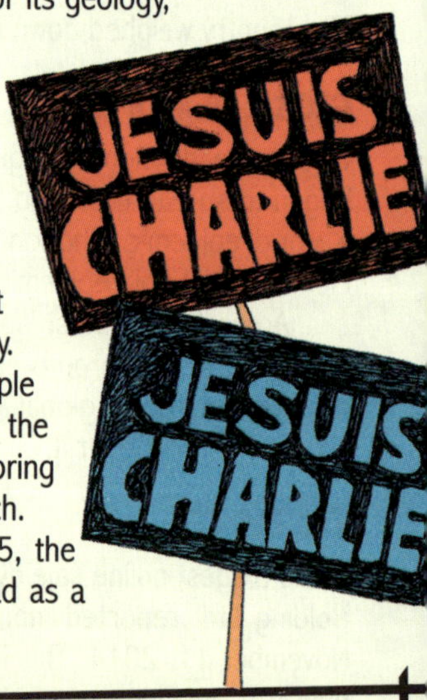

I AM CHARLIE

French satirical magazine *Charlie Hebdo's* attack of January 7, 2015 is perhaps one of the profoundest indicators of the tussle between free spirit and anarchy. When brothers Chérif and Saïd Kouachi massacred 12 people inside the magazine's editorial room, they did not expect the killings to trigger a worldwide debate on free speech or bring 4 million people onto the streets of France in a unity march.

Undeterred, in its next edition on January 13, 2015, the magazine carried another cartoon of Prophet Muhammad as a call to forgive the terrorists who carried out the attack.

- Leftist leader Alexis Tsipras won the Greek prime ministerial election.
- Iran and six world powers reached a nuclear deal in April 2015.
- While Russia attacked Crimea, Saudi Arabia led attacks on Houthi rebels in Yemen.
- Malcolm Turnbull was elected as the 29th Australian Prime Minister, replacing Tony Abbott.
- On November 9, 2014, Germany celebrated the 25th Anniversary of the Fall of the Berlin Wall.

SAARC

The South Asian Association of Regional Cooperation (SAARC) includes India, Pakistan, Bangladesh, Nepal, Afghanistan, Sri Lanka, The Maldives and Bhutan.

PAKISTAN

* A suicide bomber killed more than 60 people and injured 110 others at Pakistan's Wagah border on November 2, 2014.
* December 16, 2014 was the darkest day in Pakistan's recent history when 145 people, including 132 schoolchildren, were killed in an attack on a school in Peshawar.
* Pakistan lifted the moratorium on the death penalty for terror-related cases on December 17, 2014.
* On January 25, 2015, 80 per cent of Pakistan grappled with cold and darkness with no electricity due to a colossal power grid failure.
* Twelve Tehrik-i-Taliban terrorists were arrested on February 13, 2015 for the Peshawar school massacre.
* Finally it was cricket-time in Pakistan as the Zimbabwe Cricket Team toured Pakistan from May 19-31, 2015; a first for any Test-playing nation after the Sri Lankan cricket team attack in 2009.

BANGLADESH

* Arafat Rahman, younger son of former president Ziaur Rahman and former Prime Minister Khaleda Zia died on January 24, 2015.
* A firebomb attack on a bus by anti-government protestors on February 3, 2015 left seven people dead.
* Forty-one people died when a ferry with 100 passengers on board capsized in the Padma River after colliding with a trawler.
* An arrest warrant was issued for former Prime Minister Khaleda Zia on February 25, 2015 after she failed to show up in court to face graft charges.
* US-Bangladeshi writer and blogger Avijit Roy, whose writings on religion angered Islamist hardliners, was hacked to death by Islamist attackers on February 27, 2015.
* Bangladeshi Jamaat-e-Islami leader Muhammad Kamaruzzaman was executed for war crimes committed during the 1971 Liberation War.
* Bangladeshi secular blogger Ananta Bijoy Das was killed by a masked gang wielding machetes in the city of Sylhet on May 12.

NEPAL

* KP Sharma Oli was sworn in as Nepal's new Prime Minister on October 12, 2015.
* Nepal introduced separate buses for women on January 5, 2015.
* Nepal was hit by a magnitude 7.6 earthquake on April 25, 2015, 34 km from

Lamjung, at a depth of approximately 8.2 km. The quake toll in the affected countries (Nepal, India, China and Bangladesh) was over 9,000 dead and 23,000 injured.

* Another 7.3 magnitude earthquake struck the town of Namche Bazaar near the Tibetan border and the base camp for Mount Everest, killing at least 66 people.
* When the earthquake struck Nepal in April, Dhana Kumari Bajracharya, Nepal's longest-serving "living goddess" was forced to do the unthinkable: walk the streets for the first time in her life.
* The Nepal quake moved Mount Everest 1.2 inches to the southwest, but did not change its height, according to a report published in July 2015.
* Nepal's new national constitution was adopted on September 20, 2015, and has been praised for including provisions like equal rights for the LGBT community and abolition of the death penalty. However, critics say it is regressive on some counts, such as citizenship rights.

AFGHANISTAN

* British base Camp Bastion and U.S. Camp Leatherneck were handed over to the Afghan Government on October 26, 2014.
* On November 29, 2014, China's Special Envoy for Afghanistan publicly acknowledged that he had met Taliban representatives in Peshawar.
* On December 13, 2014, gunmen assassinated the head of the Secretariat of the Supreme Court Atiqullah Rawoofi on the outskirts of Kabul.
* On December 28, 2014, the International Security Assistance Force formally ended its combat mission and the Afghan war.
* On January 5, 2015, a suicide car bomber hit the HQ of EUPOL Afghanistan in Kabul killing one person and injuring five.
* Avalanches killed at least 187 people in north-eastern Afghanistan on February 25, 2015.
* On March 24, the US President announced that US forces in Afghanistan would not be reduced from 9800 troops to 5000 as had been indicated earlier.
* On March 25, 2015, the Afghan National Army killed 29 insurgents in a series of anti-terrorist operations.
* Secret talks were held in China in May 2015 between Afghanistan's peace envoy and the Taliban in an effort to negotiate a solution to the insurgency. The meeting was reportedly facilitated by Pakistan's ISI.
* June 22, 2015, saw the Taliban use car bombs, assault rifles and RPGs to attack the Afghan Parliament, killing two civilians and injuring 40 others.

SRI LANKA

* On October 29, 2014, a three-km long landslide in Badulla killed 16 people and left 200 missing.
* Lanka went to the polls on January 8, 2015, to vote for a new President, in a tightly contested election between President Mahinda Rajapaksa and challenger Maithripala Sirisena. Sirisena has since been appointed President.
* India and Sri Lanka pledged closer ties during Prime Minister Narendra Modi's Lanka visit on March 13, 2015.

THE MALDIVES

* This popular tourist destination was in a "state of crisis" after the capital's only desalination plant was destroyed in a fire on December 5, 2014.
* There was massive civil unrest after the high-profile prosecutions of the country's first democratically elected president and former Defence Minister Mohamed Nazim. In March 2015, Nasheed was convicted under the Anti-Terrorism Act of Maldives. He was sentenced to 13 years in prison.
* India expressed concern on Maldives' July 23, 2015 decision to open up the islands to foreign buyers, which may enable countries like China gain a foothold in the Indian Ocean.
* Four islands in The Maldives claimed that wreckage from Malaysia's MH370 crash had washed up on their beaches in August.
* Human rights lawyer Amal Clooney will represent ousted President Nasheed, who has been in jail since February, after his local lawyer was stabbed.

BHUTAN

* In one recent project, US company Matternet joined hands with the WHO and the Bhutanese government to deliver medical material to remote hospitals in the Himalayan nation with the help of drones.
* A team of Japanese social metrics experts measured the happiness of citizens in Bhutan in June. The phrase Gross National Happiness was coined in 1972 by Bhutan's fourth king, Jigme Singye Wangchuck.

By **CHETNA SINHA**

5000 BC
Sumerian civilisation in Mesopotamia (present day Iraq) established in this period.

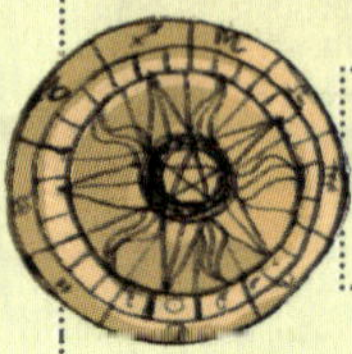

2700 BC
Egyptians create 365-day calendar with the new year starting in June.

2300 BC
Astronomy established as a science.

2000-1200 BC
Iron Age begins with the discovery of iron. Iron replaces bronze in implements and weapons

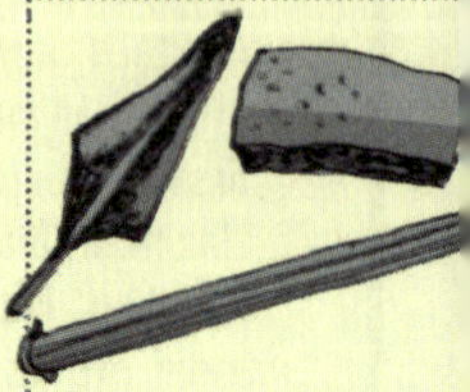

3500 BC
Wheel used for the first time.

5000 BC | 3500 BC | 2500 BC | 2000 BC | 1800 BC

3100 BC
Work begins on the Stonehenge.

2500 BC
City of Mohenjo-Daro established in the Indus Valley.

2700-2600BC
Pyramids built in Egypt.

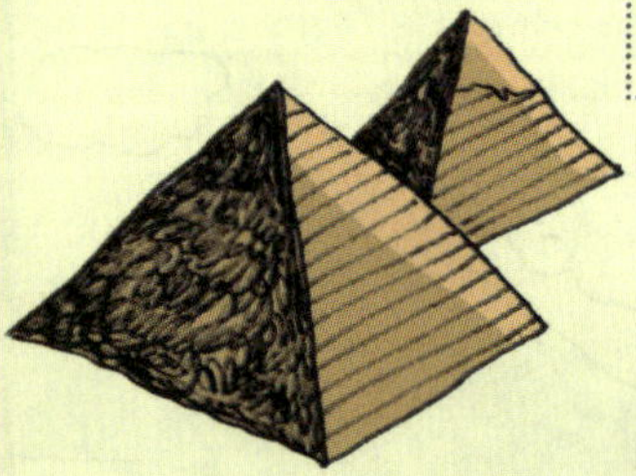

2000 BC
The Bronze Age reaches Europe; Britain invaded by Scandinavian tribes for the first time.

1500 BC
Rise of the Ganges civilisation in northern India. The Rig Veda, the oldest book in Sanskrit or any Indo-European language, compiled around this time.

753 BC
Rome is founded by Romulus. Twelve birds circled overhead during the founding ceremony and legend had it that the city would survive for 12 centuries.

509 BC
Founding of the Roman Republic. The great architecture of Rome can be traced back to this period.

776 BC
First Olympics held in Olympia, Greece.

433 BC
Parthenon in Athens completed after 40 years of work.

1000 BC
The Maya civilisation established.

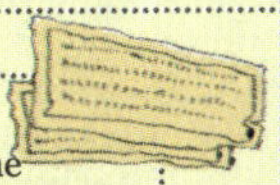

1000 BC
Hindu epics, the *Mahabharata* and the *Ramayana* composed.

430 BC
Democritus theorises that matter is composed of tiny grains called 'atomos' that cannot be subdivided.

44 BC
Julius Caesar assassinated by Brutus and other conspirators.

1120 BC
Magnetic compass invented.

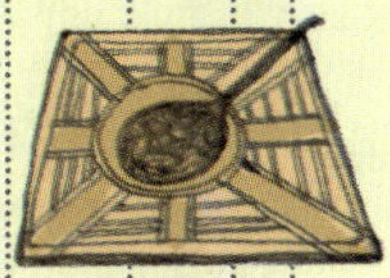

1500 BC ---- 1000 BC ---- 500 BC ---- 250 BC ---- 0 BC

1185 BC Trojan war fought.

347 BC
Death of Greek philosopher Plato.

55 BC
Julius Caesar conquers Britain, having already captured Gaul, what is now modern France.

1100 BC
Phoenicians develop alphabetic script.

560 BC
Gautama Buddha, founder of Buddhism, born in India.

1000 BC
Chinese develop gunpowder

215 BC
Building of the Great Wall of China commences.

850 BC
Iliad and *Odyssey* composed by Homer.

586 BC
Fall of Jerusalem to the Babylonians.

264 BC
Ashoka crowned, marking the beginning of the Golden Age in India.

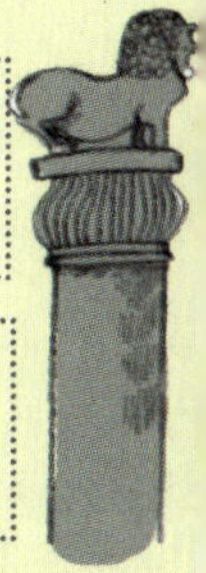

660 BC
Birth of Zoroaster, the founder of Zoroastrianism, in Medea, Iran.

650 BC
Earliest coins appear.

336 BC
Accession of Alexander the Great at the age of 22 to the throne of Macedon in southeastern Europe.

Not to scale.

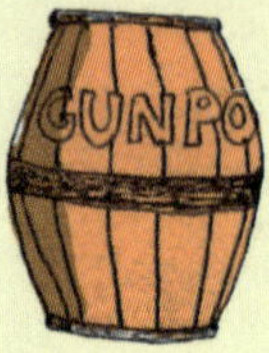

1300 AD
Gunpowder used for warfare in England after being introduced to Europe in 1242.

1285 AD
Spectacles for the farsighted are invented in Italy.

1 AD
Since the scholars who designed the new calendar did not have the concept of zero, the new Gregorian calendar is calculated to start at year 1.

5 BC—6 AD
Jesus born.

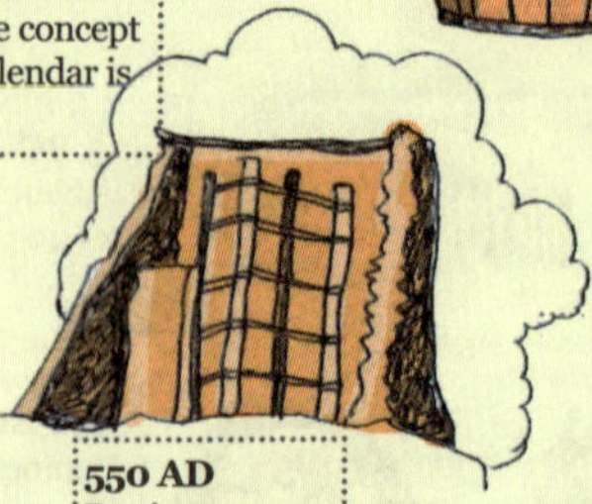

1215 AD
King John of England seals the Magna Carta, giving more power to the Barons. Mongols under Genghis Khan conquer Beijing.

64 AD
Great Fire of Rome lasts for six days. Emperor Nero does nothing to stop it.

550 AD
Persians use windmills to power irrigation pumps.

1096-99 AD
First Crusade.

1140 AD
Angkor Wat, a huge temple complex, built in Cambodia.

570 AD
Birth of Prophet Mohammad, the founder of Islam, in Mecca.

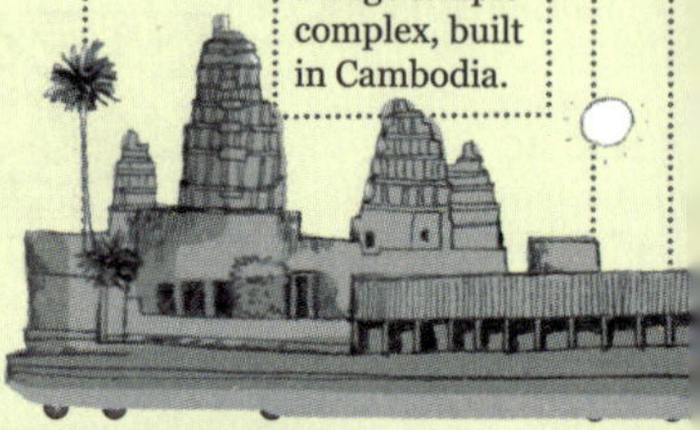

0 AD ---- 500 AD ---- 1000 AD ---- 1200 AD

70 AD
Romans under Titus destroy Jerusalem; 1.5 million Jews die. Gold taken from the temple finances the Colosseum in Rome.

1024
The Chinese invent paper.

1163 AD
Oxford University founded in Oxford, England.

68-69 AD
Civil War in Rome after Emperor Nero dies.

754 AD
Beginning of the state of the Vatican City.

1187 AD
Ships begin to use the magnetic compass.

50 AD
Buddhism reaches China.

1275 AD
Marco Polo starts on his trip to China. He returns in 1295 to Venice.

29 AD
Crucifixion of Jesus Christ.

1315 AD
Great Famine of 1315-1317.

1337 AD
Beginning of the Hundred Years' War between England and France, resolved only in 1453.

1347-50
The Great Plague, popularly called Black Death, in Europe.

1431 AD
Joan of Arc, who is credited with leading the French to victory over the English, is burnt at the stake for allegedly practising witchcraft.

1438 AD
The Inca Empire established in Peru.

1498 AD
Vasco da Gama reaches India. He becomes the first European to travel to India by sea.

1558 AD
Commencement of the Elizabethan era in England.

1564 AD
Birth of poet and playwright William Shakespeare in England.

1588 AD
The Spanish Armada is defeated by an English naval force.

1619 AD
Johann Kepler finally solves the mystery of the motion of the planets.

1350 AD — 1500 AD — 1550 AD — 1700 AD

1455 AD
First Bible printed after the invention of the printing press by German goldsmith Johannes Gutenberg.

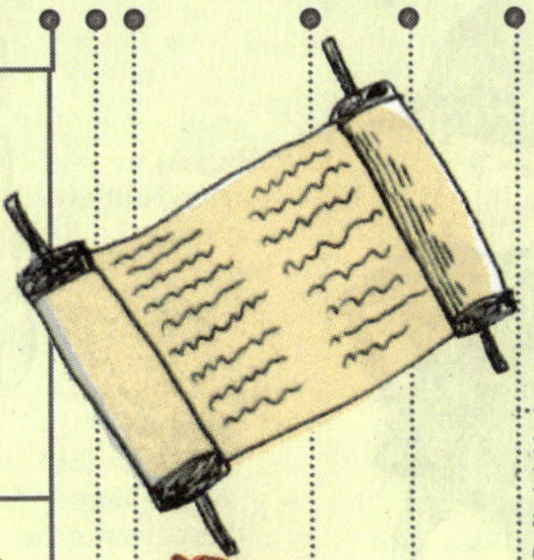

1455-85
The civil wars or the Wars of the Roses, in England.

1488 AD
Bartholomew Diaz rounds the Cape of Good Hope.

1492 AD
Christopher Columbus lands on the Americas. He dies in 1506 believing he had landed in Asia.

1504 AD
Mona Lisa painted by Leonardo da Vinci.

1519 AD
Ferdinand Magellan starts what would be the first circumnavigation of the globe.

1534 AD
King Henry VIII breaks apart from the Roman Catholic Church and appoints himself as the head of the English Church.

1556 AD
Earthquake in China kills 830,000.

1666 AD
London engulfed by the Great Fire.

1689 AD
Constitutional Monarchy established in England.

1750 AD

1770 AD
Captain James Cook discovers Australia.

1776 AD
US Declaration of Independence is signed on July 4. American colonies declare themselves independent of Great Britain.

1783 AD
First manned hot air balloon flight in Paris by Jean Francoise Pilatre de Rozier and Marquis D'Arlands.

1789 AD
On July 14, the French Revolution begins with the storming of the Bastille to free prisoners and end monarchy. Oddly enough, the Bastille was empty of any real prisoners.

1795 AD
Metric system of measurement introduced in France.

1800 AD

1801 AD
Joseph-Marie Jacquard invents a loom that uses punched cards to create designs in fabric.

1804 AD
Napoleon Bonaparte crowned Emperor of France.

1812 AD
On June 24, Napoleon takes Moscow, but it is a hollow victory. The city is burned to the ground, yet the Tsar does not surrender. Napoleon and the French army retreat.

1814 AD
Battle of Trafalgar; British fleet under the command of Horatio Nelson defeats a combined Spanish French fleet.

1815 AD
Napolean is finally defeated after many attempts in the Battle of Waterloo.

1816 AD
The year without a summer. Mount Tambora erupts and throws up so much dust in the air that it causes 10 inches of snow to fall in June in New England (US). Crops fail and famine is widespread.

1833 AD
England outlaws slavery and frees more than 780,000 slaves.

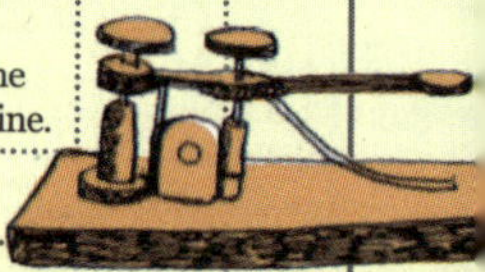

1838 AD
On January 24, Samuel Morse demonstrates the telegraph machine.

1840 AD

1840 AD
The *Nemesis*, built by a Scottish shipbuilder, becomes the first ironclad to round the Cape of Good Hope.

1839-1842 AD
The First Opium War: Hongkong becomes a British colony.

1905
While working as a patent clerk, Albert Einstein, publishes his theory of relativity and also states energy equals matter (e= mc²). This is his 'miracle year'.

1845-48
The Great Hunger (aka the Potato Famine) in Ireland. Over 1.5 million die of starvation and disease while Ireland continues to export grain to England to pay rents.

1898 AD
Spanish-American War starts. Reports of atrocities by the Spaniards against Cubans compels the US to intervene.

1837-1901 AD
Victoria is Queen of the United Kingdom.

1883
The light bulb is invented by Thomas Edison.

1876 AD
Telephone invented by Alexander Graham Bell.

1848 AD
Karl Marx and Fredrich Engels publish the Communist Manifesto.

1860 AD — 1875 AD — 1900 AD

1895
In France, the Lumiere Brothers showcase films for the first time in the history of the world.

1859 AD
Charles Darwin publishes *The Origin of Species*.

1903
Orville and Wilbur Wright invent, build and fly the first aircraft.

1896 AD
The first modern Olympic Games in Athens, Greece.

1856 AD
Louis Pasteur shows that disease is spread by tiny organisms. Modern germ theory born.

1869 AD
Suez Canal opened.

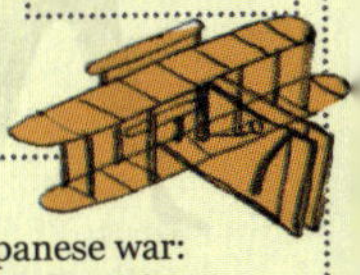

1904
Russo-Japanese war: Russians underestimate the modern Japanese fleet, which a year later destroys most of the already depleted Russian navy.

1866 AD
Prussia invades Austria.

1854 AD
Lord Cardigan leads the British cavalry against the Russians in what would become known as 'The Charge of the Light Brigade'.

1861-65
American Civil War; President Lincoln bans slavery; some states attempt to break the Union.

1912–13
The Balkan Wars. Two short wars, fought over the possession of the European territories by the Ottoman Empire.

1914
First World War, commonly known today as World War I. Germany declares war on France and begins the war.

1912
The *Titanic* which was touted to be the largest luxury liner to sail the open seas, sinks with over 1,500 passengers.

1917
In this year, the US enters World War I against Germany. Ten million people die in the war.

1917 AD
The Russian Revolution destroys the Tsarist autocracy and leads to the creation of the Soviet Union.

1944
On June 6, 1944, a date known ever since as D-Day, a mighty armada crosses from England to Normandy, France, and breaks the Nazi grip on western Europe which marks the end of Hitler's Third Reich.

1945
On August 6 an atomic bomb drops on Hiroshima, Japan, killing an estimated 80,000 civilians. On August 9 another bomb is dropped on Nagasaki. On August 14, Japan surrenders and World War II is officially over. The UNO is established.

1910 AD — 1930 AD — 1945 AD — 1950 AD

1916 AD
Easter Rising in Ireland.

1918
At the 11th hour of the 11th day of the 11th month, World War I is officially over.

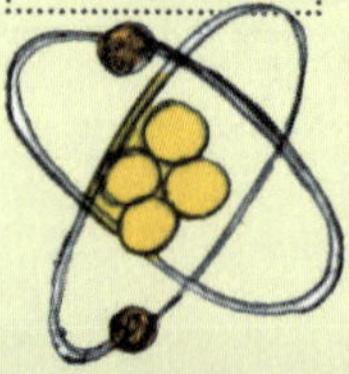

1919 AD
Ernest Rutherford splits an atom for the first time.

1928
British bacteriologist, Sir Alexander Fleming, after many years of research on antibiotics, discovers penicillin.

1930
Planet Pluto is discovered.

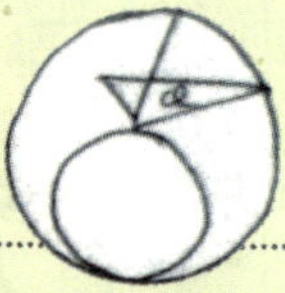

1942
At the University of Chicago, Enrico Fermi conducts the first nuclear reaction and thereby demonstrates the controlled release of nuclear energy.

1939
Hitler invades Poland on September 1. The British Commonwealth and France declare war on Germany, starting World War II.

1938
Adolf Hitler, Chancellor of Germany, launches 'Kristallnacht', a night of terror visited upon the Jews by the Nazis. Hundreds of Jews are killed and the glass from synagogues and businesses is shattered onto the streets.

1950 AD — 1975 AD — 2000 AD — 2011 AD

1950-53
Post-World War II division of Korea leads to the Korean War in which China supports North Korea and the US lends support to South Korea.

1957 AD
Sputnik I becomes the first man-made satellite.

1960 AD
On January 23, Jacques Piccard and Don Walsh travel to the bottom of the Marina Trench, the lowest point on earth, in the Bathsyscaphe Trieste. Oddly, no one has ever gone back a second time.

1961
On April 11, Yuri A. Gargarin becomes the first human in space.

1965-73
Vietnam War.

1969
On July 20 Neil Armstrong lands on the surface of the moon.

1982
Falklands War fought between Argentina and the United Kingdom over the disputed Falkland Islands, South Georgia and South Sandwich Islands.

1989
In November, the Berlin Wall that divided West Berlin from East Berlin is torn down. Berlin united for the first time since World War II.

1990
Apartheid ends in South Africa. Nelson Mandela becomes the President of South Africa in the country's first free elections.

1990
First Gulf War begins when the US attacks Iraq in response to Iraq's invasion of Kuwait.

1991
The Soviet Union dissolves, and with it the Cold War.

1994
Rwanda is engulfed in a huge and bloody civil war.

2001
On September 11, terrorists attack the World Trade Centre in New York and the Pentagon in Washington DC by flying planes into their targets.

2003
US and British forces invade Iraq. Saddam Hussein is eventually caught, and executed in 2006.

2004
A huge earthquake near Indonesia on Christmas Day causes a tsunami in the Indian Ocean that kills thousands in Indonesia, Thailand, Sri Lanka, India and other countries.

2007
Benazir Bhutto, the exiled former Pakistani Prime Minister, assassinated on her return to Pakistan.

2008
Nepal abolishes monarchy. King Gyanendra vacates the Royal Palace and Nepal becomes a democracy.

2009
Barack Hussein Obama becomes the first African-American President in the history of the US. He wins the Nobel Peace Prize.

2010
Volcanic eruptions under a glacier in Iceland cause the biggest disruption of international air traffic in recent times.

2011
Osama bin Laden, the mastermind behind the September 11, 2001, terror attack in the U.S. is killed near Islamabad.

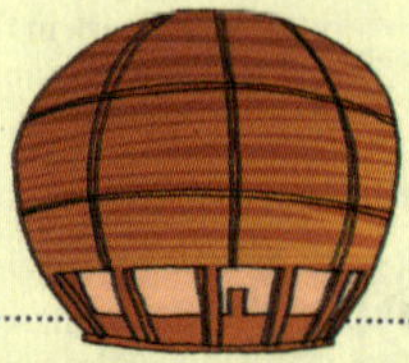

2012
Higgs Boson, the particle that is said to give matter mass, is found by scientists at CERN, the European laboratory for particle physics.

2012
Mars rover Curiosity finds landforms that point towards flowing liquid. Had there been life on Mars?

2013
A near-earth asteroid entered the earth's atmosphere, bursting over Chelyabinsk in Russia, producing many fragmentary meteorites, a powerful shock wave and damaging more than 7200 buildings.

2014
Malaysian Airlines flight MH370, carry
239 people on board, disappeared o
the South Chi
Sea and MH-1
was shot dowr
over war-torn easte
Ukraine, killin
all 298 on boa

2012 AD — 2013 AD — 2015 AD

2012
Arab 'spring': Pro-democracy protests overthrow military governments in Egypt and Yemen. In Bahrain and Syria they challenge the monarchy and the establishment.

2012
Indian American Sunita Williams takes the longest space walk for a woman.

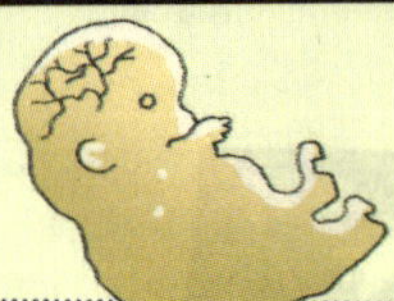

2013
US scientists successfully created a cloned human embryo, using the same technique used for developing the cloned sheep in 1996.

2014
The Ebola Virus, one of the most virulent viral diseases known to mankind, was detected in Guinea. The virus causes haemorrhagic fever and has resulted in over 4000 deaths so far.

2015
Scientists have found water on Mars, the first indication that there is possibility of life on the red planet.

TOP TEN

- ☑ WONDERS OF THE WORLD
- ☑ TOP TEN LISTS OF THE BIGGEST, LONGEST, TALLEST AND MUCH MORE

Seven natural wonders of the world

Grand Canyon, Colorado River, Arizona
Rio de Janeiro harbour, Brazil
Great Barrier Reef, Australia
Paricutin Volcano Michoaćan, Mexico
Mount Everest, on the border of Tibet and Nepal
Victoria Falls, borders of Zambia & Zimbabwe
Northern Lights, especially from northern Canada and Alaska (Aurora Borealis)

Ten man-made wonders of the world

Pyramids of Egypt, Egypt
Great Wall of China, China
Taj Mahal, India
Machu Picchu, Peru
Temples of Bali, Indonesia
Angkor Wat, Cambodia
Forbidden City, China
Bagan Temples & Pagodas, Burma
Karnak Temple, Egypt
Teotihuacan, Mexico

Ten famous monuments in India

Taj Mahal, Agra
Qutub Minar, Delhi
Gateway of India, Mumbai
Gwalior Fort, Gwalior
Fatehpur Sikri, Uttar Pradesh
Khajuraho, Madhya Pradesh
Sanchi Stupa, Madhya Pradesh
Sun Temple, Odisha
Jantar Mantar, Jaipur
Meenakshi Sundareshwar Temple, Tamil Nadu

Longest mountain ranges

Andes, South America—7242 km
Rocky Mountains, North America—6035 km
Himalayas / Karakoram / Hindu Kush, Asia—3862 km
Great Dividing Range, Australia—3621 km
Trans Antarctic, Antarctica—3541 km
Brazilian East Coast Range, South America—3058 km
Sumatran / Javan Range, Asia—2897 km
Tien Shan, Asia—2253 km
Eastern Ghats, Asia—2092 km
Urals, Eurasia—2012 km

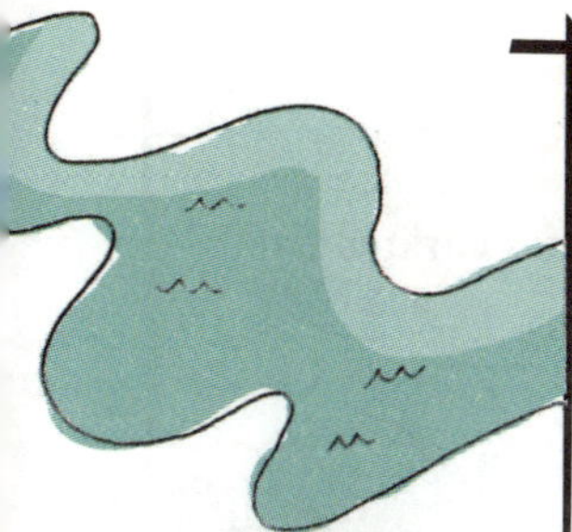

Longest rivers

Nile, Africa—6727 km
Amazon, South America—6296 km
Mississippi, North America—5970 km
Yangtze, Asia—5797 km
Ob, Russia—5567 km
Huang Ho, Asia—4667 km
Yenisei, Asia—4506 km
Parana, South America—4498 km
Irtysh, Asia—4438 km
Zaire, Africa—4370 km

Highest waterfalls

Angel, Carrao River, Venezuela—Drop: 979 m
Tugela, Tugela River, South Africa—Drop: 850 m
Utigard, Jostedal Glacier, Nesdale, Norway—Drop: 850 m
Mongefossen, Monge River, Mongebekk, Norway—Drop: 774m
Mutarazi, Mutarazi River, Zimbabwe—Drop: 762 m
Yosemite, Yosemite National Park, California—Drop: 739 m
Ostre Mardola Foss, Mardals River, Eikisdal, Norway—Drop: 656 m
Tyssestrengane, Tysso River, Hardanger, Norway—Drop: 646 m
Cuquenan, Arabopo River, Venezuela—Drop: 610 m
Sutherland, Arthur River, South Island, New Zealand—Drop: 580 m

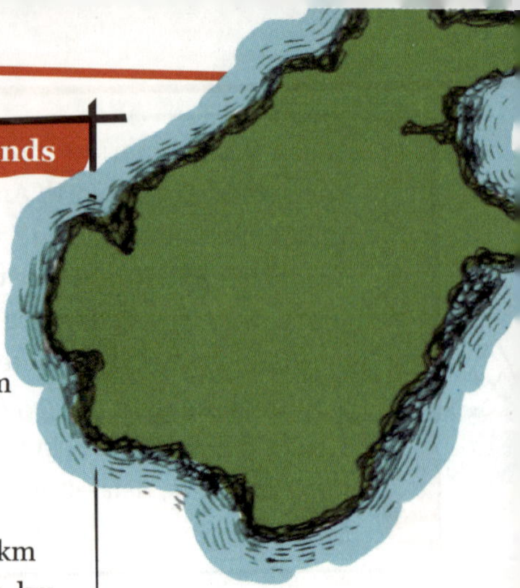

Largest islands

Greenland—2,175,600 sq. km
New Guinea—785,753 sq. km
Borneo—748,168 sq. km
Madagascar—587,713 sq. km
Baffin Island, Canada—503,944 sq. km
Sumatra, Indonesia—443,065 sq. km
Great Britain—229,957 sq. km
Honshu, Japan—225,800 sq. km
Victoria Island, Canada—220,548 sq. km
Ellesmere Island, Canada—183,964 sq. km

Largest freshwater lakes

Caspian Sea, Azerbajian/Iran/Kazakhstan/Russia/Turkmenistan
Superior, Canada/US
Victoria, Kenya/Tanzania/Uganda
Huron, Canada/US
Michigan, US
Aral Sea, Kazakhstan/Uzbekistan
Tanganyika, Burundi/Tanzania/Zaire/Zambia
Baikal, Russia
Great Bear, Canada
Great Slave, Canada

Biggest deserts

Sahara Desert, North Africa—3.5 sq. million miles
Australian, Australia—1.47 sq. million miles
Arabian, Southwest Asia—0.5 sq. million miles
Gobi, Central Asia—0.4 sq. million miles
Kalahari, Southern Africa—0.2 sq. million miles
Turkestan, Central Asia—0.174 sq. million miles
Takla Makan, China—0.125 sq. million miles
Namib, Southwest Africa—0.120 sq. million miles
Sommoran, US/Mexico—0.120 sq. million miles
Thar, India—0.1 sq. million miles

Largest oceans and seas

Pacific Ocean
Atlantic Ocean
Indian Ocean
Arctic Ocean
South China Sea
Caribbean Sea
Mediterranean Sea
Bering Sea
Sea of Okhotsk
Gulf of Mexico

Most deadly volcanoes

Year of their most famous eruption

Laki, Iceland—1783
Mount Vesuvius, Italy—79 AD
Tambora, Indonesia—1815
Krakatoa, Indonesia—1883
Mount Pelee, Martinique—1902
Ruiz, Colombia—1985
Unzen, Japan—1792
Kelut, Java (Indonesia)—1919
Papandayan, Java (Indonesia)—1772
Lamington, Papua New Guinea—1951

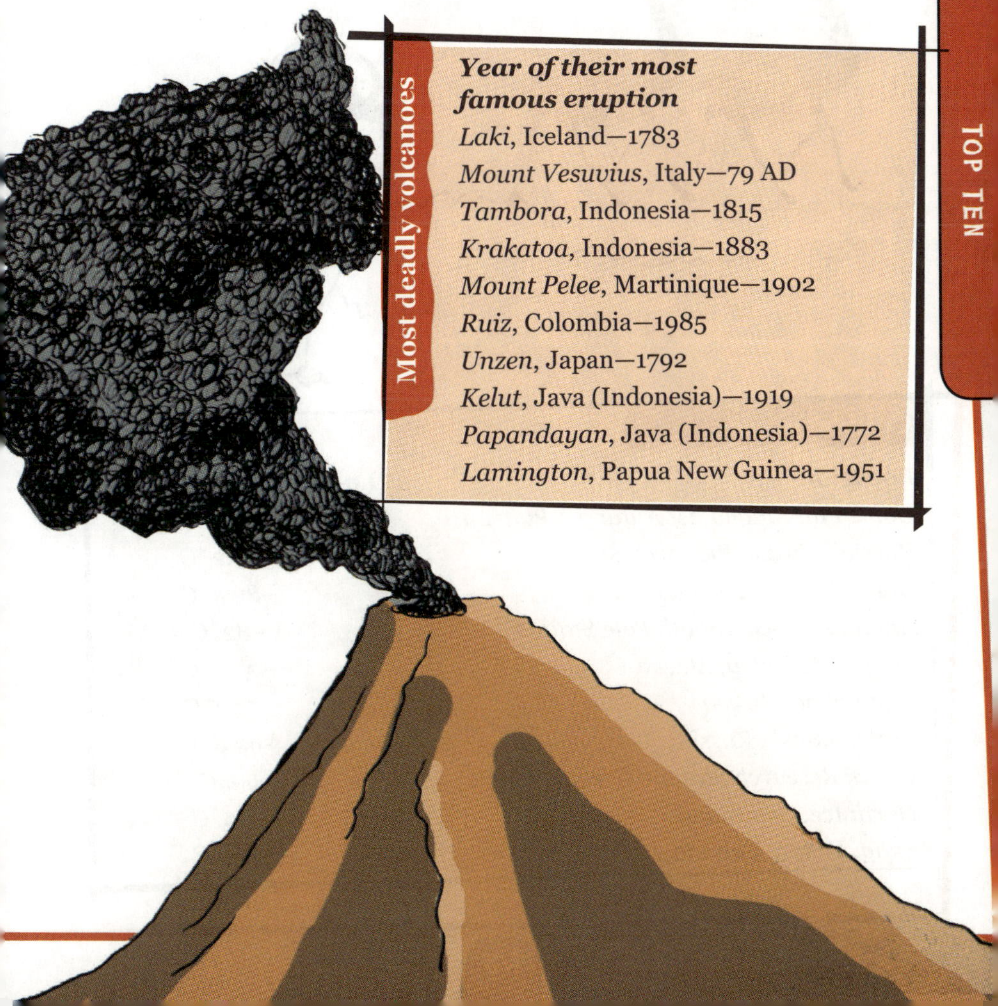

Hottest places

Location	*Highest Temperature*
Death Valley, USA	56.7° C
Tirat Zvi, Israel	54° C
Sulaibya, Kuwait	53.6° C
Mohenjodaro, Pakistan	53.5° C
Dehloran, Iran	53° C
Jeddah, Saudi Arabia	52° C
Mexicali, Baja California	52° C
As-Samarah, Western Sahara	50.7° C
Oodnadatta, Australia	50.7° C
Aydingkol Lake, China	50.2° C

Coldest places

Location	*Lowest Temperature*
Dome Fuji Ridge East Antarctic Plateau	–93.2 °C
Russia's Vostok Research Station	–89.2 °C
Dome A, Antarctic Plateau	–82.5 °C
Amundsen-Scott South Pole Station	–82 °C
Mount McKinley, Alaska	–73.8 °C
Oymyakon, Russia	–71.2 °C
Verkhoyansk, Russia	–69.8 °C
Klinck Research Station, Greenland	–69.4 °C
North Ice, Greenland	–66 °C
Snag, Yukon, Canada	–63 °C

Wettest places

Location	*Total Rainfall*
Mawsynram, Meghalaya State, India	*11,871mm*
Cherrapunji, Meghalaya State, India	*11,777mm*
Tutendo, Colombia, South America	*11,770mm*
Cropp River, New Zealand	*11,516mm*
San Antonio de Ureca, Bioko Island, Equatorial Guinea	*10,450mm*
Debundscha, Cameroon, Africa	*10,299mm*
Big Bog, Maui, Hawaii	*10,272mm*
Mt Waialeale, Kauai, Hawaii	*9763mm*
Kukui, Maui, Hawaii	*9293mm*
Emei Shan, Sichuan Province, China	*8169mm*

Countries with the lowest population densities

	People per square km
Mongolia	1.76
Namibia	2.56
Australia	3.05
Iceland	3.15
Suriname	3.26
Mauritania	3.36
Botswana	3.48
Libya	3.5
Canada	3.56
Guyana	3.65

Countries with the highest population densities

	People per square km
Macau	20,497
Monaco	18,005
Singapore	7,540
Hong Kong	6,544
Gibraltar	4,959
Vatican City	1,877
Bahrain	1,646
Malta	1,282
Bermuda	1,212
Sint Maarten	1,100

Richest countries

GDP per capita (in billion)	
Qatar	$227.101
Luxembourg	$66.013
Singapore	$320.245
Norway	$523.188
Brunei Darussalam	$17.536
United Arab Emirates	$440.181
United States	$18,286.69
Hong Kong	$312.394
Switzerland	$680.112
Netherlands	$891.549

Most populous cities

Tokyo, Japan
Delhi, India
Shanghai, China
Mexico City, Mexico
Mumbai, India
São Paulo, Brazil
Osaka, Japan
Beijing, China
New York City
Cairo, Egypt

Countries with the lowest HDI*

Country	HDI
Niger	0.337
Democratic Republic of the Congo	0.338
Central African Republic	0.341
Chad	0.372,
Sierra Leone	0.374
Eritrea	0.381
Burkina Faso	0.388
Burundi	0.389
Guinea	0.392
Mozambique	0.393

***HDI = Human Development Index**

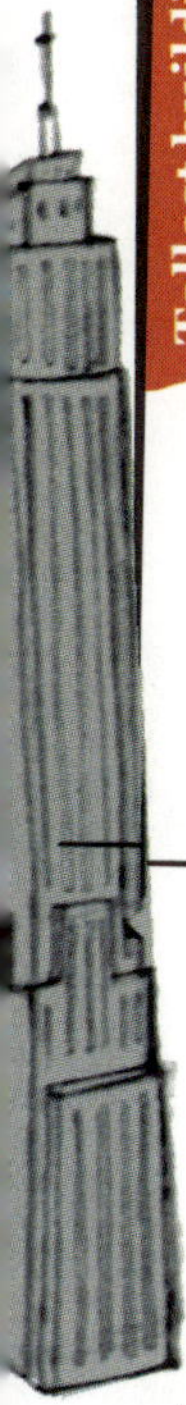

Tallest buildings

Burj Khalifa, Dubai (UAE) - 2717 ft, 163 storeys
Makkah Royal Clock Tower Hotel, Mecca (SA) - 1972 ft, 120 storeys
One World Trade Center, New York City (US) - 1,776 ft, 94 storeys
Taipei 101, Taipei (TW) - 1667 ft, 101 storeys
Shanghai World Financial Center, Shanghai (CN) - 1614 ft, 101 storeys
International Commerce Centre, Hong Kong (CN) - 1588, 108 storeys
Petronas Tower 1 & 2, Kuala Lumpur (MY) - 1483, 88 storeys
Zifeng Tower, Nanjing (CN) - 1476 ft, 66 storeys
Willis Tower, Chicago (US) - 1451 ft, 108 storeys
KK100, Shenzhen (CN) - 1449 ft, 100 storeys

Longest bridges

Weihe Grand Bridge, China—79732 m
Bang Na Expressway, Thailand—54000 m
Lake Pontchartrain Causeway, US—38442 m
Manchac Swamp Bridge, US—36710 m
Yangcun Bridge, China—35812 m
Hangzhou Bay Bridge, China—35673 m
Runyang Bridge, China—35660 m
Donghai Bridge, China—32500 m
Shanghai Maglev line, China—29908 m
Atchafalaya Basin Bridge, US—29290 m

Countries with the highest HDI

- Norway
- Australia
- Switzerland
- Netherlands
- United States
- Germany
- New Zealand
- Canada
- Singapore
- Denmark

Languages

- Chinese Mandarin—1 billion
- Spanish—399 million
- English—512 million
- Hindi—501 million
- Russian—285 million
- Arabic—265 million
- Bengali—245 million
- Portuguese—196 million
- Malay-Indonesian—140 million
- French—130 million

SCIENCE

- ☑ SCIENCE
  - ☑ SPACE
  - ☑ SCIENCE AND TECHNOLOGY
  - ☑ GADGETS
  - ☑ THE INTERNET

The biggest space success story of the year 2015 was the NASA space probe *New Horizons*. The space probe hit the bullseye after a journey of 4.8 billion kilometres, lasting nine years, as it zoomed past Pluto with uncanny precision. The year also saw the possible discovery of water on Mars, the first ever spacecraft going into orbit around a dwarf planet and astronauts on ISS tasting the first space-grown food. India kept up its space momentum by launching nine satellites, including five from the UK, and testing its most powerful rocket. During the year, ISS astronauts manufactured the first object, using 3D printing technology in space. Read on for more.

CHINA RETURNS TO THE MOON

In what is said to be the first mission of its kind in almost 40 years, China's unmanned lunar probe *Chang'e* 5-T1 completed a flyby of the Moon before swinging back toward home. Launched on October 23, 2014, the probe landed in north China's Inner Mongolia Autonomous Region on November 1, 2014. The data gathered during the mission would help researchers design and build a capsule that will bring lunar rocks and soil to Earth, something China hopes to accomplish by 2017.

COMETS SMELL LIKE ROTTEN EGG

Scientists at the European Space Agency announced in October 2014 that comets smell awful —like rotten eggs, urine and formaldehyde. They found this out after 'sniffing the fumes' of comet 67P/Churyumov-Gerasimenko using instruments on board the *Rosetta* orbiter. This foul smell can be attributed to a curious mix of water and pungent gases like carbon monoxide, carbon dioxide, ammonia, methane, formaldehyde, sulphur dioxide and others present on the planet.

FIRST 3D PRINTED OBJECT IN SPACE

In November 2014, the International Space Station achieved a first by manufacturing the first object through 3D printing in zero-gravity. This paves the way for future long-term space expeditions by providing an on-demand machine shop capability away from Earth. According to NASA, parts made in space using 3D printing technology appear to be better, with stronger bonding than similar parts manufactured on Earth using the same technology.

DAWN ORBITS A DWARF PLANET

In March, NASA's *Dawn* became the first spacecraft to go into orbit around a dwarf planet–Ceres–the largest object in the Solar System between Mars and Jupiter. In August, the spacecraft sent back the closest views of *Ceres* till now, showing its features in unprecedented detail, including a tall, conical mountain, crater formation features and narrow, braided fractures. *Dawn* is also the first spacecraft to orbit two worlds after leaving Earth. After its launch in September 2007, it was the first spacecraft to go into orbit around the giant asteroid Vesta from 2011 to 2012.

THE MOST EARTH-LIKE PLANET DISCOVERED

In July, NASA announced the discovery of the 'most Earth-like' alien planet orbiting a star just like our Sun at about the same distance that the Earth circles the Sun. Named Kepler-452b, it is said to be the first 'possibly rocky, habitable planet around a solar-type star'. The planet lies at a distance of 1,400 light-years from Earth and completes one orbit every 385 days.

ISS LIFE EXTENDED UNTIL 2024

The 15-year-old International Space Station got a new lease of life after Russia's space agency Roscosmos announced that it will extend its support to it until 2024. A multinational project, the ISS is divided into two sections—the Russian Orbital Segment (ROS) and the United States Orbital Segment (USOS)—and has been continuously occupied since 2000. The space station provides the only platform to conduct scientific research in a zero-gravity environment. Currently, the Russian *Soyuz* series of spacecraft are the only means of transporting humans to and from the ISS.

SATURN'S LARGEST RING

In June, astronomers announced the discovery of a hitherto unknown huge ring around Saturn—ranging in diameter from 14 million to 25 million kilometres; that is, about 10 times bigger than the planet's previously largest known ring—the 'E' ring. The new ring, named the 'Phoebe ring', is not visible in optical telescopes because it emits only infrared wavelengths. It was discovered by NASA's Spitzer Space Telescope.

Close encounter with Pluto

Eighty-five years after its discovery by Clyde Tombaugh, Pluto had its first space visitor— the NASA space probe *New Horizons*—which flew by the dwarf planet on July 14. Launched in 2006, *New Horizons* travelled for more than nine years and covered a distance of more than 4.8 billion kilometres, only to spend under three minutes near Pluto, as it sped past its target at a speed of more than 58,000 kilometres per hour. But it was the most rewarding brief encounter in space history. It discovered icy mountains, nitrogen glaciers and many other interesting features on Pluto and its moon Charon.

SPACE-GROWN FOOD IS YUMMY!

In August, three astronauts on board the International Space station—Kjell Lindgren, Scott Kelly and Kimiya Yui—achieved a first by tasting space grown food in orbit. They munched on a freshly harvested crop of a variety of blood red-coloured lettuce grown in the space station. The vegetable was grown without soil in the zero-gravity environment of space in an innovative "Veggie" plant growth system, housed inside the European Space Agency's *Columbus* laboratory in the ISS.

ROSETTA COLLECTS COMETARY DEBRIS

The European space probe *Rosetta*, which went into orbit around the comet 67P/Churyumov-Gerasimenko a year ago, achieved a significant milestone in August. It collected valuable scientific data as the comet started giving off gas and dust while moving closer to the Sun. The data could help scientists understand the origins of life on Earth better.

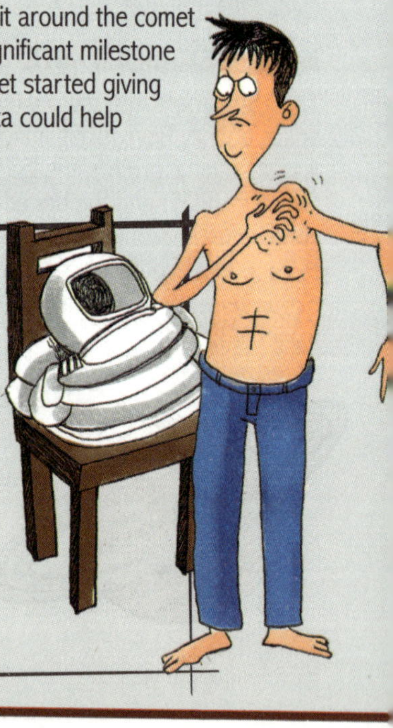

Skin gets thinner in space

In a startling revelation in July, NASA and European Space Agency scientists announced that astronauts' skin gets thinner in space, by as much as 20 per cent. It is similar to the aging process. Though scientists have known about the physiological changes like disorientation, muscle atrophy, bone loss, etc., due to prolonged stay in space, the effect of zero-gravity on human skin is a recent finding. Several astronauts returning from long stay in space had skin problems such as skin dryness and itching, in the past. Now we know why!

India's space achievements

India's space programme made significant progress, during the year. The third and fourth satellites of India's satellite-based navigation system INRSS were launched on October 16, 2014 and March 28, 2015. On July 10, Indian Space Research Organisation (ISRO) achieved a landmark by placing five UK satellites—its heaviest commercial payload—in orbit in one go. Two communication satellites, *GSAT-16* and *GSAT-6*, were launched on December 7, 2014 and August 27, 2015, respectively. *GSAT-6* is the 25th geostationary communication satellite built by ISRO. On December 18, 2014, ISRO carried out the first sub-orbital test flight of its most powerful rocket *LVM3*, which also tested a Crew Module for future manned flights.

India's first space observatory Astrosat was successfully placed in a 650-km, near-equatorial orbit on September 28, 2015 making India the fourth nation, after the US, European Space Agency and Japan, to have an astronomical observatory in orbit. Astrosat is a multi-wavelength astronomy telescope that can image objects simultaneously, in several wavelengths, giving it a unique capability in astronomical observations.

WATER FLOWS ON MARS

In September, NASA announced that its Mars Reconnaissance Orbiter has found dark streaks on the Red Planet's surface that could be evidence of flowing water. The dark streaks that appear and disappear with the seasons are believed to be created by salty water that runs down steep hills during warm months and freezes during colder times.

IS THE UNIVERSE DYING?

An international team of astronomers announced in August 2015 that the rate of energy production in the universe is slowly decreasing—stars that populate countless galaxies are slowly burning themselves out. The team arrived at this conclusion after studying more than 200,000 galaxies. But that does not mean the Universe is going to die any time soon. Even with diminishing energy generation, it will be at least 100 billion years before the Universe fizzles out. Life may be wiped out from the face of the Earth, long before that, as the Sun expands and swallows our planet in about 5 billion years.

By **Biman Basu**

PORTABLE POWER BANKS

Power banks (i.e. external batteries) used to extend the battery life of smartphones, MP3 players, tablets and laptops have become popular in recent times. Along with a profusion of substandard portable power banks from non-brands the year saw a number of established companies like Sony, Asus, Xiaomi, and OnePlus enter this segment. The glut in the market saw prices fall drastically and it was possible to buy a 10,000mAh for about Rs. 1,000.

4G LTE

4G is a mobile communications standard intended to replace 3G as it allows up to 10 times faster wireless internet access. Even as 3G services and coverage were beginning to settle down, it was time for 4G LTE. The first off the block was Airtel, followed by Reliance. Vodafone also plans to launch its 4G services by the end of 2015.

REFURBISHED SMARTPHONES

While the sale of refurbished electronics is not new, 2015 saw the organised sector selling refurbished smartphones. Refurbished goods are restored to their original working condition by the manufacturer and come with a limited warranty from the manufacturer. Global e-commerce giant Amazon kicked it off by selling refurbished Xiaomi and Samsung smartphones. Overcart and e-Bay also had refurbished offerings up for sale.

RISE OF CHINESE PHONES

The year was marked with the Indian smartphone market deluged by the Chinese Dragon. Established players like Lenovo, Xiaomi, Gionee, Huawei, OnePlus, ZTE,

Oppo, Vivo etc., vied with each other along with the likes of Samsung, HTC, Intex and Micromax for the attention of the Indian customer.

MAKE IN INDIA

In line with Prime Minister Narendra Modi's 'Make in India' project to attract world-class manufacturing and design, we had two Chinese companies setting up units in the country. First off the blocks was Xiaomi (in partnership with Foxconn) with the Redmi 2 Prime smartphone. The factory for this is based in Sri City, Andhra Pradesh. Lenovo has also started local manufacturing of the 4G variant of Moto E smartphone through a contract manufacturer at Sriperumbudur near Chennai.

AFFORDABLE 4K TVs

Even as 4K (supporting a resolution of 3,840 x 2,160 pixels, also known as ultra-high definition or UHD) is being touted as the next big standard in television broadcasting, there is an acute shortage of content. However, this hasn't deterred several TV manufacturers from launching low cost models of this future-proofed panel. What would easily have cost a couple of lakhs a year ago dropped to below Rs. 50,000 in the last few months.

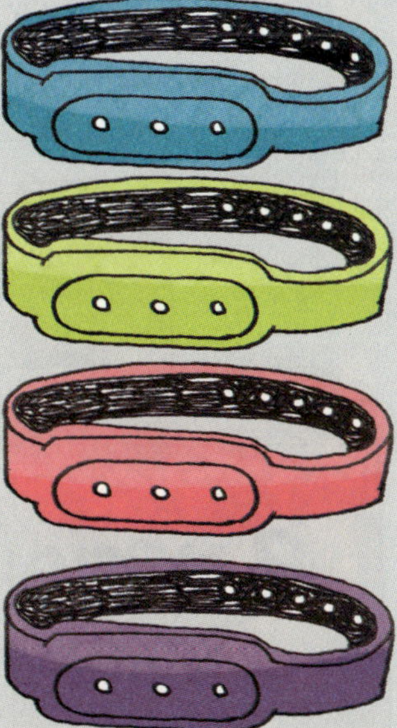

FITNESS BANDS

While fitness bands and activity trackers have been around for several years now, there has been a recent spurt in their popularity in India. One of the prime reasons for this is the availability of affordable alternatives like the Xiaomi Mi Band and the Micromax YuFit Fitness Band at Rs. 999. Meanwhile, seeing the potential of this product in India, global fitness wearable leaders like FitBit and Jawbone also made their entry. Smartwatches however were conspicuous by their absence.

MID-RANGE SMARTPHONES COME OF AGE

The onslaught of Chinese and other phone manufacturers in the Indian market in 2015 has seen the emergence of excellent value-for-money smartphones in the budget and mid-range category. You no longer need to shell out Rs. 40,000 or more for a good smartphone experience. Offerings from OnePlus, Gionee, Xiaomi, Asus, Micromax, Lenovo, Micromax and Huawei among others held their own against the big boys.

VOICE CALLS OVER INTERNET

The last couple of years has seen the emergence and popularity of free Voice over Internet Protocol (VoIP) calling. Even with Skype, Facebook Messenger and BBM Voice offering this, WhatsApp voice calling dominated. In fact, it changed the way India calls on the phone in 2014-15. WhatsApp messaging has also been truly life-changing in the way people interacted for work and pleasure over the year.

E-COMMERCE, DIGITAL SHOPPING AND SERVICES

Driven by large scale global investments, entry of leading players, Internet penetration and the growth of the smartphone market, the e-commerce market and digital shopping market in India is expected to touch Rs. 1,25,000 crore by the end of 2015. While Flipkart, Amazon, Snapdeal, Myntra etc., rule the shopping experience, the year also saw the emergence of convenience apps like Grofers, Good Service, Fasoos, Urban Clap and many more. Right from getting your car towed to getting a plumber/carpenter/electrician, to getting a cake or phone charger delivered, these online personal apps helped the connected urban Indian do just about everything this year.

By ASHISH BHATIA

Windows 10

WINDOWS 10

September saw the launch of the latest version of Microsoft Windows operating system for over 14 million PCs globally. A major highlight of the world's most popular OS is that for one year Windows 10 will be available free of charge for users of genuine copies of Windows 7 or 8.1. Feature-wise, Windows 10 is head and shoulders above its previous avatars in terms of polish and performance. Among other things it offers a brand new Edge browser instead of the aging Internet Explorer, a revolutionary DirectX 12 graphics technology, new Task View virtual desktops, Windows Hello biometric authentication, and the voice-based Cortana digital assistant.

MIRRORLESS CAMERAS

Mirrorless cameras have been fast catching on in the world of amateur photography. This class of shooters is smaller and lighter than DSLRs with fewer moving parts. As their nomenclature suggests, these cameras eliminate the need for a mirror and optical viewfinder. However, like DSLRs they permit interchangeable lenses and therefore are able to produce images that rival their brawnier siblings. This makes them ideal for traveller-tourist photography as they are smaller than DSLR but deliver the same quality. On the downside, mirrorless cameras are not as fast and powerful as their bigger brothers. Fewer lens options, poorer battery, and slower LCD screen refresh rates also make them fall short of expectations.

APPLE WATCH

The most awaited gadget of 2015, the Apple Watch has been a resounding success so far. Launched in April, 2.5 million Apple watches were sold in the first quarter of the financial year. Even though the demand for the watch petered out later, it remained one of the most aspirational devices this year. Available in three models, the Watch runs iOS, and pairs with the iPhone (5 or later) over Bluetooth and WiFi for calling and Web services. There is a built-in mic and speaker too. Beyond messages, notifications, calls, mail, scores, etc., it allows you to "sketch your feelings" onscreen—say a heart to indicate love—that you can send contacts. It incorporates a heart-rate monitor and accelerometer to track fitness and activity with the calories burnt, intensity of workout and period of idleness. Unlike most smartwatches, the NFC (Near Field Communication) fitted Watch supports one-tap payments via a new digital-wallet feature dubbed Apple Pay.

LIVE STREAMING APPS

The year saw the introduction of personal live broadcasting via streaming apps like Periscope, Meerkat and Rhinobird. These apps allow people to use their smartphones or tablets for broadcasting videos, as they shoot them in real-time, to the entire world over Twitter. Likewise, you could use the service to "explore the world through someone else's eyes". Periscope currently even allows the videos to be replayed for up to 24 hours. Apart from the power of real-time access to such personal broadcasts, the USP of these apps is that they allow viewers to interact immediately with the individual beaming the video live.

DASHCAMS

Even though not hugely popular yet, the year showed many motorists are installing a car dashboard camera to constantly record their journey as they drive. These recordings can come in handy specially in case of accident disputes. Typically, a dashcam is mounted onto the car windscreen and records the video in front of the car. For dual coverage, a second camera can also record rear video footage simultaneously. These dashcams help provide proof for insurance claims and safeguard you from 'crash for cash' scams. In addition, some models come with additional features like a Forward Collision Warning System (FCWS) to monitor the distance from the vehicle in front.

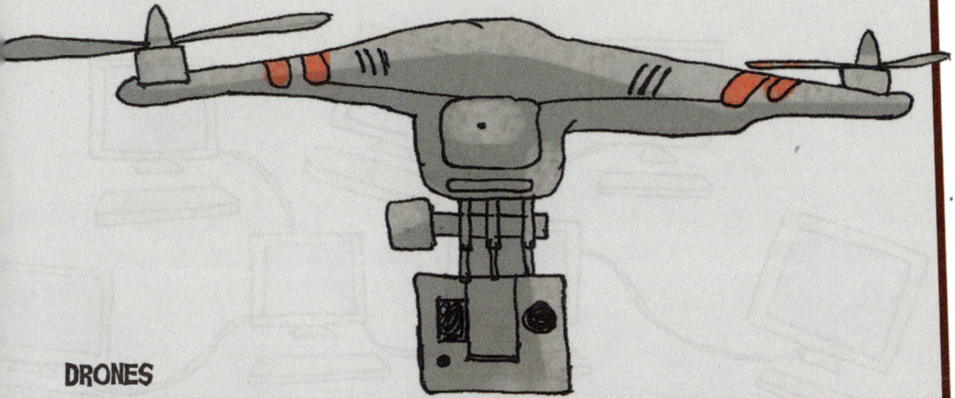

DRONES

2015 saw increased flying of small, unmanned, radio-controlled flying vehicles or quadcopters called drones by the public the world over. Used by and large for sport and aerial photography, drones are being employed for several purposes. The military arms drones with missiles or uses them for spying. They are used in war and disaster zones for dropping food and medical supplies besides aerial surveillance, spotting and rescue during disasters and natural calamities. The police in developed countries are actively deploying them for traffic management, accidents and crime scene investigations. Firefighters have started using these unmanned UAVs (unmanned aerial vehicles) as "incident commanders" to give them an overview of fire outbreaks. And Amazon and Google are itching to use drones for automated delivery of goods!

GOOGLE CARDBOARD

Cardboard as a device is a simple cardboard enclosure that embeds a pair of 40mm focal distance lenses and employs an open source Software Development Kit (SDK) to turn your phone into an inexpensive virtual reality headset. To make it work, the phone must be at an optimal distance away from the lenses. With Cardboard compatible apps, the lenses create a 3D effect when held up to your eyes. The images respond according to the position of your head when you move it around just as they would in a full blown expensive VR headset. Developed at the Google Cultural Institute in Paris, the importance of Cardboard lies in the fact that it is the first complete virtual reality platform that provides rich VR experiences at a negligible cost (Rs. 200 to Rs. 950)—unlike others which cost a few hundred dollars at least. Cardboard has since served as a reference design for several companies to create their own super cheap and simple VR headsets for compatibility with their smartphones.

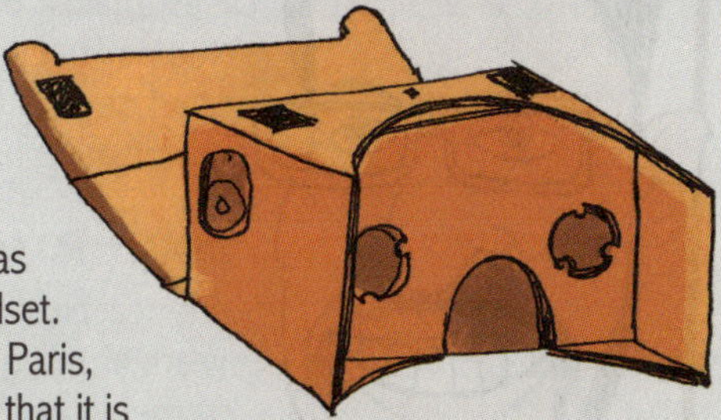

By **ASHISH BHATIA**

If someone said to you that this was an immensely exciting year for the internet in India, they'd be lying. It was a lot more than that. It was the year when just about every third person in every second garage was working on a startup, bank rolled by Venture Capitalists who asked no questions before writing cheques.

It was also the year when more people died taking selfies than by shark attacks and trolling almost became a full-time job. But neither one of these were the most exciting things happening in India.

This was also the year an app was floated for everything from delivering hot coffee to fixing doctor's appointments and finding a house. Between Uber, Ola and the like—urban mobility and how India travelled was quickly reinvented. This happened despite the several complaint cases against each of them. Such was the charm and the pay packets attached to driving for these start-ups that several MBA-grads are now driving taxis instead of pushing papers. But that wasn't it either.

INDIA—NO LONGER THE BACKROOM BOY

The real change was happening in Silicon Valley. After years of being the backroom boys, the brains, the engineers and the coders, Indians were stepping into the limelight front, right and centre. What started with Sathya Nadella taking over as the CEO of Microsoft suddenly acquired a feverish pitch as IIT-Kharagpur alumni Sundar Pichai took over as CEO of Google Inc.

Needless to say, Twitter went completely bonkers. Indians did everything short of taking their shirts off and dancing on the street. We had the Sathya,

Sundar—we just needed a Shiva to complete the trinity—well that was until the internet en masse remembered HCL CEO Shiv Nadar!

While Indians taking over two of the biggest tech companies was a matter of national pride—it was only a part of the whole story.

INCREASE IN INTERNET USERS

The number of internet users in India grew much faster than anywhere in the world and is predicted to grow from 350 million to 500 million in 2017. But it's the mobile internet which the world is most excited about. In the next two years, estimates say India will have 314 million mobile internet users and be the world's second largest mobile market after only China. Suddenly it all starts to add up, doesn't it?

ENTER THE START-UP MILLIONAIRE

India was always the land of self-made businessmen, but it was the IIM graduates and the investment bankers that were pulling in the big salaries—till it all changed very suddenly. 2015 was the year when the geeks stepped up to control the economy and national conscience!

Flipkart's Sachin Bansal and Binny Bansal are the newest billionaires out of India, while Snapdeal's Kunal Bahl too has earned himself a spot on a millionaire's list. Flipkart and Snapdeal were valued at $15 billion and $5 billion, respectively.

But the e-commerce guys were not the only ones making millions—Ola founders Ankit Bhati and Bhavish Aggarwal and PayTm's Vijay Shekhar Sharma are all notable tech bosses who made millions in 2015! But that wasn't the only exceptional thing going on—more than 85 per cent of those tech bosses who made the millionaire lists were homegrown businesses—showing that the time for start-ups in India has well and truly arrived.

BUT WAS EVERYTHING ROSY THIS YEAR?

In one word—No. It wasn't all about garage startups and billion dollar evaluations— the year also saw probably the biggest discussion on internet freedom in India's short but significant

Airtel ZERO

digital history. The #NetNeutrality debate reached a crescendo—in part driven by Airtel Zero that claimed to be creating a platform for internet in rural India. Unfortunately for the companies (Airtel and others), the internet audience didn't buy into the PR spiel. Such was the opposition to the measures that one after the other, brands that had signed on for the platforms—specifically Airtel Zero pulled out. The first one to go was Flipkart which decided the sheer volume of bad PR didn't justify being on the platform, other brands followed en masse soon after.

THE FAD OF THE YEAR: DUBSMASH

If there was one app that became the app of the year or came very close to, it was dubsmash. From Shah Rukh Khan to Salman Khan, Sonakshi Sinha to Virat Kohli to Sonam Kapoor—everyone made a dubsmash video set to the tunes of everything from Ram Lakhan to Mogambo's dialogues. For a brief period of three months, India's most talked-about app with its short videos was the internet's most talked-about and endorsed app. And then almost as suddenly as it started out, it lost steam leaving behind thousands of short videos with no real value.

#WEAREFAMILY

While there were zillions of hashtags that trended throughout the year, the main social buzz remained around family-oriented topics. #ShahidKiShaadi #RaniMukherjiBump #ViratAnushka and the like kept everyone going on social media for weeks. The fact that earlier in the year FB adopted the hashtags helped populate them much further then the hashtag's birthplace—Twitter. Why the family hashtags? Well, we are family people, aren't we?

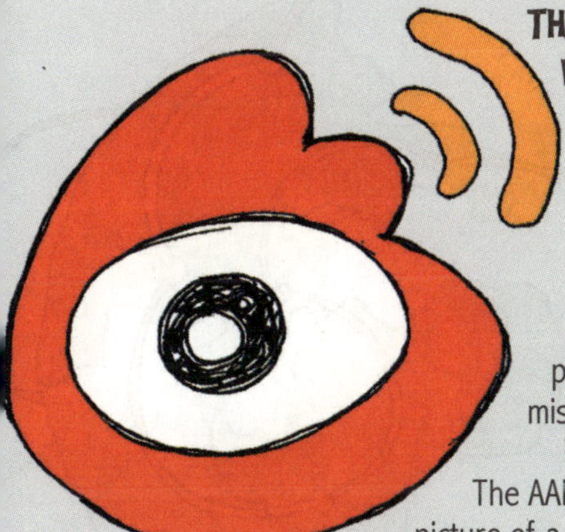

THE TIMES WHEN THE NET WENT HORRIBLY WRONG

As internet and TV competed with each other to be the first to put out a piece of news– it gave rise to a strange version of vigilante journalism that went wrong almost as often as it went right. While social media is increasingly getting mobilised to act as a pressure group to fight injustice, 2015 saw its misuse going just as viral as its benefits.

The freshest one was the Jasleen Kaur case. The AAP activist shared a Facebook post with the picture of a man who allegedly eve-teased her at a traffic signal in Delhi. Her post went viral till it emerged that there might have been more to the story. The denial too went viral. The man in question angrily denied the accusation after having his face shared on millions of Facebook timelines—others corroborated his side of the story. Politicians who were quick to heap praise on Jasleen slowly slunk away—leaving her to justify to the cameras what had really happened. The case is now in court.

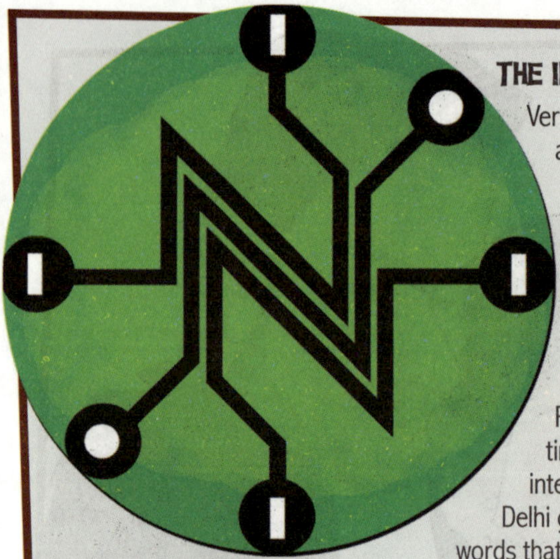

THE INTERNET AND POLITICS

Very rarely before has the internet played as integral a part in Indian politics as it does now. While a significant chunk of the General Elections last year was fought on the internet, it was only this year that the Prime Minister and his office used the internet to promote his many many foreign visits. He even made an account on China's answer to Facebook—Weibo. It was also the first time that the internet, specifically free internet featured as an election promise in Delhi government's election manifesto. Two words that were loudly and repeatedly uttered were: smart cities. Plans are afoot to create 100 such connected cities in the next three to five years.

All in all, a hectic year for the internet. And it managed to accomplish all this without any video of Alia Bhatt or dancing cats going viral! How's that for growing up?

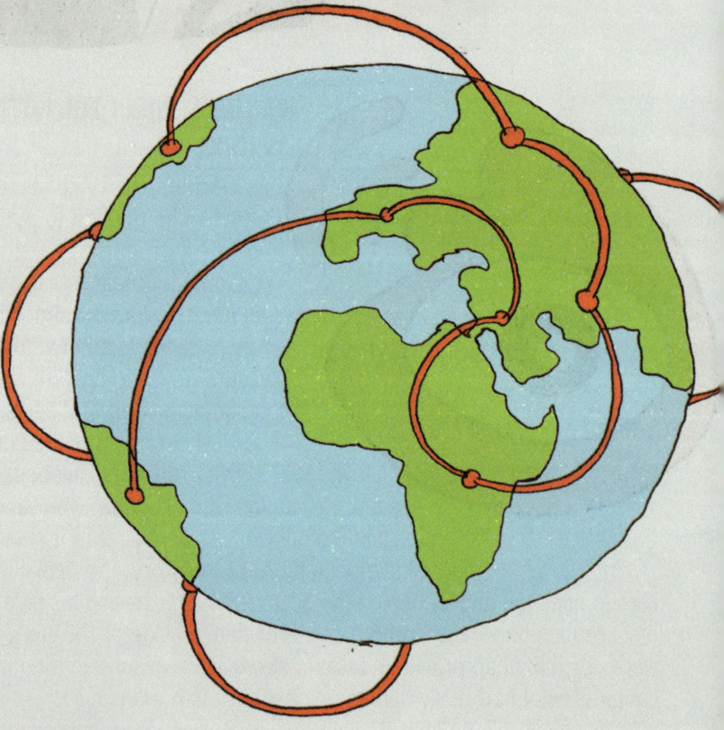

By **Kabeer Sharma**

ENVIRONMENT

- [x] ENVIRONMENT NEWS
- [x] ENVIRONMENT EXTRAS

From a rather controversial rise in the tiger population to the grandiose announcement of achieving the target of building toilets in all schools to being declared the country with the worst quality of air in its capital—there is a lot that India witnessed in the year gone by. Here's taking a look at a few important environmental developments from across the globe.

THE BIG ROAR!

India reportedly witnessed a rise in its tiger population. According to the Status of Tigers in India, 2014 report, there has been a 30 per cent rise in the number of big cats! That's not it. Apparently, India now has 70 per cent of the world's tiger population.

Reason enough to cheer? Well, not really, if a section of experts is to be believed. They have questioned the methodology adopted for the census and its accuracy.

India's Tiger Trail

- Karnataka scores the highest number with 408 tigers!
- Uttarakhand follows second with 340.
- Madhya Pradesh comes at the third position with 308.
- Tamil Nadu is fourth with 229.
- And finally, Maharashtra stands at the fifth spot with 190.

WATER WORRIES

According to a UN report, "By 2025, more than 2.8 billion people living in 48 countries will face water stress or water scarcity." The recently revised United Nations population projections go on to declare, "By 2050, the number of countries which will face water stress or scarcity will rise to 54, and their combined population to 4 billion people—40 per cent of the projected global population of 9.4 billion."

In reality, these are not just numbers. This is a peek into the harsh truth of our collective lives in the coming years. And drinking bottled water won't really help then.

Yes, Earth is a wet planet with something like 1.5 billion cubic kilometres (that is 15,00,000 billion litres) of water. But most of this water, by the way, is salty.

Some parts of the world have more water than they need, while others do not have any. Ground water reserves are not distributed evenly. In India,

for instance, Rajasthan with 8 per cent of the country's population has only 1 per cent of the water, and Bihar with 10 per cent of the population has 5 per cent of it!

EL NIÑO: NOTHING EXOTIC ABOUT IT

El Niño, a devastating weather phenomenon, is back in the news after a long halt of over 20 years. The last time it raised its head in the Pacific Ocean in 1997-98, more than 20,000 people died, causing damage worth billions of dollars due to increased global average temperatures. Currently, the sea temperature anomalies in the central Pacific Ocean are now at their highest since 1997-98, which can ultimately lead to large-scale damage.

What is an El Niño?

Simply put, it is a natural, tropical, ocean temperature phenomenon. A part of the El Niño-Southern Oscillation cycle (ENSO), its occurrence involves periodic warming and cooling of the tropical Pacific Ocean. The warm air and ocean currents bring warm weather and raise global average temperatures. This impacts weather patterns around the world and is known to cause floods in the eastern coast of Australia and droughts in Papua New Guinea.

LIGHT IT UP, BABY!

2015 was proclaimed as the International Year of Light and Light-based Technologies (IYL 2015) during the 71st Plenary Meeting of the United Nations General Assembly's 68th session. This is to intensify global awareness on how light and light-based technologies promote sustainable development. It aims to provide solutions to global challenges in energy, education, agriculture and health.

CLIMATE CHANGE GOES SOCIAL

The 20th United Nations Conference of Parties on Climate Change (COP 20), held at Lima, Peru, witnessed the 10th Conference of Youth on Climate Change (COY 10), and brought together over 1,000 youngsters from around the world.

During the conference, UN climate chief Christiana Figueres urged participants to exploit the power of internet and social media.

Figueres also proposed setting up a section on the UN's climate website dedicated to young people, called Voices of Youth.

GREEN TAX FOR TOURISTS, ANYONE?

In an unprecedented move, Maldives has introduced a new green tax for tourists from November 2015 at a rate of \$6 per bed per night. Maldives Minister of Environment and Energy even called on the international community to give due consideration to the challenges faced by Small Island Developing States (SIDS).

FLUSH AND FORGET?

The Prime Minister, during his Independence Day speech in 2014, promised that every school in India would have separate toilets for boys and girls by August 15, 2015, as part of the Swachh Vidyalaya initiative. The Ministry of Human Resource Development recently announced that the target had been achieved with the building of 4,17,000 toilets in 2,61,000 schools. But it is still to be seen whether these toilets will be maintained or become just another job simply done and forgotten.

10 new species discovered in 2015

- **Feathered Dinosaur (*Anzu wyliei*)** has origins in a bird-like group of dinosaurs that lived in North America.
- **Coral Plant (*Balanophora coralliformis*)** is a parasitic plant, discovered and almost immediately considered endangered.
- **Cartwheeling Spider (Cebrennus rechenbergi)** is an agile arachnid that lives in the desert and cartwheels its way out of danger.
- **The X-Phyla (*Dendrogramma enigmatica*)** are multicellular animals that look like mushrooms, with a mouth at the end of the "stem" and the other end like a flattened disc.
- **Bone-house Wasp (*Deuteragenia ossarium*)** is an insect, about half an inch (15mm) long with a unique way of protecting its offspring.
- **Indonesian Frog (*Limnonectes larvaepartus*)** is the newest species of fanged frogs found in Sulawesi Island, Indonesia.
- **Walking Stick (*Phryganistria tamdaoensis*)** belongs to a family of stick insects that are about nine inches long.
- **Sea Slug (*Phyllodesmium acanthorhinum*)** is a strikingly beautiful inch-long sea slug found in the waters of Japan.
- **Bromeliad (*Tillandsia religiosa*)** is a plant with red and green leaves that grows up to five feet in rocky habitat in the northern regions of Morelos, Mexico.
- **Pufferfish *(Torquigener albomaculosus)*** is a new aquatic species with geometric designs that is about six feet in diameter. They are found on the seafloor off the coast of Amami-Oshima Island.

Every year, the International Institute for Species Exploration (IISE, Arizona State University) convenes a meeting of taxon experts (i.e., experts in classifying organisms) to select the 'top ten new species' discovered in the preceding year. The list was made from nominations by the public, scientists, scientific journal editors, IISE staff, and by the committee members themselves.

By **PRACHI GURON**

Top 10 most endangered species

Black Rhino
Giant Panda
Tiger
Beluga Sturgeon
Golden Seal
Alligator
Snapping Turtle
Hawksbill Turtle
Big Leaf Mahogany
Green Cheeked Parrot

Ten worst natural disasters of the 21st century

Haiti earthquake—January 12, 2010
Estimated death toll: 316,000
Indian Ocean earthquake and tsunami—December 26, 2004
Estimated death toll: 230,000 in 14 countries including Indonesia, India, Sri Lanka, Bangladesh, Myanmar and Thailand.
Cyclone Nargis (Myanmar)—May 2, 2008
Estimated death toll: 146,000
Kashmir (POK) earthquake—October 8, 2005
Estimated death toll: 86,000
Sichuan (China) earthquake—May 12, 2008
Estimated death toll: 69,197
Russian heat wave—May to August 2010
Death toll: 56,000 (affected the United States, Canada, Russia, Central Asia, Northern Europe and China)
Iran earthquake—December 26, 2003
Estimated death toll: 43,000
European heat wave—2003
Estimated death toll: 40,000
Tōhoku (Japan) earthquake and tsunami—March 11, 2011
Estimated death toll: 18,400
Gujarat earthquake—January 26, 2001
Estimated death toll: 19,727
Gujarat earthquake—January 26, 2001
Estimated death toll: 19,727

WORLD'S WORST ENVIRONMENTAL DISASTERS OF ALL TIME

CHERNOBYL

Chernobyl is one of the greatest environmental disasters of all time. On April 26, 1986, one of the reactors at the Chernobyl power plant in Ukraine exploded, resulting in a nuclear meltdown that sent massive amounts of radiation into the atmosphere.

BHOPAL

The Bhopal gas tragedy is one of India's worst environmental disasters. Around midnight on December 2, 1984, an accident at a Union Carbide pesticide plant in Bhopal resulted in 45 tonnes of poisonous methyl isocyanate escaping from the facility. Thousands of people died within hours.

KUWAITI OIL FIRES

The end of the Gulf War in 1991 did not signal the end of all troubles. As the War drew to a close, Saddam Hussein sent men to blow up Kuwaiti oil wells. Approximately 600 were set ablaze, and the fires burned for seven months. The Gulf was covered completely in poisonous smoke, soot and ash.

LOVE CANAL

For years, Love Canal, located near the Niagara Falls in the US was a developed and well-settled neighbourhood with hundreds of houses and a school. But by 1978, thousands of tonnes of toxic industrial waste that had been buried underground in the 1940s and 50s had begun to bubble up into backyards and cellars. The inhabitants were compelled to sell their houses and relocate.

THE *EXXON VALDEZ*

One of the worst environmental disasters at sea has been that of *Exxon Valdez*, the oil tanker that ran aground on Bligh Reef in Alaskan waters on March 24, 1989. Millions of gallons of oil spilled out into the cold waters and eventually spread to an almost 500-mile distance. Thousands of birds, fish and other sea life perished as a result of the spill.

TOKAIMURA NUCLEAR PLANT

The Tokaimura disaster is Japan's worst nuclear accident and happened at a uranium-processing facility northeast of Tokyo on September 30, 1999. Three workers at the plant improperly mixed a uranium solution with disastrous consequences. Hundreds of workers were affected by the resultant radiation.

THE ARAL SEA

The Aral Sea, situated between Uzbekistan and Kazakhstan, was once the fourth largest lake on earth. However, it has now shrunk to 90 per cent of its original size because of its source waterways being diverted for various Soviet irrigation projects. Over time, it has been reduced to a massive desert.

SEVESO DIOXIN CLOUD

An explosion at a chemical plant near Seveso, north of Milan in Italy, on July 10, 1976 released a thick, white cloud of dioxin that quickly settled on the town. Once the ill effects began to be felt by the residents, the town had to be evacuated.

MINAMATA DISEASE

Industrial poisoning of Minamata Bay, located on a southwesterly island in Japan, due to pollution from a local industrial unit, caused behavioural changes in animals, particularly cats. By 1956, humans were being afflicted too, with what soon became known as the Minamata disease. Symptoms of the disease included convulsions, slurred speech and uncontrollable limb movements.

THREE MILE ISLAND

The Three Mile Island nuclear reactor near Harrisburg, Pennsylvania, in the US partially melted down on March 28, 1979. Although there were no casualties, this is still considered one of America's worst nuclear accidents.

AL-MISHRAQ

A fire at an Iraqi sulfur plant at Al-Mishraq in 2003 burned for about a month, releasing sulfur dioxide into the atmosphere. Sulfur dioxide kills people by causing respiratory problems and also creates acid rain that destroys crops.

BP OIL SPILL

The Deepwater Horizon or BP Oil spill of April 2010 is the largest accidental marine oil spill in the history of the petroleum industry. This oil spill was caused by an explosion of an oil well at a drilling platform operated by British Petroleum (BP) in the Gulf of Mexico. The explosion killed 11 people working on the platform and injured 17 others. It flowed for three months, releasing 4.9 million barrels of oil in the surrounding sea. The oil caused extensive damage to the coast along the Gulf. It affected the livelihood of hundreds of shrimp farmers and fishermen along the coast of the US states of Mississippi, Alabama, Florida and especially Louisiana. Hundreds of marine species were also killed or deformed.

THE GREEN CALENDAR

Important environmental dates to celebrate:

February 2	World Wetlands Day
March 20	World Sparrow Day
March 22	World Water Day
April 22	Earth Day
May 3	International Migratory Bird Day
May 22	World Biodiversity Day
June 5	World Environment Day
June 8	World Oceans Day
June 15	Global Wind Day
June 17	World Day to Combat Desertification and Drought
July 11	World Population Day
July 29	International Tiger Day
September 16	International Day for the Preservation of the Ozone Layer
September 18	World Water Monitoring Day
September 28	Green Consumer Day
Last Sunday in September	World Rivers Day
October 4	Animal Welfare Day
First Monday in October	World Habitat Day
Second Wednesday in October	International Day for Natural Disaster Reduction
October 22	World Planting Day
October 22	International Day of Climate Action
November 6	International Day for Preventing the Exploitation of the Environment in War and Armed Conflict
December 2	Bhopal Gas Tragedy Day
December 5	World Soil Day
December 11	International Mountain Day

Other important dates

October 1-7 World Wildlife Week

United Nations Decade of Education for Sustainable Development—2005-2014

Water for Life Decade—2005-2015

United Nations Decade on Biodiversity—2010-2020

ENTERTAINMENT

- ☑ ENTERTAINMENT
  - ☑ CINEMA
  - ☑ BOOKS
  - ☑ ART
  - ☑ INDIAN THEATRE
  - ☑ DANCE
  - ☑ MUSIC
  - ☑ TELEVISION

The success of Bollywood, every year, is measured not only by the number of box-office hits it delivers, but also by the trends it sets, the rules it breaks and the surprises it throws up.

If last year, Bollywood reigned supreme with the queens of the industry doing a victory *thumakda*, then this year the trend continued. The women broke rules, embraced cinema that spelt SENSIBLE and SENSITIVE and walked away with acclaim and Box Office numbers. More about that later!

REIGN OF THE QUEENS

The gorgeous Aishwarya Rai Bachchan has made her much-awaited comeback as a lawyer who is also a passionate 'Ma', with Sanjay Gupta's legal-thriller, *Jazbaa*. Aishwarya's last outing was five years ago with Sanjay Leela Bhansali's *Guzaarish*.

If *Jazbaa* is about a Ma protecting her daughter, Shoojit Sircar's *Piku* had Deepika Padukone, looking after her father, Aishwarya's Pa Amitabh Bachchan, whose sole preoccupation is his 'motions.'

NOT THE USUAL FORMULA

Not your regular film, *Piku* was beautiful in many ways. It had a career woman who not only revels in her 'single' status but also shows how it's all about loving your parents, even when all they are obsessed with is their motion! The credit actually goes to another woman, writer Juhi Chaturvedi who seems to have a thing going for

Dum Laga Ke Haisha

In the day and age of 'perfect' heroines, along came a 'fat' protagonist in the Yashraj production, *Dum Laga Ke Haisha*. The unusual story proved to be a sleeper hit. Showing once again, that content is king even if it comes in an XL size!

off-beat subjects—whether it is *Vicky Donor* or *Piku*—that are far removed from Bollywood formula.

Deepika was earlier seen riding on the success of Farah Khan's *Happy New Year* starring Shah Rukh Khan. The film released in Hindi, Tamil and Telugu. While the film and the story left a lot to be desired, it nevertheless bolstered Deepika's position as a bankable, successful actress, and *Piku* cemented it.

BY GOD'S GRACE

Interestingly, before *Piku* made a splash, a similar sounding film, *PK*, hit theatres and broke records. The Aamir Khan film directed by Rajkumar Hirani made the right noises about God and religion. It was a delicate subject but handled with Hirani's trademark humour.

If Aamir wooed the audience as a 'cute alien' in *PK*, then his fellow Khan, Salman, turned peacemaker in Kabir Khan's *Bajrangi Bhaijaan. BB* was about Pavan, a simple ardent Hanuman devotee, who takes it upon himself to 'deliver' a small Pakistani girl home! The star, for once, was shorn of his 'Salmanisms' (read no cheesy lines or hands-in-pocket dance movements) and had audiences sniffing into their handkerchiefs.

PK

The movie released last year and was eventually shown in an astounding 6000 screens worldwide! It was released earlier this year in China, where it made Rs. 100 crores. It had Ranbir Kapoor in an interesting cameo.

LARGER THAN LIFE

If *Bajrangi Bhaijaan* had Salman fans satiated till his next release, SS Rajamouli's magnum opus, *Bahubali—The Beginning* had everyone flocking to the theatres. Not to forget the popular 'Katappa ne Bahubali ko kyun maara' jokes, which are still doing the rounds! A bilingual Tamil-Telugu film, *Bahubali* was dubbed into Hindi, Malayalam and French. The film was hailed for its massive sets, breathtaking war scenes and larger than life production values. Made on a budget of Rs. 120 crores, it has already made something to the tune of 600 crores and still counting. The sequel is slotted for release in October 2016.

BIG BOMB

If *Bahubali* came as an unexpected bolt from the south, Bollywood got a jolt in the form of *Bombay Velvet*, an Anurag Kashyap-Ranbir Kapoor, 120 crore collaboration. The film was long in the making and had everyone in the industry rooting for it. Sadly, when it released it not only squashed the audience's massive expectations, it was

also dubbed an "epic disaster" and almost sealed Kashyap and Kapoor's fate and careers.

BOOM TIME FOR SOME

While Ranbir went into a shell after *Bombay Velvet* and came out only to make noise about his next, *Tamasha* with director Imtiaz Ali and ex Deepika, another star-kid, Varun Dhawan strengthened his footing in the industry with five hits in a row including Sriram Raghavan's angsty *Badlapur* and Remo D'souza's *ABCD 2*.

DOUBLE DOSE OF SUCCESS

It was a year of sequels as Anand Rai's *Tanu Weds Manu* returned with Haryanvi Kusum aka Datto, also played by Kangna Ranaut who was still riding the *Queen* wave. The film— *Tanu Weds Manu Returns*— turned out to be an entertainer and brought more cheer to Kangna's soaring career.

CRITICALLY ACCLAIMED

While Kangna's double role in a sequel got her acclaim, Tabu whose films are always eagerly awaited shone on the big screen as Ghazala Meer (Gertrude from Hamlet) in Vishal Bhardwaj's *Haider*, as Salman Khan's sister in *Jai Ho* and a ruthless cop in *Drishyam*.

MULTI-LINGUAL

Speaking of *Drishyam*, which had its roots in the Malayalam original, the Mohanlal-starrer, the film made most noise as it was remade in Telugu, Tamil (as *Papanasam* with Kamal Haasan), in Kannada (as *Drishya* starring Ravichandran), in Telugu (as *Drushyum* starring Venkatesh) and in Hindi with Ajay Devgn playing the naïve but crafty common man, whose family unwittingly gets involved in a murder. Though Devgn's effort didn't quite set the film on fire, it was still a decent effort.

REAL ON REEL

It was also the year of real life stories taking birth on celluloid. *Manjhi - The Mountain Man* was about Dashrath Manjhi a poor labourer in a village in Bihar, who had a tussle with a mountain for 22 years as he chipped at it with just a hammer and chisel to make way

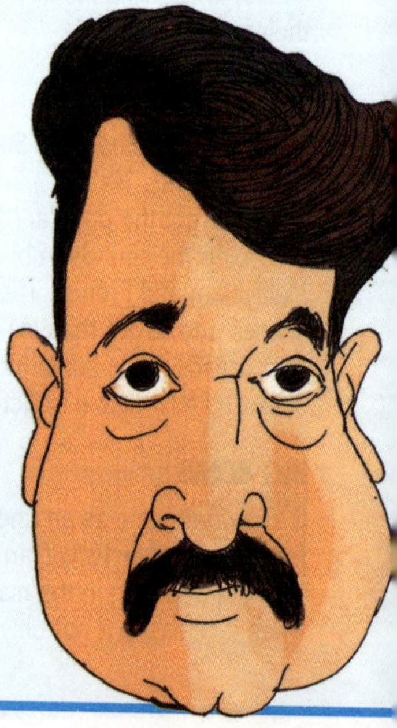

for a road. Nawazuddin Siddiqui played the title role with poignant honesty.

Aarushi Talwar's mysterious murder was also the plot behind two films—*Rahasya*, starring Kay Kay Menon and Tisca Chopra, and the recently released *Talvar*. The latter, directed by Meghna Gulzar, who returns to direction after eight years, has already garnered praise on international film circuits.

Also coming up are three films—one in Bengali and two in Hindi—based on the sensational Sheena Bora murder case.

While this was more or less how the year went by, the coming 12 months look equally exciting. There is a lot to look forward to: Shah Rukh Khan's *Raees* and *Dilwale*, Salman Khan's *Sultan*, Ranbir's *Tamasha*, Alia Bhatt and Arjun Kapoor's *Ki And Ka*, Hansal Mehta and Manoj Bajpai's *Aligarh*. So, good, bad, ugly, there is never a dull moment at the cinemas!

Women on a high!

Yet another instance of women continuing their success run was Zoya Akhtar's *Dil Dhadakne Do* which explored relationship dynamics in a super-rich family. The ensemble cast was top-lined by Anil Kapoor (who actually put white in his hair), Shefali Shah, Priyanka Chopra, Ranveer Singh, Farhan Akhtar and Anushka Sharma. A fun film with some great moments and sharp performances.

Another woman who came out unscathed from the *Bombay Velvet* debacle was the charming Anushka Sharma. She had *PK* and *Dil Dhadakne Do* to her credit and also made headway as producer with the edgy and the reasonably successful *NH10*.

Hollywood Blockbusters

Jurassic World

Reboot of the Jurassic Park series, starring Chris Pratt, who is the flavour of the month. The movie was well-received and critically acclaimed.

Furious 7

First movie after the death of Paul Walker, and the last which had him in a starring role. The film was a high grosser in India.

Avengers: Age of Ultron

Sequel to the first *Avengers* movie, it did not perform as well as the first, but was highly anticipated.

Minions

Spin off from the *Despicable Me* series, the movie featured only the side characters—the Minions. The Banana dialogue in the trailer was a big hit.

Inside Out

This is the Disney movie that no one thought would do well but gained a lot by word of mouth publicity.

Mission: Impossible – Rogue Nation

Latest installment of the *Mission Impossible* series, this Tom Cruise starrer was a critical and commercial success.

Terminator Genisys

Terminator series reboot, the film also starred Arnold Schwarzenegger and Emilia Clarke, the actress from the *Game Of Thrones*. The movie was highly anticipated and made for good social media conversation.

By KSHAMA RAO

Landmark film festivals around the world

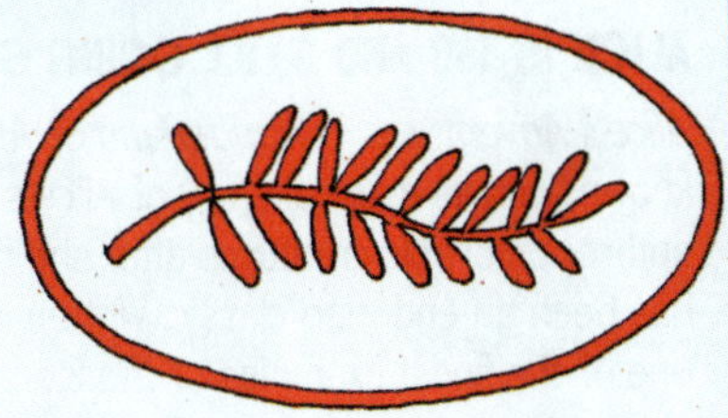

Venice Film Festival
Held in August/September in Venice, Italy since 1932.
The oldest film festival in the world.

The Cannes Film Festival
Held in May in Cannes, South of France, since 1939.

Berlin International Film Festival (Berlinale)
Held in February in Berlin, Germany, since 1951.

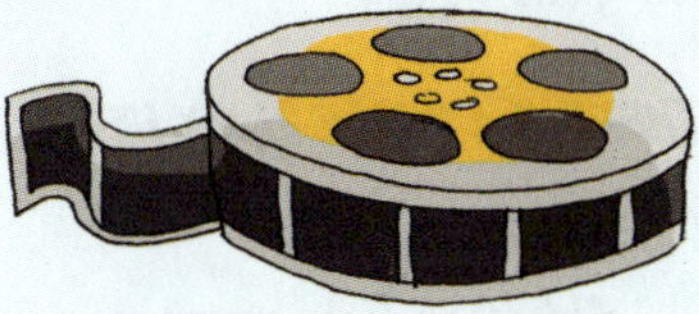

The New York Film Festival
Held in October in New York, USA, since 1963.

The Sundance Film Festival
Held in January in Park City, Utah, USA, since 1978. It has been the world's largest showcase for independent films.

The Tribeca Film Festival
Held in April in New York, USA. Founded by Robert De Niro, Jane Rosenthal and Craig Hatkoff, following the 9/11 attacks on the World Trade Center.

The Toronto International Film Festival
Held in October in Toronto, Canada, since 1976.

Hong Kong Film festival
Held in March/April in Hong Kong, China, since 1977.

SXSW
Held in Austin, Texas, USA, since 1994. A premier event for cutting-edge technology and interactive films and multimedia.

International Documentary Film Festival
Held in November in Amsterdam, Netherlands, since 1988.

The International Film Festival of India (IFFI) was founded in 1952 and is one of the oldest in the world. It is now held annually in Goa.

BOOKS

ALICE IS 150 AND STILL GOING STRONG

Alice's Adventures in Wonderland or *Alice in Wonderland* as it is more commonly known, with its magical story of Alice's encounter with various anthropomorphic creatures after she falls down the rabbit hole, has been an enduring classic. Written in 1865, the book is one of the finest examples of the literary nonsense genre and even 150 years after it was written continues to charm young and old alike.

THERE'S A VOICE IN MY HEAD

> *The End.*
> *At last, Sir Terry, we must walk together.*
> *Terry took Death's arm and followed him through the doors and onto the black desert under the endless night.*

This is how Sir Terry Pratchett's assistant Rob Wilkins tweeted the writer's death in March 2015. Pratchett, who published over 40 books in the Discworld series, was suffering from Alzheimer's. From creating a world where a disc is being balanced by four elephants to the many fascinating characters that people the series, such as Rincewind, the cowardly witch, Granny Weatherwax, the grumpy one, and many other such memorable characters, Pratchett was a master storyteller.

SCOUT GROWS UP, AND HOW

Harper Lee, now 88, had only one book to her name—the immensely popular Pulitzer prize-winning *To Kill a Mockingbird.* So when it was announced earlier this year that a sequel to her first book was in the offing, it caused quite a stir. Lee had always maintained that she would never publish another novel.

As it turns out, this second book, *Go Set a Watchman*, is a sequel by release date only since Lee is believed to have actually written 'Watchman' before Mockingbird. *To Kill a Mockingbird* had won Lee millions of fans as it exposed the racist attitude of adults through the eyes of two children, a theme relevant even today.

It was little surprise then that fans lined up at midnight on July 14, 2015 to buy her second book, which has the adult Scout or Jean Louise Finch revisiting Maycomb to see her father, Atticus, and is believed to be the first draft for Mockingbird.

NO ROOM FOR DISCUSSION

The ban on Wendy Doniger's book, *The Hindus, An Alternative History,* and the murder of writer M. M. Kalburgi all seem to indicate that Indian society is plagued with extremist views on religion. Kalburgi was murdered for his non-conventional views on Hinduism, much like his contemporaries Govind Pansare and Narendra Dabholkar. The three were also non-believers, and strived to expose black magic and superstitions. Kalburgi was a scholar and studied the literature of the Lingayat community called Vachana. He emphasised that literature was against caste, class and gender biases.

APP-Y INDIAN LITERATURE

In what is being seen as a revolution in the world of books in India, a newly launched publishing house is all set to create phone books. With so many apps buzzing 24x7, this new one promises to deliver the best of Indian literature, right on your phone.

Called Juggernaut (meaning unstoppable, in a way), this digital publishing house is being led by Chiki Sarkar, the ex-editor of Penguin Random House India, and hopes to release 25 titles by next year.

Not only books but even storytellers are moving online. So there is the never-done-before website called StoryWeaver that has published 800-plus stories online and lets anyone change the beginning, middle and end to suit them. Excitingly, the stories are told in Kannada, Hindi, Afrikaans, French, Khmer, Marathi, Sanskrit, Spanish and many more languages. You can translate the stories to any language, read them in any language and bond with other readers/ storytellers on this uber-cool website.

THE STORY LIES IN THE CLUE

Sleuths with a pen lined up for India's first Crime Writers Festival held in January 2015. The festival had filmmakers, writers and experts coming together to decipher what it takes to write the perfect crime novel. One of India's bestselling detective fiction writers in Hindi, Surendra Mohan Pathak, was also present. Other writers of the crime and detective genre spoke of how Scandinavian crime fiction or Nordic Noir leads the world in stories that make readers nervously bite their fingernails. Think Stieg Larsson's Millennium trilogy, each book of which was made into an exciting film.

OH-SO-POETIC

"The world is never the same once a good poem has

been added to it," said Dylan Thomas. Indian poetry in English is becoming popular, and how. This year Arundhathi Subramaniam won the Khushwant Singh Memorial Prize for Poetry for her collection *When God is a Traveller* at the Jaipur Literature Festival. News of the institution of this new award was greeted with a great degree of enthusiasm by new and established poets alike. Adil Jussawala, Jeet Thayil, Vijay Nambisan, Arvind Krishna Mehrotra, Sridala Swami, Vivek Narayanan, Ranjit Hoskote, Meena Kandasamy and many others are stocking bookshelves all over the country or reading aloud at cafés. Performance poetry and slam poetry has also begun to generate a faithful following through groups/events such as The Poetry Club (Mumbai), Poetry at Toddy (Delhi), Bring Back the Poets (Delhi), Airplane Poetry Movement (Delhi, Mumbai, Bangalore and Pune) and Delhi Poetry Slam, among others.

ALL ABOUT GOING BIG

The popularity of children and Young Adult fiction has been spilling onto the silver screen. Though the trend started off with the Jennifer Lawrence-starrer, *Hunger Games*, the year blazed high and bright with films like *Insurgent* based on Veronica Roth's eponymous novel. *The Maze Runner: The Scorch Trials* by James Dashner, *Paper Towns* by John Green, *Mockingjay* by Suzanne Collins (the final installment of *The Hunger Games* franchise) had calendars marked before their release. Classics like *Goosebumps* by RL Stine will get a contemporary makeover after the Tim Burton film and so will JM Barrie's *Pan*, which is a prequel to Peter Pan and has young and young-at-heart fans squealing with delight. Classics like Mary Shelley's *Victor Frankenstein* starring James McAvoy (of X-Men) and Daniel Radcliffe (Harry Potter, duh!) had its moment in the theatre.

THE READ QUARTERLY

And finally, there is good news for everyone associated with the children's publishing industry, whether it is publishers, authors, illustrators or readers. Children's literature enthusiasts Sarah Odedina and Kate Manning will be launching a magazine called *The Read Quarterly* in January 2016. The Quarterly will be a forum in which global children's literature will be discussed and celebrated and will be published four times a year in January, April, July and October. It will contain articles from global writers about global issues.

LITERARY AWARDS

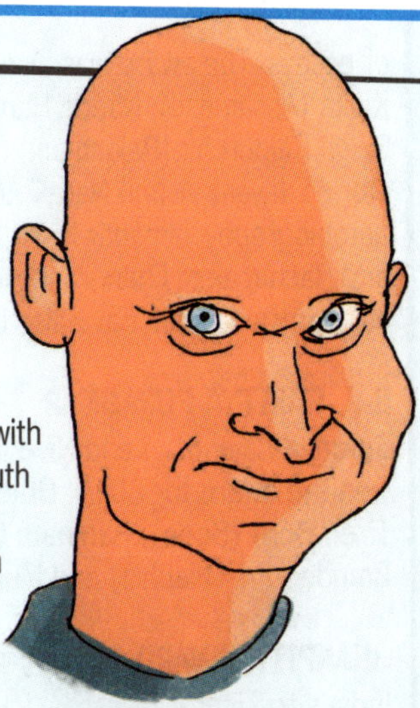

NATIONAL HUMANITIES MEDAL: Indian-origin writer Jhumpa Lahiri was awarded the 2014 National Medals of Arts and Humanities by the American president Barack Obama.

THE DSC PRIZE FOR SOUTH ASIAN LITERATURE 2015: In its last year of association with the Jaipur Literature Festival, the DSC Prize for South Asian Literature was awarded to *The Lowland* by Jhumpa Lahiri. The award received 75 entries from South Asia and countries like the UK, US, Canada, Australia and South Africa. The Jaipur Literature Festival's parallel b2b platform Jaipur BookMark announced a new award, the Oxford Bookstore Book Cover Prize, this year.

CROSSWORD BOOK AWARDS: *The Blind Lady's Descendants* by Anees Salim won the award for Best Indian Fiction 2014. In the non-fiction category, the award was accorded to *This Divided Island: Stories from the Sri Lankan War* by Samanth Subramanian. Translator Lakshmi Holmstrom was presented with the Best Indian Language Translation award for the book, *Children, Women, Men,* written by Sundara Ramaswamy. *Bankerupt* by Ravi Subramanian emerged as the most popular book and the Kotak Junior Children's writing award was given to *Timmi in Tangles* by Shals Mahajan.

COMIC CON AWARDS: *World War One* was given the Best Graphic Novel/Comic Book of the Year award along with *Simian* by HarperCollins. A complete classic, *Tinkle's Dental Diaries* won the Best Continuing Graphic Series. In the Children's Illustrated Book category, *The Fox & the Crow* by Karadi Tales was adjudged the best. Scholastic's *Bookasura* and Ruskin Bond's *With Love From the Hills* won the Best Publication for Children and Best Children's Writer award respectively. Writer-painter-cartoonist and much more rolled into one, the 80-year-old Aabid Surti received the Lifetime Achievement Award for 2015.

SAHITYA AKADEMI: The country's most eminent awards that promote Indian writing in English and Vernacular Literature with equal aplomb were dominated by poets this year. For poetry, Utpal Kumar Basu (Bengali), Urkhao Gwra Brahma (Bodo), Adil Jussawalla (English), Shad Ramzan (Kashmiri), Gopalkrushna Rath (Odia), Jaswinder (Punjabi), Gope Kamal (Sindhi) and Munawwar Rana (Urdu) were presented with the award. For fiction, Shailender Singh (Dogri), Ramesh Chandra Shah (Hindi), Subhash Chandran, (Malayalam) Asha Mishra (Maithili) and Poomani (Tamil) received the honour. (Late) Ashvin Mehta (Gujarati), GH Nayak (Kannada) and Madhavi Sardesai (Konkani) have got the award for their collections of essays. The award was also given to Arupa Patangia Kalita (Assamese), Nanda Hankhim (Nepali) and Rampal Singh Rajpurohit (Rajasthani) for their books of short stories. Jayant Vishnu Naralikar (Marathi) for his autobiography, Jamadar Kisku (Santali) for his play and Rachapalem Chandrashekara Reddy (Telugu) for his literary criticism have also been honoured.

BAL SAHITYA PURASKAR: English novelists Sowmya Rajendran and Niveditha Subramnian won the award for 2015. Other recipients included Tiren Boro (Bodo), Ramnath G. Gawade (Konkani), Ramdeo Jha (Maithili) and Mukti Upadhyay 'Baral' (Nepali).

JNANPITH AWARD: Marathi writer Bhalchandra Nemade is the 50th recipient of India's top literary awards, for his novel *Kosala* (Cocoon, 1963).

PUBLISHING NEXT INDUSTRY AWARDS 2015: An award that includes both print and digital publishing, the Publishing Innovation of the Year was bestowed on Pratham Books' Donate-a-book initiative. *A Clutch of Indian Masterpieces: Extraordinary Short Stories from the 19th Century to the Present* by David Davidar won the award for Printed Book of the Year. Other awards this year were: HarperCollins Publishers India (Publisher of the Year award); *Disaibon Hul* – Adivaani and *The Boy and the Drum* – Pratham Books (Printed Children's Book of the Year); *Korma, Kheer and Kismet* – Aleph Book Company and *The Dramatic Decade* – Rupa Publications (Digital Book of the Year); and *The Sibius Knot* designed by Arati Devasher (Book Cover of the Year).

By KANIKA SHARMA

OVER THE YEARS

Celebrating 25 years of its existence Gallery Espace mounted a blockbuster exhibition in Delhi as part of its anniversary celebrations. The exhibition featured drawings by Indian artists over the last seven decades, ranging from the more conventional pencil and ink drawings to video works.

WATER, WATER EVERYWHERE

Artist Atul Bhalla took his fascination with water to another level with *Ya Ki Kuchh Aur!* his show at Vadehra Art Gallery. The artist explored water in all its forms—it's environmental, sociological, political and even religious associations. It serves as a site of myth and memory, history and knowledge. In the show, a burning boat in his video appeared to herald the death of a river by sheer neglect.

PINK POWER

India's premier art institution, the Lalit Kala Akademi at Delhi, hosted *Other Narratives/Other Structures* an exhibition that showcased paintings done over half a century by Arpita Singh, one of India's foremost women artists. A motif that keeps cropping up in her works are pink flowers, which make their way into carpets, the decorative borders of her paintings or even lend a hint of colour to the cheeks of her male protagonists.

DOMESTIC TRAP

Guns in refrigerators, meat cleavers in ovens and the torso of a woman in a box bed hinted at the violence that often underlies scenes of domestic bliss. These house-hold objects were covered with camouflage material, which made spotting the booby traps all the more difficult in Anita Dube's solo show *Yours Disparately.*

ART EXPLORATION

The Kochi Muziris Biennale was the most awaited event on the country's art circuit and artist-curator Jitish Kallat did not disappoint. Titled *Whorled Explorations*, the various sites in Kochi played host to art works and site specific installations that ruminated on themes ranging from time and space to dreams and myths. Boats, celestial bodies and maps made an appearance as did 'Black Pearl', a pirate played by performance artist Nikhil Chopra.

TIME STANDS STILL

There was no shortage of clocks in Raqs Media Collective's solo *Asamyavali/ Untimely Calendar* at the National Gallery of Modern Art (NGMA). This came as no surprise given the group's preoccupation with time. However, these clocks were not the usual tick-tock variety. In one work the numbers on a clock face were replaced by emotional states allowing visitors to swing between "fear" and "ecstasy."

FAREWELL MRINALINI MUKHERJEE

In a tragic turn of events artist Mrinalini Mukherjee, passed away on February 2, 2015, shortly after the opening of her retrospective at the NGMA. Mukherjee is well known for her monumental hemp creations which straddle the human and animal world. Several of them could be spotted at the show, which also brought together her works in ceramics and bronze.

FUN AND FAIR

The 7th edition of the India Art Fair in Delhi gave artists, collectors, galleries and art lovers a chance to immerse themselves in a dizzying display of artworks. The art projects section brought together Indian and international artists and art forms, which included performance art, ceramics, site-specific installations and photography.

BONES AND BLOSSOMS

Anju Dodiya juxtaposed bones and blossoms in her show *Imagined Immortals* in which she explored death and its relationship to art. Pages from medical books with detailed anatomical drawings served as the basis for her collages. She also used self-portraiture to articulate her inner artistic struggles.

UNDER SURVEILLANCE

In Delhi an abandoned house in Jor Bagh played host to the group CAMP's *As If – II Flight of the Black Boxes*. Site specific installations and video works focussed on how CCTV cameras can be used both as mechanisms of surveillance by the state and also subverted to foster exchanges between people in a community. Different avatars of the show travelled to Kolkata and Mumbai.

CLICK! CLICK!

In his *7000 Museums: A project for the Republic of India* at Mumbai's Bhau Daji Lad Museum, Atul Dodiya presented three bodies of works: a series of watercolours with tongue-in-cheek depictions of imaginary museums in mofussil towns; a group of cabinets with objects and images and finally canvases that drew on news photographs clicked during the Independence movement.

Famous painters/sculptors

Painter/Sculptor	Period	Famous works	Painting/Sculpture
Donatello	1386-1466	Mary Magdalene	Painting
Jan Van Eyck	1390-1441	Ghent Alterpiece	Painting
Leonardo Da Vinci	1452-1519	The Last Supper; Mona Lisa	Paintings
Michelangelo Buonarroti	1475-1564	Genesis; Last Judgement; David	Paintings, Sculpture
Peter Paul Rubens	1577-1640	Samson and Delilah	Painting
Rembrandt van Rijn	1606-1669	Jacob Blessing the Children of Joseph	Painting
JMW Turner	1775-1851	The Fighting Temeraire	Painting
Claude Monet	1840-1926	Impression: Sunrise	Painting
Auguste Rodin	1840-1917	The Thinker	Sculpture
Pablo Picasso	1881-1973	Garcon a la Pipe; Guernica	Painting

Names ordered according to year of birth.

CELEBRATING CONTEMPORARY ART

Ahmedabad's Kanoria Centre for Arts commemorated three decades of its existence with a show at the Jehangir Art Gallery in Mumbai. At a time when there was little patronage of contemporary art, the centre served as an important hub for printmakers and other art forms. Among the art works were sculptures by K.S Radhakrishnan and G. Ravinder Reddy.

UNSEEN FORCES

Alwar Balasubramaniam's show *Layers of Wind, Lines of Time* at Delhi's Talwar Gallery demonstrated that Alwar is a magician with materials. He sculpts granite and sandstone as if it were mere dough, to be shaped at will. His works spoke of the unseen forces, such as air and magnetic fields that shape the material world around us.

BARTER SYSTEM

In a unique initiative artist couple Shreyas Karle and Hemali Bhuta decided to create a barter system for artworks. Titled *Len Den* or *Bartered Collections*, it involved 16 artists and the not-for-profit Mumbai Art Room. Visitors could view both the e-mail correspondence between the participants and the art works at the gallery.

MATERIAL WORLD

The Kiran Nadar Museum of Art in Delhi mounted *Constructs/Constructions*, a thematic show of 30 artists curated by Roobina Karode. Constructions in myriad materials abounded. These ranged from the terracotta tile works by L.N. Tallur to the jute rope forms by Manisha Parekh.

ART HUB

Every July, the Experimenter Curators' Hub injects a frisson of excitement into Kolkata's art scene. For the fifth year, running curators from around the world flocked to the city to discuss curatorial practices among themselves and with art lovers.

HAIR-RAISING TALES

Renowned German artist Rosemarie Trockel's drawings, photographs, mixed media works

and sculptures were on display at Apeejay Arts in Delhi. She lent the term "hairbrush" a completely different meaning in one of her installations, which showed hanging paint brushes that ended in locks of human hair!

SPACE FOR ART

Bangalore's arts space 1 Shanthi Road celebrated 12 years of its existence by launching a book titled *Making Space for Art.* A hub of artistic activity in the city, it offers residency space to visiting artists from abroad besides hosting lectures, performances and art shows.

Famous Indian Artists

Painter/Sculptor	Period	Famous works
Raja Ravi Varma	1848-1906	*Village Belle; The Orchestra*
Rabindranath Tagore	1861-1941	*Self Portrait; Dancer*
Abanindranath Tagore	1871- 1951	*Avisarika; Passing of Shah Jahan*
Nandlal Bose	1882-1966	*Umar Tapasya; Sati*
Jamini Roy	1887-1972	*Bride and Two Companions; Dual Cats with one Crayfish*
Amrita Sher-Gil	1913-1941	*Young Girls; Hill Women*
M.F. Hussain	1915-2011	*Battle of Ganga and Jamuna: Mahabharata; Mother Teresa*
Syed Haider Raza	b. 1922	*Cityscape; Baramulla in Ruins*
F.N. Souza	1924-2002	*Head of Christ; Landscape at Night*
V.S. Gaitonde	b. 1924	*Homi Bhabha Study*
Satish Gujral	b. 1925	*Fantasy; Brunt Wood*
Tyeb Mehta	1925-2009	*Celebration; Kali*
Anjolie Ela Menon	b. 1940	*Goat Herd; Ram, Rahim—Two Faces of India*
Jatin Das	b. 1941	*Man-Woman; Working Woman II*
Rameshwar Broota	b. 1941	*Metamorphosis; Man-1*
Manjit Bawa	1941-2008	*Ranjha; Kali and Shiva*

Names ordered according to year of birth.

By MEERA MENEZES

AS THE CURTAINS ARE DRAWN

There was a time when theatre was one of the few sources of entertainment in our country. But with the advent of cable TV, cinema, social media and the internet, the competition has turned fierce. The short-film-YouTube mobile-flashing people refuse to sit through a two-hour narration of historical events or literary monologue. But theatrewallahs too are not ready to give up. Many production companies and directors are leaving no stone unturned to woo their audiences with everything, from mythology to satire, original plays to musicals and adaptations to lavish settings.

FESTIVAL OF ART

While theatre festivals like National School of Drama's Bharat Rang Mahotsav, Kolkata Youth Festival, Prithvi Theatre Festival, International Theatre Festival of Kerala and NCPA's Centrestage, continued to enthral the audiences this year too, it was the collaboration of a corporate house with the stage that stole the show. Aditya Birla Group brought five new plays from Rage Theatre, QTP, Masque Theatre, Akvarious and Arpana Theatre under Aadyam. Almost 45 shows of *The Sidhus of Upper Juhu* (Rahul da Cunha), *The God of Carnage* (Nadir Khan), *The Merchant of Venice* (Vickram Kapadia), *The Hound of the Baskervilles* (Akash Khurana) and *Mere Piya Gaye Rangoon* (Sunil Shanbag) were unveiled in Mumbai and Delhi across eight months.

ADAPTATIONS

Other than regular annual fests, the year gone by also saw many groups and companies celebrating works of writers and poets—some popular and some fairly unknown. Among them Motley's celebration of Krishan Chander's stories was commendable. While few plays were revised to suit the younger audiences, many new plays were premiered during these fests to bring literature back into vogue.

Though the works of Saadat Hasan Manto continued to remain a favourite for adaptations, the birth centenary of writer Ismat Chugtai too was celebrated with an adaptation of her plays and discussions on her works. Another writer who would have turned 100 this year is Bhisham Sahni. The month of August saw NCPA Mumbai celebrate the Bhisham Sahni Festival where his stories like *Saag Meat, Oob, Sir Ka Sadka, Dholak, Yaddein* and *Samadhi Bhai Ramsingh* come alive with tributes from stalwarts like Benjamin Gilani, Naseeruddin Shah, Ratna Pathak Shah, Yashpal Sharma, Seema Bhargava and Manoj Pahwa.

Begum Qudsia Zaidi Centenary Festival celebrated the life and work of this often forgotten figure of Indian theatre, with a series of events across India from December 2014 to December 2015. Zaidi adapted and translated over 20 plays. Her most popular works include Urdu translations of Brandon Thomas's *Charley's Aunt* as *Khalid ki Khala*, and GB Shaw's *Pygmalion* as *Azar Ka Khwab*.

New children's plays

Krishna Kidding

James Aur Ek Giant Peach

Wolf

Googli Jhanak Jhayein

The Clowns

IT'S PLAY TIME!

Many theatre companies have been trying to promote drama among youngsters. While Nadira Babbar's Ekjute, Raell Padamsee's Ace, Sayeed Alam's Pierrot's Troupe and Om Katare's Yatri Group held workshops throughout the year at different intervals, special training programmes like Summertime@Prithvi and Summer Fiesta at NCPA also helped children interested in the field of art and drama showcase their talent. Cities like Jaipur, Kolkata, Delhi and Pune held many children's workshops during the summer vacations. Divya Palat's YouTheatre festival was a unique kids' training programme which not only brought out new talent but also raised funds for NGOs. Though many theatre groups staged plays only for the young audiences this year, the one which deserves a special mention is *Googli Jhanak Jhayein* written by Gulzar and

directed by Salim Arif. Although, the play—a musical based on Satyajit Ray's *Gupi Gayen Bagha Bayen*—was a children's play, it had no child artiste. Also, Naseeruddin Shah's adaptation of Krishen Chander's satirical story *Gadh-ha aur Gadd-Ha* **won accolades from children of all age groups.**

BACK ON STAGE

If actors like Paresh Rawal and Naseeruddin Shah are to be believed, it is not easy to stay away from theatre. And despite tasting success on small and big screens, many theatre artistes keep coming back to the stage. Sharman Joshi made a comeback on stage after almost a decade with *Raju Raja Ram Aur Main*. While he had acted in the Gujarati version of the same play in the initial years of his career, the actor produced the play in Hindi, touring many cities, witnessing packed halls and standing ovations. Sonali Kulkarni too, who returned to theatre with *Night Lily aani Night Rider* (Marathi), wooed the audiences with her performance in Saif Hyder Hasan's *Gardish Mein Taare*—a play loosely based on the lives of Guru Dutt and his singer wife Geeta Dutt.

Famous festivals

- Bharat Rang Mahotsav
- Kolkata Youth Festival
- Prithvi Theatre Festival
- NCPA's Centrestage
- Bhisham Sahni Festival

BOLLYWOOD ENTRY

Twelve years after its first production, Divya Palat revised her popular play *The Verdict* with actress Tanishaa Mukerji debuting on stage as one of the protagonists. Kalki Koechlin, who had already worked in Manav Kaul's *Colour Blind*—a play based on the relationship between Rabindranath Tagore and his muse Victoria Ocampo—debuted as a director with *The Living Room*. The play opened in Bangalore in July this year and is a conversation between death and an old woman who is about to die but unwilling to exit the world. Ashvin Gidwani produced the next chapter in *Bottoms Up*, a show much loved in the 1980s, with a new look and an evolving script directed by Bharat Dabholkar.

FOR THE LOVE OF LANGUAGE

The year also saw a slew of new vernacular entries in the theatre world. While the various fests in different regions of the country continue to promote new talents in Malayalam and Bengali theatre, Marathi and Gujarati witnessed a lot of new shows on stage this year. Saumya Joshi's *Aaj Jaane Ki Zid Na Karo* saw packed houses wherever it went. The unconventional love story of a prostitute and a policeman won accolades even from non-Gujarati speaking audiences. Rohit Tiwari's *Inspector Pandey Phir Marr Gaya*, which encouraged audiences to look at a policeman from a different perspective, received rave reviews from both the viewers and critics. Another new play which is worth mentioning for this year's entry is *Jaise Sookhe Huey Phool Kitaabon Mein Milien*, not only for its symbolism but for Nadira Babbar's indefatigable efforts to bring the younger generation closer to our languages. The play urges audiences to stay connected to languages like Hindi, Urdu and other local languages, with the plea that when a language perishes, its literature is lost as well.

Popular new entries

Mere Piya Gaye Rangoon

Gardish Mein Taare

Parey

The Song of the Swan

The Hound of Baskervilles

By **Boski Gupta**

What was the highlight in the world of Indian dance, in 2015? Tiger trails, cat walks and frog jumps! Sounds like an Orwellian Animal farm? No, no, I mean Tiger Shroff shone like a boneless wonder in Bollywood-style dancing; TV reality shows were like cat walk—more fashion than dance—and leaps and jumps in popular dancing made many look like frogs. Seriously speaking, Indian dance can be divided into 3 broad categories: classical, non-classical and Bollywood.

SOLO NO MORE

In classical forms, group work dominated, similar to previous years. Solo performances are becoming less frequent with stage and events getting bigger and grander. Group dances not only cover empty spaces on the stage but are also an opportunity to include dancers of all levels of proficiency. Solo dancers are also marginalised now because few in the audience understand Sanskrit or literature texts in this age of SMS or MMS.

MOVERS AND SHAKERS

Leela Samson was among the biggest classical dance newsmakers in 2014-15. Samson was removed from all posts (Chairperson Sangeet Natak Akademi and Chairperson Central Film Censor Board). She was previously removed as Director Kalakshetra too. Kathak icon Aditi Mangaldas made the mighty government agency—the Sangeet Natak Akademi (SNA)—give her the award she wanted, for

Kathak and not modern dance! She had refused to accept the coveted SNA award in 2014 when it was given under the Modern Dance category saying all her work was based in classical Kathak. The Akademi had to eat humble pie and go back on the decision. The power of conviction was shown by this iconic contemporary Kathak dancer.

MORE NEWSMAKERS

Male solo dancers—Rahul Acharya, Sinam Basu Singh, Suresh K. and Sunjoy Shanbagh— made their mark. As did quiet couples—Tushar-Puja Bhatt, Parshwanath-Shruti Upadhye and Anuradha-Sridhar.

However, nothing spectacular happened in the world of the other classical dance forms like Odissi, Mohiniattam, Manipuri and Kathakali.

SOUL SISTERS

Nrutyarutya, a dance group that is best in creative outputs—make that consistent creative output—made waves in 2015. Sisters Mayuri and Madhuri Upadhay were chosen to regale PM Modi at the Hannover fair, with their contemporary dance performance, making over 500 dancers dance to their tune, read choreography. The sisters were the only dancers at Big B's 70th birthday celebrations in Bangalore where they danced to the tune of Dr. Harivansh Rai Bachchan's iconic poem *Madhushala* sung by Amitabh Bachchan. In 2015, they won the coveted Attendance-Uday Shankar award for Choreography.

Dance India Dance

According to recent studies, Bharatanatyam is emerging as the most popular Indian classical dance form with nearly 60 per cent students learning it. Around 20 per cent learn Kathak, 10 per cent Odissi and the remaining 10 per cent opt for an assortment of other forms.

DIFFERENT STROKES

Other dance groups that gave stellar performances in the year include Daksha Sheth Dance Co. (Trivandrum) and Attakalari (Bangalore). On the downside, the worst performances were by Bharat Sharma/Bhoomika (Delhi); Samudra (Kerala) and many in Kolkata (since Bengal has no classical form of its own!).

GYMNASTICS OR DANCING?

Gymnastics seems to be fast replacing dancing in Hindi films. No wonder then that dancing for mainstream films requires learning skills like horse riding, swimming, jumping from ships and helicopters and fighting gangsters. Gone are the days when actresses— Rekha, Hema, Meenakshi Seshadri or before them, Madhubala, Waheeda Rehman, Vyjayanthimala and Helen—spent time learning the nuances of classical Indian dance forms. Thus dancing in yesteryears had beauty and elegance, as compared to some thrusts and moves by a wooden-faced actress or shedding clothes to music by another. But then all are cheering. We are fast approaching the IPL of dance, i.e. Indian Popular Leering.

TV TALK

Among the new TV /film choreographers who made it big this year are *ABCD's* Remo D'Souza and Terence Lewis for TV. But the karan(t) or the current flavour of dance on TV was indisputably Karan Johar, who neither has films nor floor to show-off his dancing skills.

TV dancing

Semi or non-classical dances mean no set grammar, structure or substance. So anything goes. This genre suits popular Indian tastes ... a leg of Chhau, a hasta of Manipuri, the costume of Odissi ... many such themes abound in the name of experimentation. On TV dance reality shows (unreal is the real word!), anything goes in the name of dance. TV shows have helped popularise dance but this is TV dance not Indian dance.

Dance-inspired movies

Famous dance-intensive films in the past include *Mughal-E-Azam, Jhanak Jhanak Payal Baaje, Pakeezah, Nache Mayuri* and *Devdas*.

FILMY CHAKKAR

2015 is also the year of dance-centric films. Besides *ABCD, Janisar* and *Bajirao Mastani* also had dance as the focal point. Muzzafar *Umaro Jaan* Ali and Sanjay Leela Bhansali need to be congratulated for their efforts in this regard.

BOOK TALES

It is sad that in a country of a billion the year saw the launch of only three books on dance. There was a book on Kathak (in Marathi) targeted towards the Marathi-reading population; one on Telugu traditions and one on Sitara Devi/Kathak.

There appears to be more serious reading and writing related to dance in South India, seen in the publication of three dance journals. *Sruti* published for the last 25 years from Chennai, *Attendance*, 18 years old and published in Bangalore and *Nartanam*, operational for more than a decade and published in Hyderabad. The best dance portal is again from the south: *www.narthaki.com.*

ON COURSE

The University Grants Commission (UGC) has devised an M.A level course on 77 subjects, including dance. The course is called e-PG Pathshala. The course will be introduced by Baroda's M.S. University, under Parul Shah, ex-head and dean of the dance department founded by iconic Mohan Khokar in 1949. The university incidentally is also India's first university to offer performing and fine arts at the B.A. level. With dance headed for cyberspace the future generation of dancers might just be able to learn Indian classical forms on the Net without spending time commuting to college.

By **Ashish Mohan Khokar**

If previous years could be summed up with a single album and artist then 2015 was the year of Adele's *Frozen* soundtrack and Taylor Swift, who became perhaps the biggest pop music act in the world, a title previously thought to be held by the likes of Justin Bieber and One Direction. Swift's close friend, Ed Sheeran also vied for the tag, and if the crowd reaction at his concert here was anything to go by, he might rival her for it soon.

SWIFT AND STRONG

Taylor Swift, the American singer-songwriter, who gained fame as a country artist, switched genres completely with her full-fledged pop music album *1989*. The record, named so after the year of her birth and because it was influenced by the sounds of the 80s, was an instant hit. In its first week alone *1989* sold over 1.2 million copies in the US, making it the fastest-selling album in that country in 12 years. Songs such as lead single *Shake It Off*, which addressed her critics and *Bad Blood*, rumoured to be about her rift with pop singer and contemporary Katy Perry, made Swift a permanent fixture on the charts and the news. She released a special remix of *Bad Blood* that featured Kendrick Lamar. The US rapper's own record *To Pimp A Butterfly*, which centred around race relations in America, was perhaps the most acclaimed album of 2015. Swift and Lamar, in all likeliness, will be vying for the Album of the Year award at the 2016 Grammy Awards.

INDIA AT THE GRAMMYS

British singer-songwriter Sam Smith was the star at the 2015 Grammys. He picked up the Best New Artist and Record and Song of the Year awards for his plaintive ballad *Stay With Me*. In India, however the news was focused on the wins in the Best New Age Album and Best Children's Album categories for Ricky Kej's *Winds of Samsara* and Neela Vaswani's audio-book version of Malala Yousafzai's memoir *I Am Malala: How One Girl Stood Up For Education and Changed the World*. Both Kej and Vaswani are Indian-origin American citizens.

Top five music markets

According to the International Federation of the Phonographic Industry, India is the 20th largest music market in the world with annual record sales for 2014 valued at a little over $100 million. The top five music markets, the US ($4,898 million), Japan ($2,628 million), Germany ($1,405 million), the UK ($1,335 million) and France ($843 million) accounted for 75 per cent of the global total revenue of nearly $15,000 million.

FROM THE SCREEN TO THE STAGE

The last 12 months also saw a new trend of Bollywood musicians performing concerts regularly, starting with composer Amit Trivedi's appearance in November 2014 at the NH7 Weekender festival in Pune. Maestro AR Rahman is scheduled to perform at the festival in Delhi, Pune and Bangalore, from November 28 to December 6, 2015, along with British producer Mark Ronson, whose song *Uptown Funk* with American singer Bruno Mars was the longest-running chart topper in both the US and the UK in 2015. Ronson's appearance will make him one of the many international acts to perform in India over the last couple of months, a list which also includes American electronic dance music trio Major Lazer, and a pair of UK acts, singer-songwriter Ed Sheeran and alternative rock band Alt-J.

VIDEO VISITS

Coldplay's frontman Chris Martin visited India twice this year. He surprised the audience at a Delhi pub by playing a short acoustic set there in July and then returned to shoot a video in Mumbai in September. India in fact proved to be a popular destination for international music video shoots. Major Lazer shot the clip for *Lean On*, which featured dancers wearing traditional Kerala saris, on the outskirts of Mumbai. The catchy track ended up becoming one of the biggest hits of 2015. Producer Diplo, who is one-third of Major Lazer, formed another musical partnership, Jack U, with Dubstep star Skrillex.

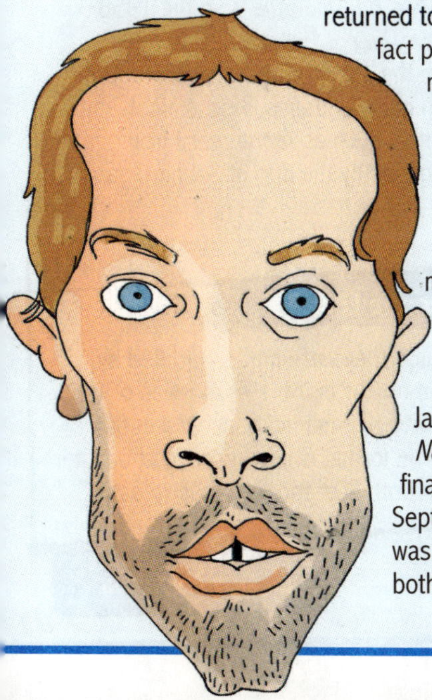

TEENAGE DREAMS

Jack U enjoyed success with the single *Where Are U Now* featuring Justin Bieber. The teenage heartthrob finally got his long-awaited first number one hit in September with the tune *What Do You Mean?*, which was among the handful of tunes to reach the top of both the UK and US charts, along with *See You Again*

Music

by Wiz Khalifa featuring Charlie Puth and *Cheerleader* by OMI. Things didn't go quite as smoothly for another set of teen icons. One Direction's Zayn Malik left the British boy band in March, while the remaining four members announced in August that they would be taking a break after the release of their fifth album.

FRIDAY IS THE NEW SUNDAY

Internationally, the music industry made a landmark decision by shifting the worldwide release date of albums from different days of the week to a global standard—Friday—effective from the second week of July. As a result, the UK and the US also changed the days on which they released their weekly music charts. UK switched from Sunday to Friday and the US from Wednesday to Monday.

STREAMING MUSIC

The end of June saw the launch of Apple Music, the streaming service run by Apple, incidentally also the company behind the largest digital music retailer in the world, iTunes. Apple Music, which rivals similar sites such as Spotify, was the tech giant's response to the increasing trend of people consuming music by streaming it on their digital devices for a monthly fee as opposed to purchasing downloads of individual songs and albums.

INDIAN IDOLS

Remixes of older hits continued to be a trend in Bollywood. Amit Trivedi's soundtrack to *Bombay Velvet* featured *Fifi*, a remake of *Jata Kahan Hai Deewane* from the 1956 Hindi film *CID* while rapper Yo Yo Honey Singh's single *Dheere Dheere Se* was a reinterpretation of the song by the same name from the 1990 movie *Aashiqui*. Unlike last year, 2015's soundtrack smashes included both party anthems like the Meet Bros's *Chittiyaan Kalaiyaan* from *Roy* and slower songs, such as *Jeena Jeena* from *Badlapur* and *Sun Saathiya* from *ABCD 2*, both composed by the duo of Sachin-Jigar. On the Indian independent music front, noteworthy albums were released by both established acts like Bangalore alternative rock band Thermal and a Quarter, Blackstratblues aka blues-rock guitarist-composer Warren Mendonsa and electro-folk-fusion duo Midival Punditz as well as newer artists such as singer-songwriter Prateek Kuhad and Aqua Dominatrix aka electronic music producer Akshay Rajpurohit.

Long live the LPs!

Even though they were made outdated by the arrival of CDs in the 1980s, sales of vinyl records have been steadily increasing this decade. The format is now growing at a faster pace than both CDs and digital downloads.

By **Amit Gurbaxani**

AIB

WILL INTERNET BE THE NEW TV?

International television seems poised at a watershed moment in its history. For the first time in the 67 years Emmy Awards history, the biggest winners were cable and streaming TV, instead of good old network television. Cable network HBO swept the awards with a grand total of 43 Emmys, whereas streaming networks like Netflix and Amazon also took home a few big ones.

With the rise of internet collectives like *The Viral Fever*, whose original fiction series *Pitchers*, has over 1.5 million views on each of its six episodes, and the launch of streaming mobile and digital platforms like Hotstar, 'television' viewing may be all set to change. In fact, Hotstar's first series is a best of both worlds; with comedy group All India Bakchod teaming up with them for a news-based series.

And for all you know, in the next couple of years, YouTube comedy groups AIB and TVF might be taking home the biggest awards over Star Plus, Colors and Zee TV at an Indian Television Awards night.

WAIT, WE ARE STREAMING

Both TV and film studios are also joining the race to be the next 'Netflix'—and there are plans for the original Netflix to come to India too—so we're up for some fun times ahead. ErosNow, the streaming platform from Eros International, has announced three big-budget TV series, with filmmakers like Rohan Sippy and actors like Bipasha Basu associated with them. Yash Raj Films, on the other hand, has already launched its first original series, *Man's World*, through its youth division, Y Films, while Balaji Telefilms, not to be left behind, has promised 'edgy' content too, to exploit the fact that there's no censorship on the internet.

By next year, it is all too likely that television may want to change its programming to keep up with all the exciting things happening on the digital front, but at the moment, just like the audiences, television network heads prefer to wait and watch.

INDIAN TELEVISION HIGHLIGHTS:

CHILDREN'S PROGRAMMES

Over the last few years, there's a new big boss in viewership segments in India, and it caters to the little ones. Children's programming has boomed of late, propelled by localisation of content on children's TV channels. Pogo TV's *Chhota Bheem* led the way with the show now spilling out to merchandising and a stage musical. And with *Motu Patlu*, *Pakdam Pakdai*, *Little Krishna* and more, television for kids is no small matter anymore.

With over 15 channels catering to children, including a new one called Baby TV or 'Television for infants', the segment now commands the largest viewership segment in India after general entertainment channels. Even as programming heads still struggle to bring quality Indian shows (as *Doraemon*, *Shin-chan* still continue to dominate), experiments like *Galli Galli Sim Sim* or the Indian *Sesame Street* are a step in the right direction, because it seems that finally young viewers are being taken seriously by adults.

POPULAR SEGMENTS

At the fag end of September 2015, the top rated shows on Indian television were: *Saath Nibhana Saathiya*, *Ye Hai Mohabbatein* and *Diya aur Baati* (Star Plus), *Sasural Simar Ka*, *Swaragini* and *Udaan* (Colors TV), *Kumkum Bhagya* and *Jamai Raja* (Zee TV) and *Taarak Mehta Ka Ooltah Chashmah* (Sab TV). Sound familiar?

Same old—Yes, if 2014 shows like Abhinay Deo's *24*, Anurag Kashyap's *Yudh* and Vipul Shah's *Pukaar* were hinting towards exciting times ahead for Indian television, 2015 showed that the more things change, the more they remain the same. Indian television seemed to be circling back to the same old formula of women-led soap operas.

Sports Leagues—The Indian Premier League may be guilty on many counts but it's certainly done great wonders for other sports in the country. The idea of 'Sports Leagues' has caught on and how, proven by the smashing, celebrity-driven seasons of The Pro Kabaddi League, The Indian Super League, Hockey India League and the Indian Badminton League.

More English channels—There has never been a better time to be a fan of English-language entertainment in India. There are already about 10 channels providing the same in India and now Viacom18 has extended its Colors' brand to start yet another general English entertainment channel Colors Infinity. With Karan Johar and Alia Bhatt curating the programming, and original English-language shows lined up, it remains to be seen whether or not it will be a game-changer.

New and improved reality shows—Dance, music, comedy and adventure-based reality shows are proven hits in India. This year too, a new entrant in each genre—*Dance Plus* in dance, *The Voice* in music, *Comedy Nights Bachao* in comedy and the upcoming *I Can Do That* in adventure—has upped the excitement about each.

Food channels—With the popularity of *Masterchef India*, *Junior Masterchef* India, *Farah Ki Dawat*, Sanjeev Kapoor, and food in general, it was only a matter of time before more channels dedicated to food popped up. Food Food has already been doing well, and now, with Living Foodz entering the segment with English and Hindi language shows, it looks like too many cooks aren't spoiling the broth, at the moment.

Fresh ideas that made an impact—The official remake of *Everybody Loves Raymond*, *Sumit Sambhal Lega*, was appreciated for re-versioning Indian sitcoms; *Chakravartin Ashoka Samrat's* fresh treatment of the show made it a big success; *Reporters* was a novel idea that got a lot of love; *Stories by Rabindranath Tagore* was a stimulating piece of work by Anurag Basu, and TVF's *Pitchers* was the first big internet series that proved that the audiences are ready for many more fresh ideas.

INTERNATIONAL TELEVISION HIGHLIGHTS:

Indian star on an American TV show—The Priyanka Chopra-starrer American TV show *Quantico* has opened to glowing reviews—but it remains to be seen how it will do ratings-wise. But with Chopra's face plastered across billboards in New York and LA, looks like American TV probably has its first big Bollywood star.

Superhit network shows—*Empire* and *How to Get Away with Murder*, were two shows that wore their diversity (behind the scenes and in front of the camera) on their sleeves and proved to critics that network TV isn't going to go away anytime soon. But the trick is fresh voices, diverse faces and dramatic content.

End of eras—David Letterman retired from *The Late Show* after 22 years, Jon Stewart moved on from *The Daily Show* after 19 years and *Mad Men* ended after eight years. American pop culture as a whole will never be the same again after 2015.

Four superheroes on the small screen—The big war between Marvel and DC comics spilled from the big screen to the small, with both DC Entertainment and Marvel Studios making a push to take over the television landscape. While DC's big wins came through *The Flash* and *Gotham*, Marvel's *Daredevil* and *Agent Carter* proved that the TV crown is still up for the taking.

Shows to prove Netflix is here to stay—With the debut seasons of three big-budget and big-cast shows with big ambitions—*Narcos, Sense8, Bloodline* and two great follow up seasons of *House of Cards* and *Orange is the New Black*, Netflix has proved this year that not only was it on HBO's trail ... it may just have surpassed it.

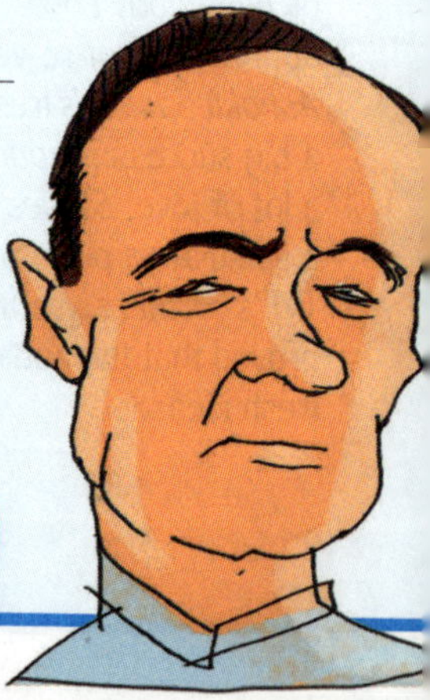

By Nikhil Taneja

SPORTS

☑ YEAR IN SPORTS

CRICKET

WEST INDIES IN INDIA

October 3 to 17, 2014

- The West Indies cricket team toured India and ended up playing just four One Day Internationals instead of four Tests, five ODIs and one Twenty20 match.
- The series got off on a wrong footing with the West Indies players threatening to pull out, right after the toss at the first ODI, due to non-payment by the West Indies Cricket Board (WICB).
- The tour finally ended abruptly with the WICB calling the tour off due to the protesting players. The Board however, washed their hands off the decision later.
- India later suspended all tours between the two countries.
- India won the four match ODI series, 2-1.
- Mohammed Shami was declared the Man of the Series.

  Winners: *First ODI (Kochi):* West Indies won by 124 runs; *Second ODI (Delhi):* India won by 48 runs; *Third ODI (Visakhapatnam):* Cancelled; *Fourth ODI (Dharamsala):* India won by 59 runs.

SRI LANKA IN INDIA ODI SERIES

October 30 to November 16, 2014

- The series was a replacement of the West Indies tour to India.
- Indian team captain MS Dhoni was rested for the series.
- Virat Kohli captained the team which won five out of the five matches, the fourth time in the history of Indian cricket.
- Rohit Sharma scored a record 264 runs, in the third match, the highest score in an ODI. He also hit 33 fours in his innings, yet another new.
- Kohli also broke the record for the fastest 6000 runs and the most runs by a batsman in a year, in the fourth match.
- Virat Kohli was adjudged the Man of the Series.

  Winners: *First ODI (Cuttack):* India won by 169 runs; *Second ODI (Ahmedabad):* India won by 6 wickets; *Third ODI (Hyderabad):* India won by 6 wickets; *Fourth ODI (Kolkata):* India won by 153 runs; *Fifth ODI (Ranchi):* India won by 3 wickets

BORDER-GAVASKAR TROPHY (TEST SERIES)

December 9, 2014 to January 10, 2015

- Australia won two out of four matches played. Two matches ended in a draw.
- The first Test in Brisbane was postponed due to Australian cricketer Phillip Hughes's death.
- The series was played without the Decision Review System, the technology used to review and challenge wrong decisions taken by umpires.
- Virat Kohli captained India in the first and last Test matches.
- Skipper MS Dhoni announced his retirement from Test cricket with immediate effect.
- Steve Smith was declared the Man of the Series.

  Winners: *First Test (Adelaide)*: Australia won by 48 runs; *Second Test (Brisbane):* Australia won by 4 wkts; *Third Test (Melbourne):* Match drawn; *Fourth Test (Sydney):* Match drawn

CARLTON MID TRIANGULAR SERIES, AUSTRALIA

January 16 to February 1, 2015

- The Tri-Nation series between India, Australia and England was hosted by Australia, close on the heels of the World Cup.
- The game schedule was tightened, with each team playing the other teams twice in the round-robin stage, instead of the usual four, due to the World Cup.
- The winning teams played the Finals. India lost the race, making it a final between archrivals Australia and England.

  Winners: Host Australia won the series, defeating England by 112 runs in the Finals played at Perth.

ICC CRICKET WORLD CUP

February 14 to March 29, 2015

- The foremost cricketing event this year saw participation from 14 teams. It was jointly hosted by Australia and New Zealand.
- Host team Australia won their fifth World Cup, defeating co-hosts New Zealand, in the finals.
- Defending champions India reached the semifinals but lost to champions Australia by 95 runs.
- Veterans Virender Sehwag, Gautam Gambhir, Yuvraj Singh, Harbhajan Singh and Zaheer Khan were excluded from the Indian team for World Cup 2015. Of the World Cup 2011 winning team only MS Dhoni, Virat Kohli, Suresh Raina and Ravichandran Ashwin made it to Team India in 2015.
- West Indies batsman Chris Gayle struck the first double ton in the World Cup, off 138 balls. It also became the fastest double-hundred in ODIs.
- In a shocker of a semi-final, South Africa was beaten by New Zealand. This was the first time that New Zealand made it to the World Cup Finals.

- The 2019 Cricket World Cup will be hosted by England.

Winners: *Semifinal 1 (Auckland):* New Zealand beat South Africa by 4 wickets; *Semifinal 2 (Sydney):* Australia defeated India by 95 runs; *Finals (Melbourne):* Australia outplayed New Zealand by 7 wickets to win their fifth ICC Cricket World Cup.

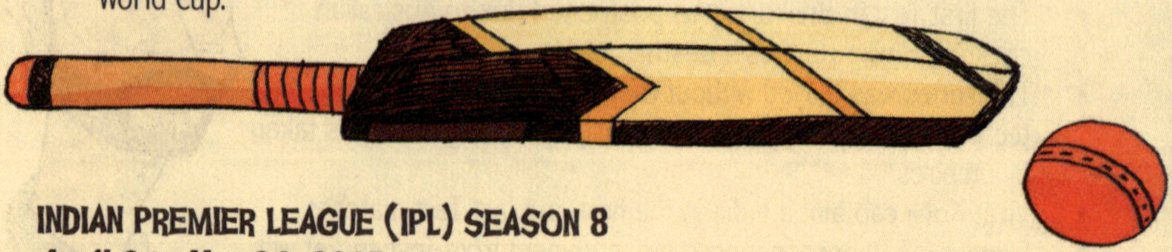

INDIAN PREMIER LEAGUE (IPL) SEASON 8

April 8 to May 24, 2015

- The IPL once again saw plenty of action—both on and off the field.
- Mumbai Indians won the league for the second time, defeating Chennai Super Kings by 41 runs, at the Eden Gardens. Rohit Sharma played a captain's knock steering his team to a win.
- The valuation of Chennai Super Kings (Rs. 5 lakhs) this year raised a lot of eyebrows, especially since it was valued at over Rs. 450 crore last year. To add fuel to the fire, the former blacklisted IPL chief Lalit Modi alleged that four CSK players were involved in match-fixing.
- Defending champions Kolkata Knight Riders, protesting the suspension of Sunil Narine, threatened to withdraw if BCCI would not lift the ban on him. The off-spinner was cleared following a retest on his bowling action.
- Warned by the umpire to shut his mouth during a Mumbai Indians and Royal Challenger's game, Kieron Pollard responded literally by putting a tape on his mouth. He drew a lot of flak for his act.
- During a RCB and Sunrisers Hyderabad game, RCB skipper Virat Kohli and teammate Dinesh Karthik lost their cool and got into a heated argument with the umpire Kumar Dharmasena, when, despite incessant rain, the officials refused to stop the match. Karthik was later fined 20 per cent of his fee for indiscipline.
- Virat Kohli breached the code of conduct when he was spotted with his girlfriend Anushka Sharma during a rain-break, in a match against Delhi Daredevils at Bangalore.

INDIA IN BANGLADESH

June 10 to 24, 2015

- The tour consisted of one Test and three ODI matches.
- India had a humiliating loss in the three-match One-Day International (ODI) series, losing two ODIs.

Close shave

A magazine in Bangladesh carried a picture of Indian cricketers, taking a dig at India's tragic defeat in the three-match ODI series. This created a furore as the caricatures showed Indian players—Rohit Sharma, Virat Kohli, MS Dhoni, Shikhar Dhawan and others—with half their heads shaved off. The picture was said to be in bad taste and drew a lot of flak.

World Cup controversies

No ball for Rohit Sharma: In the quarter finals between India and Bangladesh, in the 39th over, Bangladeshi bowler Rubel Hossain threw a full-toss which Rohit Sharma struck and was caught. But the ball was adjudged a 'no-ball' by umpire Aleem Dar, thus saving Sharma's wicket. Sharma went on to score 137. ICC President and Bangladesh official Mustafa Kamal criticised the 'poor umpiring'.

Shikhar Dhawan's catch: Shikhar Dhawan's spectacular catch that led to the dismissal of Mahmudullah, in the India-Bangladesh quarter finals, came under attack when the replay showed that Dhawan's foot may have touched the boundary line while the ball was in his hands.

Virat Kohli sees red: Virat Kohli unleashed his infamous temper and a volley of choicest abuses on a stunned Indian journalist, who he thought was behind stories about his private life. Kohli, however, had to eat humble pie when it turned out to be a case of mistaken identity, forcing him to apologise.

A gamble that didn't pay off: Pakistan's chief selector Moin Khan was forced to return home unceremoniously after he was spotted in a casino two days before the all-important match against West Indies. The incident caused a furore back home in Pakistan where it is illegal to gamble.

No century for Taylor: Yet another bad umpire decision robbed the English batsman James Taylor of a chance to complete a World Cup century, in the opening Australia vs England match at Melbourne. Taylor was at 98 runs when he was declared LBW out even as he ran for a single.

At the other end, Glen Maxwell knocked down the bails, running out the 11th batsman James Anderson. Taylor challenged the decision and asked for a review for his LBW call, following which he was declared not out. However, Anderson was given run-out, leaving Taylor two short of his century. A day later, ICC accepted the mistake that the ball should have been deemed dead when the batsman was originally given out.

- India suffered their first series loss to Bangladesh in history.
- Shikhar Dhawan emerged as India's shining star, scoring 158 runs, making him the top scorer in the series.
- Left-arm pacer Mustafizur Rahman had a dream debut when he walked away with five wickets to 50 runs in the first ODI at Mirpur. He surpassed the dream run taking six wickets and conceding only 43 runs in the second ODI. He made history by taking 13 wickets in a three-match ODI series.
- Mustafizur Rahman was also declared the Man of the Series.

Winners: *One Test (Fatullah)*: Match drawn; *First ODI (Mirpur)*: Bangladesh won by 79 runs; *Second ODI: (Mirpur)*: Bangladesh won by 6 wickets; *Third ODI (Mirpur)*: India won by 77 runs.

INDIA IN ZIMBABWE

July 10 to 19, 2015

- The two teams played three One Day International matches and two Twenty20 matches.
- India won the ODI series 3–0. The T20 series was drawn with both the teams winning a match each.
- Chamu Chibhabha of Zimbabwe was declared the Man of the Series.
- Ajinkya Rahane led the Indian team for the tour as most of the senior players were rested.
- Harbhajan Singh made a comeback after four years but failed to spin his magic.
- The second T20 match marked Zimbabwe's first win against India in a Twenty20 match.

Winners: *First ODI (Harare):* India won by 4 runs; *Second ODI (Harare):* India won by 62 wickets; *Third ODI (Harare):* India won by 83 runs; *First Twenty20 (Harare)*: India won by 54 runs; *Second Twenty20 (Harare):* Zimbabwe won by 10 runs.

INDIA IN SRI LANKA

August 6 to September 1, 2015

- The series included a tour match and three Test matches.
- India won two matches in the three-match series, for the first time in 22 years. It was also India's first overseas Test series win, in the last four years.
- Virat Kohli captained the Indian side.
- Sri Lankan batsman Kumar Sangakkara announced his retirement from international cricket during the series.
- All-rounder Ravichandran Ashwin was judged the Man of the Series.

Winners: *First Test (Gale):* Sri Lanka won by 63 runs; *Second Test (Harare):* India won by 62 wickets; *Third Test (Harare):* India won by 83 runs; *First Twenty20 (Harare):* India won by 54 runs; *Second Twenty20 (Harare):* Zimbabwe won by 10 runs.

TENNIS

CHENNAI OPEN

January 5 to 11, 2015

- The first ATP event each year and India's only ATP World Tour stop, the Chennai Open is the only ATP world tour event in South Asia.
- The tournament, often seen as a springboard for champions, provides an opportunity for Indian players to compete with the best talent in the world.
- The tournament, which was first held in 1996, celebrated its 20th year this year.

Winners: *Men's Singles:* Stanislas Wawrinka successfully defended his title by beating Slovenian Aljaz Bedene, 6-3, 6-4.
Men's Doubles: Jonathan Marray and Lu Yen-Hsun outplayed top seeds Leander Paes and Raven Klaasen, 3-6, 6-7, to win the tournament.

AUSTRALIAN OPEN

January 19 to February 1, 2015

- One of the most prestigious tournaments and the first Grand Slam of the year, it is also one of the toughest tournaments.
- Serb Novak Djokovic continued his winning streak, lifting the Men's Singles, his fifth Australian Open title. This was also his eighth Grand Slam win.
- Serena Williams won her 19th Grand Slam singles title, second only to Steffi Graf's 22 titles in the Open Era of tennis. This was also her sixth Australian Open title, making it an Open Era record.
- India's own Leander Paes and tennis partner Martina Hingis bagged the Mixed Doubles title.

Winners: *Men's Singles:* Djokovic retained the title by defeating Murray, 7–6, 6–7, 6–3, 6–0.
Women's Singles: Serena Williams defeated Maria Sharapova, 6–3, 7–6.
Men's Doubles: Simone Bolelli and Fabio Fognini defeated Pierre-Hugues Herbert and Nicolas Mahut, 6–4, 6–4.
Women's Doubles: Bethanie Mattek-Sands and Lucie Šafářová beat Chan Yung-Jan and Zheng Jie, 6–4, 7–6.
Mixed Doubles: Leander Paes and Martina Hingis defeated Kristina Mladenovic and Daniel Nestor, 6–4, 6–3.

FRENCH OPEN

May 24 to June 7, 2015

- The French Open is the second Grand Slam of the tennis calendar.
- The highlight of the tournament this year included Rafael Nadal's loss against Novak Djokovic, in the quarter finals. Nadal has been the champion for the past five years consecutively. Djokovic was finally defeated by Stan Wawrinka in the finals.
- In the women's section, Serena Williams knocked down Lucie Šafářová, to win her third French Open. This was Williams's 20th Grand Slam singles title.

Winners: *Men's Singles:* Stan Wawrinka defeated Novak Djokovic, 4–6, 6–4, 6–3, 6–4.

Women's Singles: Serena Williams beat Lucie Šafářová, 6–3, 6–7(2–7), 6–2.

Men's Doubles: Ivan Dodig and Marcelo Melo bagged the title defeating Bob Bryan and Mike Bryan, 6–7(5–7), 7–6(7–5), 7–5.

Women's Doubles: Bethanie Mattek-Sands and Lucie Šafářová outplayed Casey Dellacqua and Yaroslava Shvedova, 3–6, 6–4, 6–2.

Mixed Doubles: Bethanie Mattek-Sands and Mike Bryan knocked out Lucie Hradecká and Marcin Matkowski, 7–6, 6– 1.

THE WIMBLEDON

June 29 to July 12, 2015

- The Wimbledon Open holds the distinction of being the oldest and also perhaps the most acclaimed tournament in the Grand Slam. The tournament which started in 1877 is the only tournament played on a grass court.
- The Serb defending champion, Novak Djokovic picked up his third Wimbledon title in Men's Singles. Serena Williams picked up her 21st Grand Slam single.
- For India, it was a double whammy, when Indian Sania Mirza won the Women's Doubles title with her game partner Martina Hingis and Leander Paes bagged the Mixed Doubles, also with Martina Hingis.

The Twirlgate

Canadian player Eugenie Bouchard found herself in the middle of a controversy when she complied with a request by reporter Ian Cohen to do a "little twirl" to show off her outfit after a win in the Women's Singles. Cohen was citing Bouchard's tweet complimenting Serena Williams for her twirl after an earlier win. What followed was a frenzy with opinions flying on social media criticising the request to be demeaning to a woman and outright sexist. The incident came to be called the "Twirlgate".

Winners: *Men's Singles:* Novak Djokovic beat Roger Federer, 7–6, 6–7, 6–4, 6–3.

Women's Singles: Serena Williams defeated Garbiñe Muguruza, 6–4, 6–4.
Men's Doubles: Jean-Julien Rojer/Horia Tecău outplayed Jamie Murray/ John Peers, 7–5, 6–4, 6–4.
Women's Doubles: Martina Hingis/Sania Mirza defeated Ekaterina Makarova/Elena Vesnina, 5–7, 7–6, 7–5.
Men's Doubles: Leander Paes/Martina Hingis beat Alexander Peya/Tímea Babos, 6–1, 6–1.

THE US OPEN

August 31 to September 13, 2015

- The US Open is the fourth and final Grand Slam event played on a hard court.
- The tournament is in its 135th edition this year.
- The highlight of the series was the epic Men's Singles final which had Novak Djokovic beat Roger Federer over four enthralling sets.
- The surprise, however, came in the form of Flavia Panetta's debut US Open win.

- Indians Sania Mirza and Leander Paes retained their winning streak, winning the Women's and Mixed Doubles, respectively, with their common tennis partner Martina Hingis.

Winners: *Men's Singles:* Novak Djokovic defeated Roger Federer, 6–4, 5–7, 6–4, 6–4.
Women's Singles: Flavia Pennetta beat Roberta Vinci, 7–6, 6–2.
Men's Doubles: Pierre-Hugues Herbert and Nicolas Mahut beat Jamie Murray and John Peers, 6–4, 6–4.
Women's Doubles: Sania Mirza and Martina Hingis won over Casey Dellacqua and Yaroslava Shvedova, 6–3, 6–3.
Mixed Doubles: Leander Paes and Martina Hingis beat Bethanie Mattek-Sands and Sam Querrey, 6–4, 3–6.

Quite an upset!

Italian Roberta Vinci's victory over Serena Williams in the first Grand Slam semifinal (2-6, 6-4, 6-4), at the US Open, is being seen as one of the biggest surprises in women's tennis history. Vinci, an unseeded player, hadn't ever won a set against Williams in four previous matches. Williams was right there near her Grand Slam win at the time of the upset. Vinci, however, later lost to country mate Flavia Panetta, who bagged her first and last US Open, before announcing her retirement.

In 2012, Williams encountered a similar upset when she lost the first round of the 2012 French Open to the French, Virginie Razzano.

ATHLETICS

WORLD CHAMPIONSHIPS, CHINA

August 22 to 30, 2015

- The 2015 World Championships was the 15th edition of the IAAF world meet. 1,781 athletes from 205 countries participated in the championship.
- Kenya topped the table for the first time ever with seven golds, six silvers and three bronze medals.
- The US won the most medals overall with 18 medals (six gold, six silver and six bronze).
- The 28-year-old Jamaican Usain Bolt continued to add to his legacy, retaining his title as the fastest man on the planet.

Winners: *Men:* Usain Bolt won the 100 metres, the 200 metres, and Jamaica won the 4x100 metres relay.
Great Britain's Mo Farah won the 5000 and 10000 metres races.
In high jump, Canadian Derek Drouin bagged the gold.
Women: Shelly-Ann Fraser-Pryce retained her gold in the 100 metres race.
In what is being called the greatest women's 200 metres final in the history of women's athletics, Dafne Schippers from the Netherlands beat Jamaica's Elaine Thompson to create a new Championship record.
Thompson, however, anchored Jamaica to a gold medal in the 4x100 metre relay.

BADMINTON

- Saina Nehwal and K. Srikanth won the China Open Super Series Premier tournament held in Fuzhou.
- While Saina Nehwal defeated Japanese Akane Yamaguch, K Srikanth clinched his maiden Super Series title after defeating Olympic champion Lin Dan (China) in the Men's Singles events. This is the first time that an Indian male player won a Super Series Premier event.
- PV Sindhu beat Korean Kim Hyo Min in the Women's Singles finals, to retain the Macau Open Grand Prix title. The Olympic bronze medallist won 21-12, 21-17.
- Kidambi Srikanth became the first Indian male player to clinch the Swiss Open when he defeated defending champion Viktor Axelsen (Denmark) 21-15, 12-21, 21-14 at St Jakobshalle.
- Saina Nehwal and K Srikanth lifted the India Open Super Series titles defeating world champion Ratchanok Intanon (Thailand) and Dane Viktor Axelsen of Denmark, respectively, on home ground.
- Ace Indian shuttler Saina Nehwal regained the number one

position in the International rankings ahead of Carolina Marin and China's Li Xuerui who dropped to third position in the Women's category.

- Indian Women Doubles pair Pradnya Gadre and N Siki Reddy triumphed at the Polish Open 2015 at Arlamow, Poland. The duo beat fourth seeds Canadian pair Alex Bruce and Phyllis Chan 21-16, 21-18.
- Indian Badminton duo Ashwini Ponnappa and Jwala Gutta reunited, after they parted ways at the end of the 2012 London Olympics, to ignite the badminton courts in the Canada Open. They upstaged the top-seeded Dutch pair of Selena Piek and Eefje Muskens, 21-19, 21-16.

CYCLING

TOUR DE FRANCE

July 4 to July 26, 2015

- Tour de France is the world's most prestigious and difficult bicycle race.
- Of the three foremost races (the other's being Giro d'Italia and the Vuelta a España), the Tour de France attracts the world's best riders.
- The Tour comprises 20 professional teams of nine riders each and covers some 3,600 km, mainly in France, with occasional and brief visits to countries such as Belgium, Italy, Germany, and Spain.
- Kenyan-born Britain's Chris Froome of Team Sky won the race, followed by former Team Sky mate Richie Porte and Colombian Nairo Quintana.

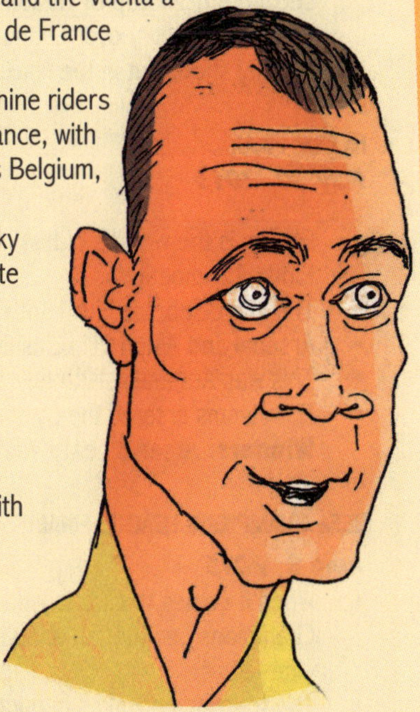

FOOTBALL

FIFA PLAYER OF THE YEAR AWARDS, ZURICH

January 7, 2015

- The FIFA World Player Gala, in 2010 merged with France Football's Ballon d'Or award to form the new 'FIFA Ballon d'Or', given annually to a player based on his performance in the previous year.
- Portugal forward Cristiano Ronaldo won the FIFA Ballon d'Or as the World Player of the Year for a second consecutive time defeating other contenders Lionel Messi and Manuel Neuer.

Winners (2014): *Ballon d'Or:* Cristiano Ronaldo
Women's World Player of the Year: Nadine Kessler (Germany/Wolfsburg)
Men's Football Coach of the Year: Joachim Löw (Germany)
Women's Football Coach of the Year: Ralf Kellermann (Wolfsburg)
FIFA Presidential Award: Hiroshi Kagawa (Japanese reporter)
Puskas Award (Goal of the Year): James Rodríguez (Colombia vs Uruguay)

AFRICAN CUP OF NATIONS
January 17 to February 8, 2015

- The Africa Cup of Nations celebrated the 30th year of the international football championship for African countries.
- The tournament was initially scheduled to be hosted by Morocco but was postponed due to the Ebola epidemic. It was later hosted by Equatorial Guinea.
- In a surprising loss, defending champions Nigeria did not even qualify for the semi-finals.
  Winners: Ivory Coast won their second African Cup of Nations with a 9-8 victory over Ghana in a penalty shoot-out in the final.

Football fever in India

The second edition of the Hero Indian Super League (ISL) for football began on October 3, 2015 in Chennai. Eight teams will play 61 matches over 79 days. The finals of the league will be played on December 20.

FA CUP FINAL
May 30, 2015

- FA Cup is the world's oldest football competition.
- The cup celebrated its 134th year of existence in 2015.
- Arsenal and Aston Villa clashed in the final at Wembley Stadium in London.
- This was Arsenal's 12th title and the sixth win for manager Arsène Wenger.
- Both teams entered the competition in the Third Round as a Premier League club.
  Winners: Arsenal beat Aston Villa 4-0 in the final to claim their maiden trophy.

UEFA CHAMPIONS LEAGUE FINAL
June 6, 2015

- When it comes to club tournaments, it just doesn't get bigger than the UEFA Champions League, an annual competition featuring Europe's best and the most elite teams.
- The tournament rakes in huge revenues and brings in both crowds and TRPs.
- This year the final was held at Berlin's Olympiastadion between Juventus and Barcelona.
- Andrés Iniesta was named the Man of the Match.

Winners: Spanish Barcelona defeated their Italian rivals Juventus 3–1. This was their fifth trophy in the cup.

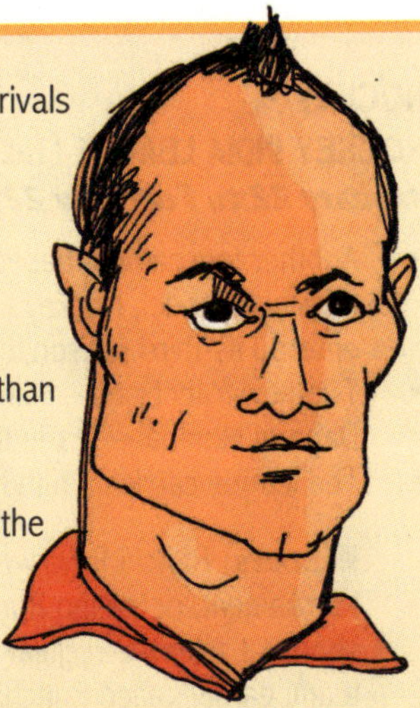

FORMULA ONE

GRAND PRIX

March 15 to November 29, 2015

- For motorsport enthusiasts there is nothing better than the adrenalin rush of Formula One, motor racing's biggest and most prestigious annual championship.
- Twenty-two drivers representing ten teams contest the 19 Grand Prix that make up the calendar for the 2015 season.
- Defending champion, Mercedes' Lewis Hamilton who was declared the 2014 Formula One Champion looks formidable in 2015 as well.
- Mercedes dominates the circuit after 14 races with Hamilton in the lead position with 41 points, followed by teammate Nico Rosberg.
- Sebastian Vettel stands in the third place till September end, and seems to have silenced the critics who questioned his skills, specially after his win at the Singapore Grand Prix. Vettel snapped ties with former team Red Bull to join Ferrari.

Tragic end

In a tragic turn of events Jules Bianchi, who was injured in a crash at the 2014 Japanese Grand Prix after he collided at high speed with a mobile crane, slipped into coma and finally passed away. The 25-year-old French motor racing driver drove for Marussia F1. Bianchi is the first Formula One driver to have died in a car crash during a race, since the legendary case of the death of Ayrton Senna at the 1994 San Marino Grand Prix.

Team changes: McLaren reunited with Honda, which came back to the circuit as an engine supplier after three years, exiting Mercedes. However, they failed to ignite the magic together.

Sebastian Vettel left the team with which he won four World Drivers' Championships, to join Ferrari.

Fernando Alonso rejoined McLaren after eight long years, leaving Ferrari. He, however, pulled out of the season following an accident. Magnussen was his temporary replacement.

Belgian-Dutch driver Max Emilian Verstappen made his Formula One debut in 2015. He is the youngest World Championship Grand Prix driver in the history of F1.

HOCKEY

HOCKEY INDIA LEAGUE (HIL)

January 22 to February 22, 2015

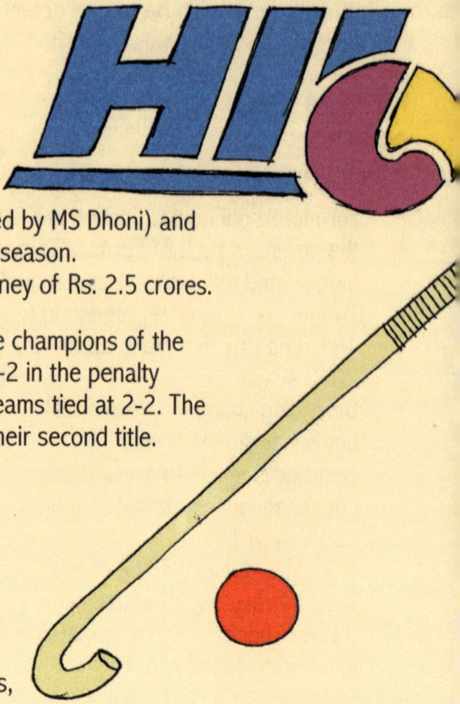

- Another tournament based on the IPL's franchise model, Hockey India League entered its third season, in 2015.
- Two new franchises—Ranchi Rays (owned by MS Dhoni) and Dabang Mumbai—made their debut this season.
- The league carries a handsome prize money of Rs. 2.5 crores.

Winners: Ranchi Rays were declared the champions of the tournament, defeating Punjab Warriors 3-2 in the penalty shootout after the regular time had the teams tied at 2-2. The team, earlier called Ranchi Rhinos, won their second title.

GOLF

MAJOR CHAMPIONSHIPS

April to August 2015

- The four most prestigious annual tournaments in professional golf jointly combine to form the Major Championships, commonly known as the Majors, and is played by elite players from all over the world.
- The players' rankings and reputation are largely based on the number of major championship victories they accumulate.
- Rory McIlroy was voted the 2014 PGA Tour Player of the Year for the second time, winning against rivals like Martin Kaymer (who won The Players Championship and US Open), Masters champion Bubba Watson and FedEx Cup champion Billy Horschel.

Winners: April – Augusta Masters (Winner: American Jordan Spieth)
June – US Open (Winner: American Jordan Spieth)
July – The Open Championship (Winner: Zach Johnson of US)
August – USPGA Championship (Winner: Australian Jason Day)

By **NAMIT ANAND**

STOP PRESS!

Vijender Singh knocked out Sonny Whiting of Britain, the crowd favourite, at the Manchester Arena, on October 11, on his pro-debut bout.

LIFESTYLE

- A Food Odyssey
- Fashion Diaries
- Travel Trends

2015'S TOP 10 FOOD TRENDS

While there is always space for the evergreen chaats, mithais and kababs, some new food trends had people eating out of their plates. Here are a few:

BAO = WOW

We have vada pavs, the French have croque monsieur, the Italians have paninis, the Spanish have bocadillos, the Vietnamese have banh mi and the Americans have po boys. And the Chinese have bao, short for baozi. Traditional Chinese restaurant-goers probably know this yeasty 'sandwich' as tia pao or pork pao. But over the last few years, we've seen this street food and breakfast basic, rise from its previously ignored status to having its own section (quite like salads and pizzas) at every fifth Oriental restaurant.

TACOS TAKE OVER

Would you agree if we say, India as a nation understands and appreciates Mexican cuisine far more than we do, say, Korean? Maybe ... it has something to do with the heavy handed way they use spice or how they cook their meat and lentils. Perhaps it's their devoted affection for soft and crispy breads. Most likely, it's all of the above. So what may have started as a 'trend for 2015' in the west has long been popping up on the menus of chic Indian restaurants and pubs. Now, the real question of the year is, which take on the taco—modern, deconstructed, *desi* or Lebanese—did you enjoy most?

THE GRID REVIVAL

Noticed how breaky staples are turning into a permanent lunch and dinner-stay? It's official. Waffles are the new black. And if that wasn't shocking enough, chefs have gone and given this usually sweet morning treat a savoury swirl. First there was the soul food special: fried chicken and waffles, but today's restaurateurs are going all out with mashups like truffle mac and cheese, pizza waffles, hash browns and even chicken tikka masala.

OF SPICES IN SIPS

Long have we quenched our inherently spicy (read: Indian) thirst with bloody or wasabi Marys. Enter: jalapeno margaritas, saffron and Kashmiri mirchi martinis, green chilli and lemon spiked gin and tonics, all made fresh for you (mocktails). And if that wasn't enough of an homage to just how much we adore all things spice, consult the barkeeps and mixologists for their latest garnish creations such as candid cardamom sticks and Sriracha sea salt rims.

KEEP CALM AND GO VEGAN

Bill (Gates and Clinton) is, Gwyneth swears by it and even Jay-Z and Beyonce tried it—if only for 22 days. Just to clarify, we're talking about adopting the green and going vegan. Simply put, while both vegans and vegetarians don't eat meat, vegans also avoid all animal and dairy-based products. That's no cheese, butter, milk, eggs, honey, wool, silk and leather. Having said that, the numbers and data are in. Turning vegan is now mainstream. So forget about the old dietary and animal rights activism and ring in the new by making a lifestyle choice for a cleaner, green and more morally sound tomorrow.

ONE GREEN JUICE A DAY, KEEPS THE DOCTOR AWAY

If your vocabulary of veggie juices begins and ends at V8, we advise an upgrade because this is one globally growing trend that's worth buying into. Made mostly of juiced—using a juicer and never a blender—green vegetables and herbs to fruits in a 70:30 ratio, this smoothie gets everybody's thumbs-up for controlling diabetes and cholesterol besides adding hard-to-find antioxidants, chlorophyll, minerals and vitamins to the daily diet. Ask your mom to make you one by picking a liquid base like lemon, water, coconut juice or green tea, then adding two leafy green vegetables and two fruits, each. Continue and add flavour-providers such as ginger, turmeric, cucumber or sprouts. End with herbs like parsley, coriander and celery.

THE FUTURE OF FOOD A LA 3D PRINTING

Statistically speaking, the 3D printer has been in the offing for quite some time. Especially if you consider all those sci-fi authors who have long been imagining and littering our childhood with cool kitchen appliances that could prep, cook and serve food, on command. Some of our most-famous fictitious food inventions/machines include *Star Trek's* replicators, *Back to the Future II's* hydrator and *The Fifth Element's* food pills, which instantly turn into a full roast chicken. As for the 'real' near future, it holds sweet treats in any imaginable shape, colour, texture and everyday ingredient. **The process basically uses ingredients to generate three-dimensional meals by layering compounded foods together.** Eventually, the final frontier of food will even allow you to customise how much fat, protein and calcium etc., constitutes your daily intake.

SAMPLE THE SMALL PLATE REVOLUTION

The Spanish are to blame. According to legend, tapas or "small snack" came into vogue in the 14th century, thanks to their King Alfonso, who declared that no wine be served in his kingdom unless it was accompanied by something to eat. If you ask us, there's nothing more exciting than teasing your taste buds by sharing small plates packed with new flavours. Because, why stick to the same taste for the full meal when you can have a new texture with every third bite, right?

SECRET, OFF THE MENU, ORDERING

Marketing trick or insider's secret revealed. We rule in favour of the latter. At home, the Taj Group of Hotels is infamous for it, in the UK, every chain from McDonald's to Subway has not only fessed up to serving off 'it' but also revealed the names and contents of creations like the Monster Mac and Pizza Sub. And then there are our local South Indian, Catholic and Calcutta Chinese eateries, whose waiters always try and deny 'their' very existence. Secret menus are actually a thing. The only exception to the rule may be a very particular chef who chooses to cite seasonality vis-à-vis ponkh poha (in Gujarati; also known as hurda in Marathi and green jowar or sorghum) and truffle capellini.

CRONUT IS SO 2014. HAVE YOU TRIED A KOLACH YET?

Mutated desserts seem to be the flavour of the decade. Last year's crowned king, the cronut crossed oceans and continents to wow everyone from India to Japan. This year's 'it' international import comes to us from Central Europe, specifically Czech Republic and Slovakia (where it was a midday snack), via Texas. Think soft but slightly flaky doughnut-like pastry with its centre left hollow for sweet and savoury fillings that span poppy seeds, cream cheese, bacon/jalapeño/ham and sausage to a generous dollop of fresh fruits or Nutella-and-banana.

The lead-noodle saga

In the middle of this year, the Government of India decided to ban one of the nation's mainstays, Maggi, after it failed a series of tests on quality. The country was immediately carved into two: one, that instantly claimed starvation after the ban of their beloved cheap and quick, anytime snack. And second, that started to ask questions like, 'Do we know what we eat?' 'Are 2-minute meals even healthy?' 'Which other brands have something to hide?' 'Why did Nestle India decide to destroy their stock after strongly defending the safety of their product?' Personally, we'd suggest, you wait and taste before deciding what works for you.

By **JHARNA THAKKAR**

Fashionably speaking the year swayed wildly between being an immensely great one to being a terrible one—depending on where you are standing. If you worked in fashion, were a fashion editor, a stylist, a photographer or any one of the Fashion Haves, with an access to the inner workings of the fashion world and trends, you would have hated it. For everyone else it was probably one of the best fashion years since humans learnt to stitch.

FASHION GETS DEMOCRATIC

Fashion suddenly became something it never was—democratic. Fashion's haves were no longer the influencers, Instagram was showing people what was happening at fashion weeks seconds after it actually did. No one wanted to wait for six months for something they could already see online.

Fashion editors who'd already begun to lose their front row seats and perks to fashion bloggers over the last couple of years, suddenly had someone even newer and younger to contend with – the social media influencer. The photographers who'd spend years cultivating their personas and composing their iconic picture styles suddenly had to compete with everyone with a smartphone and an Instagram account. The covers that for decades had been defining fashion trends for the months ahead suddenly found they were competing for influence with vine videos.

The breed of influencers could be anyone—photographers, filmmakers, celebrity managers, restaurant owners, musicians—just about anyone with a good Twitter/Instagram following and having a unique perspective on fashion. Suddenly the voices dictating fashion trends were a lot more diverse and fly-on-the-wall.

INSTA-FASHION

Insta-coffee, stop-gap relationships, short-vacations ... fashion joined the race. Fashion designers who were used to sending out collections to stores up to six months after a show realised people no longer wanted to wait six months. A brand like Topshop Unique was telecasting their show on FB and even offering people the option of buying it on the spot. It couldn't get more empowering if it wanted to.

So far the power to make or break a fashion brand remained in the hands of the fashion press, suddenly there was a wave of brands that didn't get much support by the press but managed to create a huge hype. And that was this year's greatest development, but not the biggest one.

THE INSTA-SHOW

During the New York Fashion Week, Bahrain-born British Designer Nonoo showed off her collection in World's First Insta-Show, on Instagram, that was telecast to the 3,000 followers of an Insta-handle, specially created for the show. While she was the first one to do a special show for Instagram, others were also beginning to organise live web streaming of their shows. Elsewhere, photographers, designers and brands were collaborating for 'Insta-shoots' and even established designers like Stella McCartney were opting for them. But while the fashion press was getting squeezed out of the equation like an unwanted wart – the only one who was winning was the consumer.

THE PLUS SIZE MOMENT

Strangely though, one of fashion's biggest trends—Plus Size pride—didn't have much to do with India. In America, Ashley Graham became the first plus size (read non-skinny) model to end up on the cover of *Vogue* and then become the first plus-sized model to star in *Sports Illustrated's* Swimsuit edition. Elsewhere brands and designers, who preferred stick-thin models or even hangars (so their curves didn't ruin how the fabric fell) too were using plus-sized models for their shows.

INDIA DIDN'T AGREE

Everyone from Sonakshi Sinha to Parineeti Chopra to Bhumi Pednekar went around losing their curves and fitting themselves into crop tops. Even a pure, all-out skinny fashionista like Alia Bhatt lost whatever little curves she had.

THE DEMISE OF THE CHOLI

There was something rather interesting exploding on the runways, though. Sonam Kapoor donned shirts with her saris for events. Manish Malhotra and about half a dozen designers too preferred cropped full sleeve tops with lehengas, making it sufficiently clear that the traditional choli was no longer enjoying its moment in the sun. The choli started disappearing not just from the runway but also from the wardrobe of some fashion conscious brides. They were replaced by what some call the 'art house' version—a shirt or a cropped long sleeved anti-fit blouse.

THE PANTS WEREN'T QUITE SO SKINNY

After a couple of years of wearing pants so skinny that a chicken nugget could make you pop a stitch, the skinny pants weren't quite as important. Whether it was neat pleated palazzos worn with kurtis, wide legged pants worn with biker jackets and other such draped versions—skinny pants' 15 minutes of fame was over. In fact not just pants, the emphasis this year shifted and stayed on easy, loose-fitting silhouettes rather than harsh form-fitting ones.

THE END OF AN ERA

Ralph Lauren, the man who dictated, decided and then prodded the world of fashion towards corporations, accessories and the like will no longer be at the head of his own brand. He stepped down as CEO of his own brand.

THE HIJAB BECAME THE SYMBOL OF DIVERSITY

In part driven by world events, the happenings in Syria, and in part just because it was its time, the hijab made an appearance on fashion runways in both New York and London Fashion Weeks. The bigger shot in the arm though came from the fact that H&M and a couple of other brands too used hijab-wearing models in their ads.

THE YEAR OF RIHANNA

Despite the fact that her daring, out there avatar debuted last year, despite the fact that Kim Kardashian posted not one but two to three controversial instagrams (one of which was in a controversial white swimsuit very soon after giving birth), Rihanna ruled 2015. Just about everything she was on, even when she was just lounging in Brazil watching parades or showing off her barely there gowns on award red carpets— everything that Rihanna did defined fashion to a huge extent. And this was no small feat. She managed to do this in a year when Kendall Jenner was still going strong and Miley Cyrus was flashing the cameras at every available opportunity!

By **KABEER SHARMA**

The year 2015 is the 'Can Do' year of travel. Indian travellers have broken several boundaries with élan, with young parents travelling with children, women holidaying alone, and families straying way off the beaten path. We've also evolved into a more ecologically sensitive breed of travellers, showing sensitivity towards the environment and making green choices whenever possible.

BE SOCIAL

If it ain't on Facebook or Twitter, it ain't real! People are sharing discoveries as they travel and having conversations with friends and family on the go. Though a bit of this exchange on social media is about showing off, it is also about sharing the wonder of a new place and enabling others at home to enjoy a bit of armchair travel. And joining the ever-increasing apps and sites is Twitter's Periscope app, which just made it easier to share live videos.

CROWDSOURCING

Technology continues to change and shape the way we travel. We've been using it to research and book our holidays, find great deals on platforms like Airbnb and make the most of airline sales. Now, we are also using it to crowd source information about lesser-known destinations on platforms like Twitter and Facebook. With advice pouring in from all quarters—locals to seasoned travellers—travel couldn't get more exciting.

LET'S TALK RUBBISH

Indian travellers care about the environment. Hiking groups regularly organise special treks on which participants not only hike to interesting places in the mountains and the Western Ghats but also return feeling extra good because they have collected rubbish along the way. Seeing a stunning place while helping to keep it clean makes a holiday especially gratifying.

CHOOSE GREEN

Travellers have also begun to ask questions about how the way they travel affects the environment. When picking a hotel or a place to stay, people now want to know how they manage their waste and resources, whether they recycle, if they use solar energy, and contribute to the local economy. Giving preference to properties that adopt green measures, is the least one can do for the environment. Let's hope more and more people catch the green bug.

HAVE KIDS, CAN TRAVEL

Modern couples who love to travel have often worried that having a child might mean a complete change in their lifestyle. And though parenthood does bring a lot of changes, one thing which continued unabated this year is travel, with more parents

The next big trip

The Wizarding World of Harry Potter at Orlando, Florida, USA

Universal Studios' Florida theme park opened its recreation of Diagon Alley in the latter half of 2014, fuelling young and adult imaginations alike. Visitors step through a gap in a brick wall to enter a magical world where they can buy wands and perform magical spells, see the fire-breathing dragon atop Gringotts Wizarding Bank, and drink delicious butter beer. They can also ride the Hogwarts Express across to the village of Hogsmeade in the Islands of Adventure theme park, which had opened a few years earlier. A must-do for fans of the series.

taking trips with infants as young as six months, building up a bank of memories that any child will be thrilled to grow into.

> **Unexpected Adventures**
>
> **Oman and Jordan**
>
> The middle-eastern countries of Oman and Jordan have becomes surprisingly popular destinations for adventure travellers during the past year. Jordan holds the promise of exciting treks and desert campsites, and thrilling canyoning trips through its narrow gorges. Oman has become popular for diving or snorkelling holidays along its 1,700 kilometre long coastline that showcases the marine life of the Gulf of Oman and the Arabian Sea.

TRAVEL TO LEARN

As any traveller knows, a journey isn't just about seeing a new place, but also about learning new things about ourselves and the world we live in. Recognising the fact that an education isn't just gained in the classroom, more and more parents are planning trips with their children to provide them exposure to different cultures from an early age. And if along the way, they manage to sneak in a lesson on physics or geography, who minds!

GET A NEW SKILL

In the competitive world we live in, it can sometimes be hard to justify taking a fortnight off just to travel. But what if you could learn a new skill? Increasingly, people are signing up for holidays with a purpose. It can be anything from a sketching holiday to learning Tibetan cooking, getting scuba diving training or even a mountaineering course. Travellers want a way to engage deeply with the destination, and what can be better than learning something new?

YEAR OF THE MINI SUV

Recognising Indian families' love for road trips, car companies are proactively launching mini SUVs. Different brands have launched cars that have great handling and safety features, some off-roaded capabilities and enough space for the whole family and the dog to pile in.

GIRLS LIKE TO TRAVEL

There was a time when girls rarely travelled alone, but that's long gone. Since the birth of women-only travel clubs that gave girls the courage to step out with a group of others like them, they have never looked back. Whether it is a young girl out of college, a female photographer on assignment or a mama of two looking for a break while daddy takes care of the kids, ladies are no longer waiting for someone else to take them on a trip.

WHAT ABOUT LASSIE?

Talking of dogs, Indian families love their pets and want to take them along on the annual family vacation. We've seen an increasing number of family-run properties and home stays opening their doors to four-legged guests. Some normal caveats apply: Your pet must be potty-trained and well behaved so other guests are not disturbed.

By NEHA DARA

About the Contributors

AMIT GURBAXANI is the co-founder and editor-in-chief of *thedailypao.com*. He has been writing about music for over a decade and a half, for publications such as *Time Out* Mumbai, *NH7* and *The Guardian*, among others.

ASHISH BHATIA is an independent technology writer and columnist for several print and online publications. He has been a member of the NDTV Gadget Guru Annual Awards Jury for the last five years. He was the Editor of *PC World India* and the Co-Founder and Editorial Director of *The Virtual Magazine*.

ASHISH MOHAN KHOKAR has authored over 40 books and 4000 articles on Indian dance and aesthetics and is a widely-read online columnist. He is associated with Indian dance at many levels—universities, government, awards, festivals, mentoring and curating, documenting and creating films.

BIMAN BASU is a retired scientist who has been writing popular science books and broadcasting on science over radio and television for more than four decades. He has more than 45 popular science books to his credit.

BOSKI GUPTA lives to read and writes to live. A journalist who gorges on words, music and art, she has worked for news organisations like PTI, *Economic Times* and *DNA*.

CHETNA SINHA'S day begins and ends with news. A journalist for more than a decade she has worked with publications like *The Pioneer, The Asian Age, Hindustan Times*. She currently resides in Cardiff, UK.

JHARNA THAKKAR lives, loves and breathes to eat. As part of her culinary journey, she has worked through the kitchens of Indigo and Mocha Coffee and Conversations. She has written on hospitality and travel for *Indian Express, Hindustan Times, Vogue, Conde Nast Traveller, Time Out* India and *Mumbai Mirror*, to name a few. She plans to continue eating her way through the country.

KABEER SHARMA is the Managing Editor at *Indiatimes.com* by day and masked vigilante by night. He covered every fashion show to happen in India for six years for *Hindustan Times, DNA* and *Open Magazine* and was the editor at *FHM* India. He continues to write on fashion, internet and other frivolous things. Follow him on Twitter at @ka_beer.

KANIKA SHARMA is a journalist with *Hindustan Times* and loves writing on books and films. She has worked at the *Mid-Day* in Mumbai, in the past. She is also a writer and has published four short stories with Hachette India.

KSHAMA RAO is a Mumbai-based journalist for the last 20 years. She loves to write on films and TV. And when she isn't writing funny FB updates, she works full-time as Senior Producer, Content, Hotstar!

MEERA MENEZES is a well-known art critic and curator. She is the Delhi correspondent for *Art India*, a magazine on contemporary art.

NAMIT ANAND has been eating, breathing and living sports since he started walking. He is now living his passion, writing about sports for various websites and publications.

NEHA DARA is the Deputy Editor of *National Geographic Traveller India*. She is happiest trotting off the beaten path. A journalist for ten years, she handled *Hindustan Times'* travel and other lifestyle sections in her previous assignment and has over 19,000 followers on Twitter.

NIKHIL TANEJA is a Mumbai based writer-producer, who runs creative and development for Y-Films at Yash Raj Films. He's creative produced Y-Films' *Man's World*, *Bang Baaja Baaraat*, MTV India's *Traffic* and MTV Films, among others, and the forthcoming film, *Bank Chor*. He also teaches at Jai Hind College and heads digital strategy for the Mumbai Film Festival. He spends the rest of his time either watching TV and films, or writing them.

PRACHI GURON is an independent communications specialist, associated with the Centre for Science and Environment, as a consulting editor. Between marketing and communications assignments, environmental writing and editing and being mom to two boys, she is striving to retain her sanity.

RAMESH RAMACHANDRAN writes about politics and foreign affairs. For someone who believes that the journey is as important as the destination, he found in journalism the perfect vehicle for indulging his personal and professional interests.

YAMINI DHALL is a senior journalist with over a decade of experience in reporting, editing and tracking financial news. She is currently the Web Director for DealStreetAsia. In her alternate avatar, she is an aspiring ceramist and studio potter, who likes to travel to the places where pottery thrives.

ABOUT THE ILLUSTRATOR

PRIYA KURIYAN is an independent animation filmmaker and illustrator based in Delhi. She has directed educational films for the Sesame Street show and has also co-directed a short animation film for the CFSI. Over the past few years, she has also been illustrating for a number of children's books and comics.

THE END